Heal Your Heartbreak

Chuck Spezzano, Ph.D.

Heal Your Heartbreak

How to
LIVE AND LOVE
AGAIN

Marlowe & Company
New York

Published by
Marlowe & Company
An Imprint of Avalon Publishing Group Incorporated
841 Broadway, 4th Floor
New York, NY 10003

Heal Your Heartbreak: *How To Live and Love Again*
Copyright © 2000, 2001 by Chuck Spezzano

First published in the United Kingdom in 2000
by Hodder & Stoughton Publishers.
This edition published by arrangement with Hodder & Stoughton

Library of Congress Cataloging-in-Publication Data

Spezzano, Charles.
    Heal your heartbreak : learning to live and love again / by Chuck
Spezzano.
    p. cm.
    ISBN 1-56924-626-2
    1. Disappointment. 2. Love. 3. Interpersonal relations. I. Title.

BF575.D57 S64 2001
158.2—dc21

00-048949

9 8 7 6 5 4 3 2 1

Designed by Pauline Neuwirth, Neuwirth & Associates, Inc.

Distributed by Publishers Group West
Printed in the United States of America

ACKNOWLEDGMENTS

Any book, in truth, is a team effort, a team gift, and it's even more so with this book. Last February, this book began with one of my editors, Donna Francis, as a small book on heartbreak written in our spare time. But, as I started writing the book, it took on a life of its own and began to grow and grow and grow. At the end of May, it became an upgraded project to finish by September 1999. Apart from traveling and teaching (I was only home three weeks from the third week of May to September), this summer was spent bringing the book to its present form. This has been a labor of love for my team of editors and typists, and for me.

First of all, I would like to acknowledge Lency, my wife and life partner, who at the end of the day, and sometimes in between, makes it all worthwhile. For all of your support, your bits of editing and valuable commentary, your inspiration, and for all of your methods of rejuvenation, I thank and salute you. It was your love that gave me the courage to heal my wounded heart. Thanks to my children, Christopher and J'aime, for your sweet and lively spirits that are such a source of tenderness, joy, and laughter for me. You keep me young.

Acknowledgments to Donna Francis and Bonnie Close for your brilliance, good ideas, devotion, organizational skills, dedication, support, and smooth editing; to Janie Patrick for indefatigable support, enthusiasm, laughter, organization, friendship, valuable comments, unwavering faith, and typing; to Peggy Chang, who also juggled the mountains of typing among a thousand other things, and did it all well; to my team at Hodder and Stoughton: Rowena Webb, Laura Brockbank, Karen Sullivan, and the many others who contributed. Acknowledgments also to Jeff and Sue Allen, and Julie Wookey from Vision Products for your friendship, support, and the shared vision and joy at getting these products out to the world; to Sue Allen for reading and commenting on the text and being a bridge for all of us, and finally to Kevin and Joy Matthews and Francine Girard for their great meals and general support in the final push to the finish.

I would like to acknowledge *A Course in Miracles*, which has had such a seminal and profound effect on my life. It corroborated concepts and principles I thought to be original discoveries, and it showed me so much more. I notice as I read through the chapters that there are almost no sections where I was not influenced or where my discoveries were not confirmed. It saved me from a great deal of pain and provided the heart and foundation of my spiritual life, for which I am profoundly grateful. I would also like to thank all of my clients who taught me so much. Thanks to Dr. Susan Campbell for *The Couples Journey*, and for her original ideas about the stages of relationship, which I used as the foundation of my relationship research on the stages. Finally to Dr. Sam Hazo, mentor and poet, for your inspiration and poetry.

CONTENTS

‖ CONTENTS ‖

|| Contents ||

The Call for Heart

Your heart is your connective tissue to life. Without it, you would wither in a seemingly eternal winter, become old and die. With it, you go through each inevitable spring, no matter what your age.

When I speak of your heart, I am not speaking about the biological organ in your chest. Just as when I talk about your mind, I am talking about more than just your brain. When I speak of your heart, I speak of your capacity to love, to feel, to enjoy, and to know beyond any scientific certainty what your purpose in life is. Your heart is the root of your courage; your mind is the sum of your soul. Together, they give meaning beyond the mere aggregate of facts.

It is important to examine the relationship that you have with your heart. How warm, open-hearted, human, compassionate, empathic, and giving are you? How well do you receive? On the other hand, how defensive, dissociated, sacrificial, scared, cynical, bitter, or naïve are you? How removed are you from life? Are you just going through the paces? Have you lost your sense of passionate giving, of passionate living? Have you lost your fire and zest: are you tired, burned out, used up?

These are signs that your heart has been lost—in part, or in whole. If you have lost heart, then it is time to rest, reflect, and commit to a course of action to win back your heart, because it is the cornerstone of emotional integrity. With the courage of truth, your heart provides the very essence of all integrity. Without your whole heart, you cannot give nor can you receive fully. When you lose your heart, there is a tendency to rationalize, cut corners, or take what you want because you cannot receive. Do you want to live anything less than a full life? Do you want to define yourself by your roles, or as your essence? Healing is needed. Unlearning is required. True learning is necessary. It is not too late. It is your life; you choose: wholeheartedness or half of a life?

Face it! You need your heart. Without it you can only live a partial existence, a half life, because you cannot enjoy it. You cannot love. You cannot receive. You cannot feel. Without your heart, you are reduced to being either predator or prey in a grey mouse-like existence. Without your heart, you are part of the problem causing—directly or indirectly—whatever was done to you. Without your heart, you cannot answer the calls for help in times of need, and this is just such a time—a time of crossroads, a time of birth. Without wholeheartedness, you will not be able to give what you promised to give. You may have promised to love another person well, to foster and bond with a child, or to save the world. To achieve these promises, you need your whole heart to gather itself up, and to give itself fully.

With your heart, you will know the blessed healing of tears—including the tears of joy. With your heart, you will know the joy of true giving, and you will be able to step forward when the need around you is great. You will hear the calls for help, and the call of your own soul to give itself to life and to those around you. With your heart, you know purpose, creativity, and vision. With your heart, you are able to appreciate, know truth, feel gratitude and openness, and receive from others. With your heart, you are an active participant in the life of the planet, and in the lives of those around you.

If your heart has been broken, it is your responsibility to yourself, to life, and to anyone you love, or will ever love, to regain it. Your willingness to regain it has led you to this book. Now be willing to let what is in it help you to get back your heart. Through this book, my heart reaches to yours. You may be in the ring, but I will be your coach in the corner supporting you toward wholeheartedness. With your heart, you will ultimately know love, and you will know grace, which is God's love for you.

Chuck Spezzano, Hawaii, October 1999

Congratulations and welcome to *Heal Your Heartbreak*! This book represents your commitment to making yourself whole again. All too little is taught about your heart, yet it is the key to love, fulfilment, and enjoyment. It is what joins you to others and also what gives you the courage—from the French *le coeur* meaning "heart"—to live your life to the fullest.

In schools today, nothing is taught about relationships and families, yet it is these relationships that underpin your life. They give direction, meaning, and fullness. Relationships are the juice of life. If you do not experience them as an elixir, then they have probably become a poison. Relationships head toward life or toward death; there is no in-between, in spite of the stasis or boredom that sometimes occurs.

Any problem is a relationship problem. Your relationship patterns direct the patterns of your health, your happiness, your money, your success, your love, your sex life, and even your art. Every poet needs his muse, and creativity is a state that love made. Yet, we know so little about relationships and how transforming they can be. You need to know how to change your relationships, because when your relationships are stuck, so are you. It is crucial that relationships are taught through nursery school to post-doctoral studies. This book is an aid to learning and, more importantly, to unlearning what we've got wrong. As we understand and remove the mistakes, we find love present.

If relationships are the chief transforming aspects of your life, and also the most important factors in health, happiness, success, and evolution, then it is time to learn about relationships. Of all the wishes I could have for my children, my deepest wish is that they be great in their relationships and that they love profoundly. Everything else that's important will follow.

This book is not only about heartbreak; it's also about relationships in the context of heartbreak. It is all about your relationship to yourself and your relationship to your God or spirit, because all relationships reflect the relationship we have with ourselves, our spirit or God, and the world around us.

I have been a counselor, a life coach, and a personal consultant for twenty-eight years. I have been in the front-line trenches of therapy, and I do not particularly care about the niceties of theory. Theory doesn't mean much when you've held someone crying out the deepest anguish and horror of their life. I am practical. If it doesn't work, it doesn't matter, regardless of how pretty the concept. I've worked too long with people to think that ideas, especially my ideas, are more important than stopping pain. But I do know that the ideas here work. The methods and techniques have worked for me and they have worked for many others. They can work for you, too, if you want them to. As a child I stood helpless before the pain of those I loved the most. I vowed that I would learn whatever it took to remove that pain and also to help others. Now I know a way out. There are other ways, I am sure. I offer you what I have learned because I am certain that it can transform your life.

If just one reader can step out of hell, then this book has served its purpose. No matter how dark things look, there is always a way out. If you and everyone around you cannot find that way, ask for a miracle. Ask your higher mind for help. It's there, waiting for an indication that you are willing. Then it can begin to inspire and to show you the way to achieve grace. *You* are too precious to lose. There *is* a way. Your *heart* is too precious to lose. There *is* a way. Without even one of you, the darkness breeds. All the pain has been a mistake. There is a way. You *can* find the way home. There is a way you can believe in yourself again—in the importance of your purpose and in the power of your mind and your healed heart that can heal others.

Forgive me, professors, if I am not as precise as you taught me. I have become as much the shaman, the artist, and the priest as the scientist. Forgive me, religion of my birth: I feel as much Buddhist as I am Christian, as much Jewish as Hindu, and all the while, my heart dances Sufi and I am singing Rumi. It doesn't matter what or in whom you believe when you have wholeheartedness. When your heart is whole you have peace and grace, which helps you and the world around you.

I have lost my heart and regained it. A thousand times between childhood and the present, I have damned myself to hell and cursed myself to death. A thousand and one times, I have walked out of hell and chosen life. I speak with a certain authority, because I have also made mistakes and found a way out. I began with heartbreak patterns and I have true love. My heart was broken a dozen times and I am neither cynical nor over-sensitive. My dreams have been shattered and I live more truly. I am healed and healing. I am on my way, like everyone else, to wholeheartedness.

I have written this book using the Psychology of Vision model, which I developed along with my wife, Lency. It comes out of the transpersonal and humanistic traditions and is meant to provide a visionary approach to healing.

The Psychology of Vision is a return to original meaning in regard to healing. The word *psychology* comes from the Greek words *psyche* and *logos*, literally meaning "soul study." This speaks to both the depth and completeness of this model. Vision is the recognition that we must go beyond the status quo that allows the pain of the past to shrink our horizons. Instead, vision allows a positive future that shows us the way back to the eternal present. The Psychology of Vision is a marriage of cutting edge psychology and grace.

The Psychology of Vision is made up of three major elements?—Relationships, Leadership and Spirituality. Relationships, because they have primordial importance in our lives, and because all problems are symptoms of relationship problems with others, with ourselves, and with God. Leadership, because the world needs leaders today; and because leadership is a response to the calls for help around us. Spirituality, because ultimately, we are spiritual beings. As evolution occurs, we move from dependence to independence, from independence to partnership, and from interdependence to radical dependence. Radical dependence is the awareness of our reliance on God, Love, or Spirit that goes beyond all religions, and seeks that which is essential to the primary spiritual experience beyond form.

The Psychology of Vision recognizes that while there are basically two minds, our ego and our higher mind, it is convenient to deal with the conscious, subconscious, unconscious, and superconscious minds. In the conscious mind, there is a common sense approach to that which is in our awareness. The subconscious mind contains everything we hide from ourselves that has occurred since our conception and is recorded in the mind. Even though it is buried, it is still affecting us. The unconscious mind contains our personal soul path, and follows the deepest parts of the mind that determine the direction of our lives. The content of our unconscious mind is inherited from our own soul agenda, ancestral patterns, and the limitations and existentials of humanity. The superconscious or spiritual mind is the most primordial, yet most hidden, aspect of our existence. It reflects our relationship to God or "All That Is" on the way back to Oneness.

For the most part, the model of the Psychology of Vision goes beyond the scope of present-day therapy. Some of its key insights and experiences came to me in 1975 as I developed an intuitive method as an alternative to hypnosis. This allowed me to explore subconscious areas all the way into the unconscious, which is the area of the paranormal and the shamanic mind. I had mind-blowing experiences with people as they shared their most hidden and repressed issues around victim experiences. This allowed me to see an alternative to current victim theory, which, for the most part, does not get past the pain, blame and rage of the victim toward the victimizer and the event. Based on work with many thousands of individuals, I began to see that, ultimately, we are all innocent, though we have made grave mistakes in what we thought would bring us happiness. People are doing the best they can, given inner and outer circumstances, but all of us could do better. I also saw that we are both responsible and accountable for everything that happens in our lives, but that our egos want to keep us in the victim role and keep us feeling guilty.

As I continued my work, I realized that victims are the most trapped and disempowered people there are. As I began helping people work through the patterns and mistaken choices they had made that caused such heartbreak, I also began understanding and healing my own heartbreaks. After opening and understanding the hidden issues of the mind, it becomes much easier to forgive others and ourselves, and completely transform the past and the painful feelings that still remain.

The Psychology of Vision model is about love, innocence, empowerment, responsibility for our lives, and our ability to respond to others. It is about freeing victims from their traps, finding the gifts and talents blocked by such traps, and empowering them to become successful leaders and healers in their own right. The Psychology of Vision is about problem solving and evolution.

The Psychology of Vision is a healing model that is not just about healing and repair, but also about vision, creativity, and living one's purpose. It is not only important to "fix the car," it is also crucial where the car is going. After ten years of work, while I was leading workshops and practicing as a Marriage, Family, and Child Counselor in California, I began to see that most problems, especially chronic problems, had, as part of their dynamic, the intention of hiding our purpose in life. This would give us an excuse not to keep the soul promises that are vital to our happiness and fulfillment. As each problem was healed or resolved, the client took another major step toward living their purpose in life. The Psychology of Vision is about being a visionary leader and leading a creative life.

The Psychology of Vision is a path of accountability, which is a path of full responsibility for our life and everything in it. In this way, it empowers us and denies that there is any truth at all to blame and guilt, and the ego's investment in them. It recognizes that when we stop blaming others for any problem, our ego then tries to make it our fault. It recognizes that blame and guilt are just two facets of the same trap. Neither are ultimately true, although we all feel them. This is what must be healed to give up guilt and self-attack and punishment. The Psychology of Vision is about accountability and innocence.

The Psychology of Vision has mostly emerged through the healing experience that my wife and I bring, after more than fifty years of combined professional experience. It is filled with many innovative ideas, methods, and techniques. It recognizes that love and the ability to live one's purpose are the basis of happiness and healing. The Psychology of Vision has been taught around the world, to all races, and most religions. It has been equally helpful in work with aboriginal people as it has been with every culture in which it was presented. It has had great success in working with general problem solving, with relationship, family and business issues, with physical and sexual abuse, and it has even been effective working with catastrophic illnesses and addictive behavior.

The Psychology of Vision presents a map of evolution, which includes the stages we all go through in our personal growth, in relationships, and finally spiritually. It demonstrates the main traps and the way through them at each stage of growth. The Psychology of Vision shows how we evolve, and the challenges we face at each step along the way. It recognizes, as stated in the book of Proverbs in the Bible, "Without vision, people perish." It is meant to provide a positive way through the challenges of today, and it is dedicated to humanity on the journey to recognize its divinity. At the heart of the Psychology of Vision is the reality of friends helping friends to make this a better world.

ABOUT THE BOOK

Everyone has felt the anguish of heartbreak, and most have searched in vain for resolution. *Heal Your Heartbreak: How to Live and Love Again* is an interactive journey filled with signposts and roadmaps to show you the way through to the other side of your suffering. It is a life-long companion and reference book. It addresses what you are facing now, any and every time you pick it up.

The four sections: *Recipes for Disaster—Things that Lead to Heartbreak*, *The Lessons of Heartbreak*, *Healing Chronic Heartbreak—The Unconscious Patterns*, and *The Tools for Healing Heartbreak* are the basic principles that prepare you to open your awareness and help you understand what heartbreak truly is. Your resulting awareness can bring new choices, attitudes, and resolutions that will lead to success in relationships.

We begin by talking about the stages of relationships, and the fundamental principles that define them. You'll be given a basic understanding of how relationships work, how and why they go wrong, and how they alter your personal evolution. Take time to read these descriptions because we call back at many points to these basic theories, which underpin our lives, our relationships, and our ability to progress.

In *Recipes for Disaster,* you are given helpful information about the most common traps that throw people into heartbreak. Principles, suggestions, choices, and exercises are also included in this section so that you can tour rather than camp here.

Your personal journey begins with *The Lessons of Heartbreak,* and you are encouraged to research your own heartbreak: how it affects you, your life, and all those around you. This section has powerful concepts that give you the opportunity to discover how the related heartbreak dynamic fits into your life. The concepts are then summarized in "heartbreak and healing principles." Rather than living by rules, these principles become a way of life, in which you get to choose either heartbreak or healing. To further help you to adopt a new attitude and promote change in your life, "healing suggestions and healing choices" are provided to assist you to move forward easily. Finally, there are the "healing exercises." By taking the time to actually practice, rather than just read these exercises, you can gracefully and easily change debilitating and painful untruths about yourself, and transform your life, even with miracle-like experiences, bringing you back to living a life filled with love and joy.

In *Healing Chronic Heartbreak* the traps and patterns of the primordial unconscious are examined. These are the ego's best, most hidden defenses as it seeks to strengthen itself through separation, fear and guilt, and by weakening love. As you bring the light of awareness to areas long hidden in your mind, you shine the darkness away. This section also has "heartbreak and healing principles," "healing suggestions," "healing choices," and powerful "healing exercises" to help you to change these deep and mistaken patterns.

The Tools for Healing Heartbreak demonstrates the major healing methods that can transform heartbreak and free us from the bondage of pain. It also includes heartbreak and major healing principles, suggestions, choices, and exercises.

This book is meant to be read from beginning to end for a fuller and richer understanding of heartbreak and its dynamics, and this part is for subsequent user-friendly reference. If you become aware of the temptation to fall into heartbreak after reading this book, intuitively pick a number between 1 and 111 to select the principles that would most help you to begin healing the situation. Just reading these principles may be enough to dissolve the temptation and move you through your pain. Whichever method is for you, it will quickly and easily open you to wholeheartedness again.

I'd like to make a final note on the issue of accountability. When I speak of the accountability of victims, I want to reassure you that I am not saying it is the victim's fault that they were victimized. I am saying that the victim and all of us are responsible and accountable for what happens. While your conscious mind had no intention of allowing anything unfortunate to happen, when you get into the levels of subconscious and unconscious, for some mistaken reason a part of you thought you'd gain happiness by making it happen. As you explore the book, you'll discover most of the key reasons why we make these mistaken decisions. Guilt is one of the most destructive forces on earth. With it we punish ourselves endlessly. But if you are responsible you can change, put your lives back together, get past the endless rage of the victim (where most counseling is caught these days), and really get on with your lives.

How to Use this Book

You can, of course, use the book any way you want, but here are a few suggestions: this book can be life-changing if you choose it to be. What do you want it to be? What do you think you can get from it? This book is both informative and transforming. It will show you the way to wholeheartedness, and the healing choices and exercises will help you regain your heart. If you like to read and digest everything before you read on, then I suggest you do each exercise completely before addressing the next stage. If you like to skim information and then come back for a slower read, I suggest you avoid looking at the healing exercises until you are ready to do them.

Some people find that if they tape-record the questions asked in the healing exercises, and then replay the tape to respond more intuitively to each question, the questions and their answers can have greater impact. Another alternative is to commit to going through the book with a friend or your partner. This way you can do the exercises together as a committed healing project.

Throughout the book I ask you to answer questions "intuitively." This means using the first answer that pops into your head, regardless of whether your "conscious" mind knows it to be true or not. Questions throughout the exercises are prefaced with the words "If I were to know...." This approach breaks through the barriers of the conscious mind and allows us to come up with our *real* perception of events, or what we believed. It bypasses memory, which can be tainted and shadowed by the ego's need to keep things as they are to maintain itself, which we will discuss in more detail in the next section. These words also prevent us from saying "I don't know" in response. The answers to these questions may not be true according to history, but they will be true for us, in that they represent our perception of the event, what we thought or believed deep down inside ourselves. We may feel like we are guessing rather than giving a realistic answer, but the answers that first come into our heads are, in fact, what is real for us. It is what we fundamentally believe, even if we were unaware of it.

At other stages of the book, I ask you to call upon your higher mind for help. The higher mind is simply the creative part of our minds—the part that knows all the answers. All of us are spirit, and we have a spiritual core that represents the part of the mind toward which we are all evolving. Our higher minds are, in essence, our spirits, and when we call for help from that spiritual core, we can receive the grace of God and of spirit. We will be given the answers and we will know what to do. It's important to understand that we all have a spiritual, healing power within us, and we have always had it. When we evolve, or move forward, we come closer to finding that power again. It is always there to help us when we need it.

Decide what you would like to achieve as you read the information and do the exercises throughout this book. In what way would you like to see your life transformed? *Choose it. See it. Feel it. Hear it.* Imagine exactly how you want to feel at the end of the book. Write down your goal, so you can re-examine it when you are finished, and see how well you have succeeded.

THE JOURNEY BEGINS

There are few things in life that can set you back as much as heartbreaks do. I have worked with thousands of individuals who have had such setbacks. For some people, heartbreak in their early twenties was the key factor for poor health in their eighties. Other folks who were heartbroken as children, never fully came back into life until a healing event occurred, where they were once again able to experience life with all its color and brightness returned to them.

The purpose of this book is to help you understand what is going on around you when heartbreak occurs. Once you understand what heartbreak is and how it has been used in your life—how it serves you and what value it has for you—you begin to understand the purpose it has played in your life. Unfortunately, too many of us have done personal research in this area without the necessary understanding, which is why it still hurts. Without understanding, this hurt will linger as you continue to defend and compensate for your heartbreak. It is extremely helpful to be aware of the elements surrounding heartbreak—the pieces that you buried away and are afraid to acknowledge. To change any heartbreak, it is crucial to see the part that *you* played in its instigation, so you can begin to make more successful choices, including successful choices in love. You will then fully resurrect yourself, and come back to life.

This book is about bonding—the rich joining that creates love and success with ease. Bonding is living fully and luxuriously, both spiritually and emotionally. The alternative is living a partial existence, a half or even a quarter of your life, because you cannot fully experience it. If you live a heartbroken life, you will be dissociated or dependent, separated and fearful, greedy and attacking, guilty and judgmental. It is a life of sacrifice and compensation, without any natural reward.

Heartbreak can cause you to lose heart, and if your heart is lost, there is no way that you will be able to achieve your purpose. You need your heart to live fully, and to be able to give yourself to life. You need your heart to experience love, and to make the profound contribution that you are here to give. As you heal your heartbreaks, you come back to life, and open yourself to once again experience the beauty and richness that life has to offer. You open yourself to love—loving and being loved by others and your God or spirit.

When you withdraw the investment of self from heartbreaks, and give yourself back to life in a true way, life becomes that much better, and truer for all of us. So, it is important to give up the illusions that have kept you suffering. The extent to which you give up your suffering is the extent to which the whole world can be freed, so it is not just your own heartbreak that you heal. You can help to end all heartbreaks—all the fractures that separate us from each other and from peace.

So, come along on this journey. What is there to lose but heartbreaks, old pain, and the excuses and justification about love not being available for you? There is no telling where this healing journey will end up, once you begin it again. What you will see is that you are only limited by your fear—your beliefs about yourself and the world. Awareness empowers you by giving you better and more educated choices. Understanding how something went wrong gives you the chance to learn the lesson and to correct the mistake.

For those of you with present heartbreak, this book can help you find a way back to life; it is a response to your desire to understand how to live and love again. This book gives you back your power to choose, and along with it, the confidence that you can have a true life partner, and be close to them. May this book bless you with understanding, the courage of acceptance, the wisdom of forgiveness, the truth of letting go, and the choice to love again.

UNDERSTANDING
RELATIONSHIPS

Every relationship is unique, with its own guiding force and pitfalls. However each relationship follows a series of evolutionary steps and stages, and if we have some understanding of these, we will be better equipped to move through them. Each stage and step also raises specific issues for us to heal, and when we learn these lessons and move forward, we can evolve both as individuals and as a couple.

There are also certain characteristics that are common to all relationships, and these are explained here to equip us to deal with problems as they occur. An understanding of how and why our relationships have reached a particular stage is crucial to finding the tools with which to heal them. Armed with this knowledge, we can identify problem areas in our relationships, realize which problems are stage specific, understand why and how they occurred, and go on with the answers common to that stage to fulfill our true purpose in life.

STEPS AND STAGES OF RELATIONSHIPS

ROMANCE STAGE

The romance stage of a relationship occurs at the beginning of a relationship, and it gives us a taste of everything our relationships can be. We experience all the beauty, fun, and sheer joy of relationships, and when things go wrong, we often look back at this period with nostalgia. The romance stage can be held up as the ideal, showing the potential and promise of our relationships, which we can reach when we fully transform them.

When we enter a relationship, we choose a person who treats us specially. We all need to believe we are special, and the romance stage is a fulfillment of that need. We treat each other well at the beginning of a relationship because of its newness, because of our belief that we have found our perfect "missing half," and because of the overwhelming feelings of infatuation. These feelings are tinged with fear, attraction, and even urgency, as we seek a missing part of ourselves in a new partner. There is a promise of being whole when entering a new relationship, and the heart of all romance is really the illusion of how we think our partner will fulfill us and *make* us whole. We often begin relationships for this reason—which is, of course, the wrong reason—but it is the glue that attracts us initially and holds our relationships together. If the relationship doesn't work out, we fear that we will be "stuck" with them. If it continues, it succeeds because we choose to be together for the right reasons. The right reasons include love and happiness as our main purpose, and they also include healing through joining, forgiveness, and letting go to rediscover the peace, love, and happiness we have and have always had within us.

Where there has been romance or illusion, there is bound to be disappointment and frustration, unless we can set a new goal to make our relationships whole. This involves a mature commitment to healing and to our partners.

Enjoy every aspect of the romance stage, but don't be surprised or disappointed when the next stage erupts. When the romance stage is over, the relationship is not over, nor is the love gone. Romance does not equate to love; it represents an idealized vision of the relationship that fills us with powerful, often passionate feelings. These are the feelings we often mistake for love, but they can power us through the more trying stages of relationships ahead.

THE POWER STRUGGLE STAGE

This stage occurs right after the romance stage, though fights can occur at any time in our relationships. It becomes evident when our fears, differences, and needs begin to surface through the cracks that have begun to appear in our "perfect" relationships. Often the very things that attracted us to our partners—their differences—become points of conflict. We begin to see that perhaps our needs aren't being met exactly how we had envisioned, and we might discover that our partners' vision of the world is not something we can share. Herein lies the struggle. As each of us battles to ensure that our needs are met, and that things are done according to the way we see the world and our lives unfolding, we reach a potential no-win situation.

The challenge in this stage is to heal the separation as it becomes evident. When things crop up in our partner that we don't like, it is because they are acting out parts of ourselves that we have hidden away or rejected. It sounds complicated, but it's not. When we enter a relationship with someone, they embody characteristics of ourselves that we subconsciously need or have hidden away. They represent a "missing part" that has the potential to make us whole. The problem is that we suppressed that missing part of ourselves for a reason. We may have been hurt as children when exhibiting that part, and vowed to hide it away on whatever level, or it may have become separated from us through pain or trauma at another point in our lives. Whatever the cause of the separation, our new relationships bring us face to face with that part once again, and we need to venture across the pain and fear in order to love our partners, and to establish a fulfilling relationship. When we join with our partners, we reclaim the lost part of ourselves, which creates an integration that combines our energy with that of our partners. But it's a difficult step to take, and the barriers we put up form the basis of the power struggle.

In this stage we fight for what we perceive to be our fears and our needs, which leads to some big conflicts. But each time we surrender, give, forgive, and join, a new bridge is created and the relationship moves forward into understanding, bonding, and trust.

Healing this stage does not mean finding a compromise, for this only leads to feelings of loss or frustration on the parts of both partners. When we compromise, we sacrifice something that we believe in, in order to find a mutually acceptable position. Real communication, however, bypasses the need for compromise. We need to learn maturity and friendship, and we need to give from the heart, without any expectation of reward. We need to let go of every attachment and defense, and to put our faith in our partners and our relationships. In this way only can we find true communication and, on its back, love and wholeheartedness. Every time we join, heal, or break through with our partners, we will experience another period of romance. We will enjoy this until the next layer of power struggle or deadness reaches the surface. This book explains how to do that.

The Shadow Step

The shadow step is the first step of the power struggle stage and it begins on the tail of romance. This step often represents the point at which many relationships and marriages break up. Some of us get through this step very easily, but for others it can be the most challenging step of the relationship. Out of the blue, we suddenly see that our heaven-made relationship is looking more like hell on earth. And if we are living in hell, then our partners must be the devil. Melodramatic, perhaps, but this stage can raise intense feelings of fury and dislike, and the reasons for these can be quite difficult to understand. When we enter a relationship, we project our ideal onto our partners. In other words, we see in them all the things that can make us whole, and we feel that our need for "specialness" is being met. In the shadow step, however, we begin to project something else, and this is often our worst case scenario. For example, if we had an emotionally disturbed mother, we may now witness the same behavior in our wife. If we had an alcoholic father with a tendency to gamble, we may find that our husband now seems to spend most of his free time drinking at the track. Whether we actively sought people to sustain an unhappy pattern from childhood, or whether we have actually used the power of our minds to make our partners become our worst nightmares, we find ourselves in untenable situations with unlovable (even actively dislikable) people.

This is where we often discover shadow figures—parts of ourselves that we have fractured off because they were so despicable, unlikable, bad, or embarrassing that we could not go on with them as part of our minds and being. These shadow figures represent our most hated aspects of ourselves, and it is these very aspects that we now see in our partners. The very fact that we can feel so outraged, angry, and disgusted by our partners proves the existence of a shadow figure that we have suppressed but then projected onto the situation and the people within it.

There are two things that can shift the situation completely. One is to heal the shadow figure, which means integrating it back into our minds by forgiving and accepting it, and the other is to forgive ourselves, our partner, or the situations or people that caused that figure to develop within us. We need to recommit to our partners, making a choice to give ourselves to them completely. This works to shift us and our partners on to the next step. It may seem unlikely that we can shift alcoholic, gambling partners back to happiness and success, but it has been proved time and again that we have the power within ourselves both to change our perception of our lives, and the lives of those around us. Whether we heal them through commitment and the power of our minds, or we just change so dramatically that we no longer project these shadows onto them, we can undoubtedly alter and heal situations and people by reintegrating the parts of ourselves that we hate, and using our newfound peace to give the gifts of love, acceptance, or whatever is appropriate to change lives.

The Independence-Dependence Step

A relationship typically begins with two independent, self-sustaining people. When we begin a relationship we might both be vying for the favored independent position. This brings the power struggle to a new level.

Relationships balance the conflicts that both partners have within them, and each partner is assigned a role in the relationship in order to resolve them. We either play the independent, or we become dependent, according to who is best suited for the position. The roles shift throughout relationships, so we are never cast in one role unless we really want to be. The fundamental concept to understand here is that the independent partner is *always* acting out the dissociation, separateness, and indifference of both partners, and the dependent partner is *always* acting out the needy sides of both partners. So when we switch and swap roles, we are still acting out our joint and individual needs.

Obviously we all want to be in control, which leads to a struggle for the independent position at the beginning of the relationship. Being independent gives us the control to direct the dependent partner to do things our way, or we won't play. We are frightened by their neediness and it is often their dependence that drives us away. We haven't come to terms with our own pain, fear, and neediness, which is hidden beneath our dissociation. What we need to do is work through this step of the relationship by valuing our partners more than our need to have our own way. This step will occur many, many times throughout the course of our relationships. For success, we must re-establish an equal footing, where we both have our needs met, and we both have the space, freedom, and security of interdependence.

As the dependent or "needy" partner, we have to let go of our needs and attachments. As the independent partner, we need to learn how to value, reassure, appreciate, reach out, and, with our love, raise up the dependent partner. The extent to which we are able to invest our time and energy in our dependent partners, no matter how jealous, unattractive, or hysterical they may seem, is the extent to which they are able to give up these unattractive qualities and become equal once again.

Needy partners need to join independent partners in love, rather than just seeing them as a source of meeting our needs. When we do this, our relationships move forward. We need trust, letting go, and communication in order to achieve this, but it will, eventually, build a bridge over the conflicts. We need to value our partners and our relationships more than our needs, and every time we are able to do so, we will bring about a new honeymoon period, until the next layer of conflict arises.

Independent partners must realize that dependent partners are working through the neediness for both of us, and the easiest way to move through our hidden needs is to join and reach back for them. When we help our dependent partners to heal their neediness and pain, we heal ourselves, too. Recognizing the reasons why people become dependent and needy within a relationship helps us to be sympathetic and compassionate and, ultimately, a good partner. If we are good partners when we are independent, we will receive the same treatment when the roles are reversed. The crisis that typically occurs when we switch roles in a relationship is bypassed by the level of partnership that we have established.

The Positive/Negative Step

This step occurs when we realize that we have different ways of seeing things. One of us in the partnership is the "positive," and the other is the "negative." First and foremost, it's important to understand that neither is wrong. We just see and approach things in a different way. Here's how it works. A positive partner is idealistic and optimistic, and has boundless energy and enthusiasm. He or she always underestimates the amount of time, money, and energy needed to finish a project. The negative partner is much more pedantic—he or she knows exactly how much it will take, and probably doesn't believe there are the resources to accomplish it. The positive partner looks at the big picture and goes for the big goal, and the negative partner pays attention to the details and doesn't want to make a mistake.

Both of these approaches are valid and effective, and, when used together, create a productive and happy partnership. The lesson of this step is that we must value the contributions of our partners and work together, which will produce all the energy required to accomplish anything on which we set our hearts and dreams. Negative partners are excellent problem-identifiers, while positives are excellent problem-solvers. Just as these two styles are complementary within a business environment, they can produce brilliant results within a relationship. The secret is to avoid fighting about who is right, who is the better person, and who is more ambitious, practical, or clever. Respect and value our differences. Focus instead on the energy that a positive–negative couple produces, and the holistic way of looking at issues that it engenders.

Just as the negative and positive poles on a battery work in tandem to produce power, two opposites within a relationship can join to become a powerful force. This force—as well as our valuing of and recommitment to our partners—propels us into a new stage of our relationship, which begins with a honeymoon period.

THE DEAD ZONE STAGE

This stage is one that most of us have experienced within our relationships, and it is characterized by boredom, feeling trapped, and the strong belief that there must be something better elsewhere. However, the important thing to remember is that this stage might be suffocating and appear to be the natural end of the relationship, but it is, in reality, the place where some of the most profound healing can occur.

The dead zone stage comes from a number of dynamics, but all of them involve withdrawal and fear. Sometimes we have withdrawn to avoid losing to our partners in power struggle and competition. Some of it comes from times that we withdraw from life because of feelings of heartbreak, failure, and guilt. Many times we compensated for these feelings by undertaking positive roles where we are doing the right thing for the wrong reason—where we give but don't receive, where we are in sacrifice, heading toward burn-out. At every point where we lost bonding, through fear, separation, or pain, we go into "fusion." Fusion is a place where boundaries between us and others are muddled. The fusion we experienced with our parents is carried into our own relationships with our adult partners. This is the stage that we face and heal the painful illusions of the guilt and failure that is present in every role and in every family dynamic. It's painful to bring up feelings of guilt or failure that we have suppressed, but a relationship is the natural forum in which to explore these feelings and heal them. We have to get past the ego in order to do so, and that means understanding the traps it has in store.

Fusion is a term that is used often throughout the book, and it is a key behavior within relationships that leads to their downfall. Fusion is effectively counterfeit bonding, and it is set up by the ego to prevent us from really joining. You can instantly tell the difference between fusion and real bonding— when we bond, our relationships are true, alive, and free. We feel balanced and we are able to join in the kind of love that brings success to all areas of our lives. When there is fusion, however, we feel dissatisfied, that we are making sacrifices, and that our relationships are a burden to us. When there is fusion we are unable to receive because we have withdrawn. When there is fusion, we cannot progress in our relationships because there is a co-dependency with our partners to hide our fear, and we are unable to accept the love that will carry us past the ego's barriers. This increases the sacrifice and throws our lives out of balance, and often shows itself by overwork, and sometimes with laziness.

We can, however, experience true bonding and heal what was lost or non-existent in our families when we were growing up by making a commitment to move past this step, and allow ourselves to experience the true emotions and feelings we are hiding, as dire as they may seem at the time. By committing to our partners, and to life, we can escape from fusion, and the fuel for this escape is the love we have for our partners.

Compensation is another ego trap that happens all the time, but particularly at this stage. When we compensate we act in a way that hides our true feelings, beliefs, and concerns. For example, if we have a poor self-image and believe, fundamentally, that we are lazy, we might work excessively hard to hide our beliefs from ourselves. Similarly, by being "over-good," we may hide a deep-rooted belief that we are bad or evil. Like fusion, compensation is a way of avoiding and suppressing our true feelings that need healing. It will never lead to a satisfactory relationship because it blocks what we have to give and prevents us from receiving. As long as we are playing roles, or acting as we think we should, we will never reach a state of real joining, which will take us into a whole new level of the relationship.

When we are aware that the ego sets these traps, we can

watch out for them, and move past them, finding peace and love in our relationships.

The Roles, Rules, and Duties Step

We talk about rules and roles in more detail later in the book, and they are very important barriers to finding lasting happiness within a relationship. This step, which normally occurs within the dead zone, is also governed by our egos. The idea here is that we act out roles and set rules to prevent ourselves from truly giving. We do all the "right" things—behaving well, doing things for others, and working hard, for example—but we are doing them for the wrong reasons. We undertake these roles in our relationships by sacrificing ourselves to compensate for feelings of guilt and failure. We set up rules that define how things should be, because we want to hide and protect places where we suffered before. Rules are meant to protect us from past pain, but they are meant to be broken. Therefore, like all defenses, they actually bring about what they are trying to prevent. While we are giving through a role, no one close to us might be able to detect the difference, but we are not giving authentically. This is because we are not giving ourselves, which is fundamental to the ultimate success of a relationship. When we give ourselves, the ego tells us that we are vulnerable, and sets up defenses to ensure that this doesn't happen. Obviously, joining, then, doesn't take place. Ultimately, however, our "compensations" bury and hide the guilt, poor self-esteem, and feelings of unworthiness and failure, deeper, which not only affect our existing relationships, but any relationships we might have in the future.

Many of our roles are the result of patterns that exist in our families—we were brought up to believe we were not useful, important, or special, and so we bury those feelings of low self-worth and compensate by making ourselves special, invaluable, and important to others. The problem is that these feelings and beliefs remain deep inside us, and unless we are able to open them up, recognize and heal them, we will be unable to receive from others. Eventually we will head toward burn-out, depression, and, ultimately, deadness, which is reflected in our relationships. The answer is to heal. By joining and recommitting to our relationships—using the methods described later in the book—we can heal ourselves, our relationships, and the family patterns that have brought about our deadness and lack of feelings. We need to live by choice rather than by roles, by truth rather than by rules, and with commitment, which brings with it a new and invigorating freedom. Giving ourselves in commitment can heal a whole step rather than going through the hundreds of points at which we must join that are typically needed to get past any step.

The Oedipus Step

This step forms part of the dead zone, but instead of the feelings of being in a rut, or nearing burn-out, which characterize the roles and rules step, we move into deeper feelings of deadness, eventually to the point of repulsion and even revulsion for our partners. We may find these feelings bewildering, and they are made even more so because they come from our subconscious. The factor at work here is called "transference." We are taking unfinished business—especially sexuality—with our siblings or parents and transferring it onto our partners. This unfinished business may be based on feelings we repressed, including the sexual attraction to a parent or sibling, or perhaps a guilty knowledge that one parent liked us more than he or she liked our other parent. If this sounds Freudian, that's because it is. This is one of the ego's best traps to smother sexuality, relationships, and success. Everyone has these traps, although they are always well hidden.

Transference is our attempt to deal with this unfinished business so that we can finally heal and lay the family problems to rest. What it does to our relationships, however, is kill romantic and sexual feelings for our partners as we transfer feelings and attitudes toward our parents and siblings on them. This is a difficult step, and requires commitment and joining to see us through it. It helps to become aware of the things that we might be burying, in order to bring them to light and then lay them to rest. Awareness and commitment, even when we least feel like it, paradoxically brings us through this step quickly and easily.

The Competition Step

At this stage we use competition as a delaying tactic, in an attempt to protect ourselves from our fear. Competition stems from broken or inadequate bonding within our families. In our relationships it leads to power struggles and then deadness, as we withdraw ourselves to avoid defeat. Competition is another hidden issue in the dead zone. We attempt to prove that we are the best, we are right, and we are important. This step marks the point at which we need to let this go. We realize that our partners' and our interests are the same, and that neither of us has to sacrifice or lose in a relationship. We must transcend our competitive thoughts to join with our partners, which encourages an honest, balanced relationship in which we both blossom.

The Fear of the Next Step

This step is defined by our fear of moving forward. We want to know what the step is before we will move forward and we delay ourselves endlessly by trying to find out. Our fear might be based on losing our sense of control, giving up too much or taking a risk that might not work out. We often fear intimacy because we are afraid of what might happen when we give all of ourselves in a relationship. There is a certain comfort in knowing where we stand, even if we are unhappy in that place. It takes great courage, trust, and confidence to take the next step, but when it is rewarded, through joining with our partners, we will experience another short romance period and a burst of confidence. We move forward by joining with our partners at any stage of our relationships, which creates a new level of intimacy. This is the point at which we realize that the fear of the next step has been the underlying issue in all the steps of power struggles and the dead zone. Finally our willingness and courage are rewarded and our flush of success carries over to all aspects of our lives which we can greet with new confidence.

The Rock and Swamp Step

On the surface this step seems to resemble the independent–dependent step of the power struggle stage, but there are several fundamental differences. We are playing roles here, too, but they are based around different kinds of feelings. We feel deadness rather than pain at this step, and there is no real question of balancing the needs of each partner by playing opposite roles. Here, each partner feels that he or she is better, and that our way and our needs are more deserving than the other, and there is a certain self-righteousness involved.

Let's define the roles. Rock figures are heroic types who normally as children felt they had to give up their lives in sacrifice for their families, and they feel that they must do the same in their present relationships. They are the "designated givers" of the relationship, and are typically romantic and generous. The feelings and needs of the rock are typically underplayed and suppressed, and their soft bellies are always protected from anything that might expose them.

Swamp figures are incredibly needy. They are likely to have felt unloved as children, and these feelings have carried on into adulthood. They need intimacy and constant confirmation of their specialness and importance. Swamps need to be loved intensely and continuously, and, despite the best efforts of the rocks, they are typically unsatisfied by what they get. On the other hand, swamps are much more in touch with their feelings and can educate the rocks about them if they don't become emotionally indulgent. This will heal the rock's dissociation.

The scenario is this: the rocks bring everything their resources allow to the relationship, but it is never enough. As the swamps become more hysterical, the rocks pull away and become more stoical. Rocks feel overwhelmed by the needs of swamps, and feel that if they venture into their territory they would literally be swallowed. Ultimately swamps behave the way they do to hide a deep neediness inside. They feel unworthy and unlovable, and so demand more and more to try to right the imbalance they feel inside. Rocks behave the way they do because of guilt, but they balance their feelings by overcompensating—becoming frenzied givers who, in the end, can't give enough and just give up.

The answer is for rocks to give themselves to the relationship wholeheartedly. This usually begins with an apology. When a rock apologizes for how the swamp is feeling, the swamp feels recognized and loved. He or she feels that he or she has been heard, and that the giver is not just giving out of habit or because it is expected, but because he or she really cares. In return, a swamp needs to give, instead of expecting, taking, and complaining. Giving gifts, arranging special dinners, doing things the "rock's" way for a change, are just some of the ways that this can be achieved. Rocks do not expect to receive anything in return for their giving, so when it occurs, they are always touched deep inside. A new level of intimacy and understanding is reached, and with humor, joining, integration, and commitment, we can heal the problems that lie beneath our behaviors, and use this step to join with our partners to move forward together.

The Sick and Self-Abuse Step

This is the last step of the dead zone, but its symptoms may have begun to appear from the beginning of the relationship. In this scenario, both partners are calling out and even competing for love in completely different ways.

The sick partner may have been ill on and off since the beginning of the relationship, and they use their ill health as an appeal for love, attention, and the need to be taken care of. Being ill becomes part of their identity, and they are frightened to move on from this step because they are fearful of giving up such a big part of themselves. It's possible that for most of their lives they were given the attention they craved by being unwell. They are not normally willing to take the risk that they will be loved and taken care of if they are seen to be fit and well.

Self-abusers don't take care of themselves, but they hope, underneath their devil-may-care attitude, that someone will care for them, or make them care for themselves. Self-abusers are normally too busy, work too hard, eat too much, drink too much, play too hard, and become injured. They choose not to take care of themselves as a kind of test to see if they can find someone who cares for them more than they do themselves. If someone loves them enough to stand up to them—although they might resist every step of the way—they will feel worthy and valued, and able to care for themselves.

Both behaviors hide patterns of fear, the need for outside approval, and self-hatred. Underneath it all, we believe we deserve to be punished, or we are setting out to wreak revenge on someone who has not given us the love and care that we deserve. By choosing to be ill, or to work ourselves to the point of oblivion, we are sending out a message that reads: "You'll be sorry when you see the state I'm in now." Both of these behaviors are an attempt to accomplish our misguided strategy, which is to attract love and attention. They don't work, and they never bring us happiness.

Healing can be achieved by integrating these opposite styles, and through joining, communication, forgiveness, self-understanding, and commitment, we can work through the pain and fear to find everything we ever wanted in our relationships.

THE PARTNERSHIP STAGE

This is a stage of rest, peace, and reward, and when we reach it, we will likely feel a sense of relief and a deep-rooted feeling of comfort and security in our relationships. We are working together and sharing with our partners, and those partnerships have become a way of life. There are always issues in relationships, and they will continue in this stage, but we see ourselves as a team now, and we have recovered enough of our hearts in order to share them as one.

Feelings of romance are common to this stage, and we may feel almost as much as we did in the first stage of our relationship. However, two challenges present themselves here. The first is the idea, or even temptation, that it might be time to begin again in another relationship, because of the feeling that we have completed our mission with this one. The second more likely issue that may rear its head is the possibility that deep fractures (deep-rooted feelings and issues that have been repressed and broken away in ourselves) may emerge, as we bask in the warmth of success. It's important to remember that this is all part of the healing that will bring us to the next stage of relationships, and that what appear to be setbacks are, in fact, opportunities for further healing. We are moving forward when we face issues in our relationships, and they are a healthy sign that the relationship is progressing.

Don't be surprised to find yourself facing power struggle and dead zone issues in this stage. With each succeeding breakthrough into a new stage, we always revisit the steps of the lower levels to review the lessons we learned from a higher perspective.

At this stage, we must have faith in our relationships, for there is a great deal more that we can contribute and heal in order to move onwards and upwards. When huge and even primordial fractures arise, we can heal ourselves to such a degree that our lives and relationships are dramatically changed. Both partners are able to move up to the next stage, and the bridge to our partner is stronger than ever before.

THE LEADERSHIP STAGE

In the leadership stage, we move on from partnership to a point where we encourage one another in leadership. The day-to-day struggles have been eliminated, and we feel a more powerful sense of peace and confidence in our relationships and in ourselves. This is a place of fun, flow, and co-creativity—a step beyond partnership into a transformational, inspirational, and intimate time of our lives. We are able to reach out beyond our relationships to help others, spreading our flow of positive energy to the world around us. Not surprisingly, however, this deep-rooted happiness brings up deep-rooted fractures, and it is only when we can reach these depths—at this stage of our relationships—that they can present themselves for healing.

These fractures are "soul fractures," which bring us back to the most chronic patterns of childhood, because these childhood patterns represent the chronic soul problems that we have been "given" to address in our lifetimes. Whether or not you believe in karma, or in the passage of the soul, you will find that buried issues relating to past events, or events that we cannot even remember in our conscious minds, do reveal themselves here.

To heal these deep patterns, we need commitment and grace. We have found within ourselves a certain core of spiritual peace, and that now makes up a fundamental part of our relationships both with others and ourselves. That spirituality, whether we call it God, heaven, or another name, is now an equal partner in our relationships, and we can call upon the grace of this spirituality to help us through this stage to reach true wholeheartedness.

In the leadership stage we are more open to using intuition and grace, and we have the faith, self-belief, awareness, and confidence necessary to tackle even the most difficult, and deep-rooted issues that arise. Where we become stuck, or when we experience situations or traumas that seem insurmountable, we are more equipped to deal with them and we have the additional benefit of being able to call upon our spiritual center, our God, or whatever we believe in, to ask for a miracle.

We talk about miracles later in the book, and while it may seem a far-fetched idea at this stage, there is no question that we can be the recipients of some divine intervention if we ask for it. We focus outwards more at this stage, because of our new inner peace, and we are responding to and helping others to the same extent that we are letting ourselves respond to and be helped by our God, or our own spiritual peace. When we allow ourselves to work through the problems that crop up at this stage, we can, with our partners, enter into the next step to become a visionary—a star, a genius, and a true artist. Here we will find total spiritual peace that will emanate through our partnerships and touch the lives of everyone around us.

There are a number of other stages in relationships that go beyond the scope of this book. In order, they include the stages of vision and mastery, and the steps in mastery of mastery, tantra, and union.

WHOLEHEARTEDNESS
AND HEARTBREAK

What is wholeheartedness? It is the giving of ourselves totally, withholding nothing. This book shows us how to heal in order to regain our wholeheartedness. It is based on many principles, which define the roles we play, the traps we fall into, the stages of life and love that we are in, the principles of healing, and our level of true happiness. When we reach beyond ourselves to join with others and to give effortlessly and wholeheartedly, we become different and fuller. We find a deep happiness within ourselves. That is the meaning of wholeheartedness. Giving ourselves fully is one of the easiest ways to move through obstacles in our lives and to succeed. To give ourselves wholeheartedly opens up creativity and vision, and through that we open doors and see with levels of awareness and understanding that conquers all pain and leads to true success in every area of our lives. We are not tied down by the pain, guilt, and sense of failure that characterize so much of our daily life now. We are able to transcend that and to find a spiritual peace within ourselves that gives us an ability to live our purpose to help others, and to give the gifts of healing and peace. Because of this, most of our problems will fall away as we used them only to hold us back from our purpose and destiny. The ones that remain are critical for learning about our purpose. These principles are based on the sound belief that we are spiritual beings. Whether or not we believe in God, we all have a spiritual energy that is our life force. It is an eternal energy that inhabits and animates us. And as we grow we grow in creativity, love, happiness, and spirit.

At the core of this force is our "giftedness," spiritual peace, and grace, which we have lost touch with in our busy, stressful lives. Heartbreak and daily problems build up layers over that core, making it more and more difficult to reach. And then the ego protects it still further by layering defenses over the top.

The ego is composed of our self-concepts that define and separate us from others. Ego is contentious and judgmental. It has agendas and strategies for success that don't include love or success but winning over others even to the point of being the worst at something. The ego is our identification with outside things, like position, possessions, and beliefs, and we experience fear and anxiety at the possibility of damage or loss. It reaches for the glitter but never for what has true or long-lasting value. In many ways, the ego is the opposite of spirituality. It fights our attempts to reach our spiritual core because the external defines the ego, and that is what we give up when we reach a state of spiritual peace. The tricks played and the traps set by our egos are only some of the barriers that arise on our way to peace, but wholeheartedness provides us with the awareness and the tools with which to redefine and to find ourselves and our spiritual core.

Success can be measured by how much we give of ourselves. When we are wholehearted, we give because it makes

us happy to give ourselves. Wholeheartedness is openheart-
edness and so we receive and enjoy the riches that life and
relationships have to offer. When we totally give ourselves,
we receive completely as well, and we open a door to time-
lessness. It is exactly this stage that we can reach when we are
enlightened. The world cannot hurt us, and we cannot hurt
others. Love and partnership are crucial to this because they
pave the way forward. Wholeheartedness is synonymous with
love, which is the essence of spirit. When we learn how to
love, how to *really* love, we reach a point where our lives, our
partnerships, and the lives of those around us are transformed. With wholeheartedness we can lift ourselves beyond
the pain of heartbreak, relationships, and the minutiae of
daily life to a kind of serene peace, where we are able to fulfill our purpose in life.

All of us are here for a purpose. Many of us achieve and recognize our purpose, and many of us do not. Our level of fulfillment is a good way to measure how much of our purpose
we are actually living. Our true purpose is to share and spread
love in the world. This brings us happiness. When we are not
happy, our purpose is healing ourselves. When we have
achieved our individual purpose, we can share what we have to
offer with the world. We all share a purpose, although it is a
unique calling that each of us has to give individually, and that
is how we can give ourselves in love.

When positive energy exists within us, we pass it on, and it
spreads. This idea can be simply described: consider how we
feel when a stranger smiles at us. We might feel surprised, but
we will always feel pleased and warmed. That is the warmth of
spirit. When it warms us, we pass it on, and it goes on and on.
We have been given a gift. Love does the same thing in an
even more profound way, and it lifts us out of heartbreak, pain,

guilt, anger, despair, and every negative emotion or situation you can think of.

That's what this book is about. It's about the journey from unhappiness and heartbreak to love and—if we persist in our healing—to enlightenment. We are all on a journey through life, and we have gifts we can share to ease each others' suffering along the way. We can accept gifts and they will grow inside us. We share with our partners, and they share with us. We are able to join truly in a way that awakens our true spirituality. This makes us happy and we are successful because we have the infinite ability to be so. We find and hold on to love because we have learned how, and it has become natural to do so. That is the kind of life that we all seek and through wholeheartedness we can achieve it.

RECIPES FOR DISASTER–
THINGS THAT LEAD TO HEARTBREAK

❧

1.
BROKEN RULES, BROKEN HEARTS

We can only suffer a heartbreak if someone has broken one of our major rules. Rules are defenses that are made when we are in pain, and they are used to protect us from future pain. All of our adult heartbreaks come from childhood heartbreaks that are buried underneath rules. As we all know, rules were meant to be broken. So when we create rules we are actually inviting others to break them. On the other hand, principles are what we can use to invite a dialogue of success for all concerned.

When a rule is broken, it brings out the hidden pain of old heartbreaks. Because they were set up in response to different types of heartbreak and pain, our relationship rules can be so contradictory that they are confusing to our partners. In most cases our rules are never stated and the first indications that they even exist occur when we react to them being broken. We mistakenly believe that if our partners loved us, they would be able to read our minds, or at least be attentive to our every signal. We assume that our partners know our rules when we have never made them clear—least of all to ourselves. Our rules along with our buried pain combine to set the stage for heartbreak. Broken rules always seem to transgress our feelings of being special. We feel insulted because our pride has been affronted.

A rule is a defense that is meant to protect us, but it has none of the flexibility of a principle, which is a guiding truth. A defense always ends up bringing about what it attempts to stop, because the "defensive" stance we hold when we have rules begs to be triggered. The pain needs an outlet in order for it to be healed. When the ego is given room to control us, we experience more misery because that is how the ego stays strong and builds itself. On the other hand, our higher mind encourages healing. If there is no healing after a trauma, we typically compound the problem by changing from being dependent with one set of rules, to being independent with a completely new set of rules. In fact, the rules of dependency are still present, but they are now buried and we compensate for them.

When we carry unresolved heartbreaks and their resulting conflicts, we never fully recover the amount of energy or enthusiasm we once had. This can cause us to live in fantasy, to become independent and cynical, or to become more dependent and foolishly idealistic or naïve. We can withdraw from life in such a way that some of our gifts and part of the brightness that we are, never quite comes back.

HEARTBREAK PRINCIPLE

A rule is a defense that invites itself to be broken and it reinforces heartbreak. A rule is an attempt to control. If it succeeds, there is deadness or boredom. If it doesn't succeed, the control leads to a fight or power struggle. A heartbreak is always the result of broken rules.

HEALING PRINCIPLE

Principles are a way of life. They invite dialogue and offer flexibility, which allows us to change and evolve, rather than living the controlled, restricted life that rules dictate.

HEALING SUGGESTION

Choose to change your relationship rules into principles. When you communicate about your rules, you can turn them into principles. Explore the areas where you have fear or old heartbreaks, in order to expose your rules. By talking about the hurt and fear that had you make them, you begin to build bridges to your partner. The sharing invites your partner's awareness, compassion, and partnership which can help to heal this area of pain.

HEALING CHOICE

I commit to living by principles instead of rules. I choose to heal the pain beneath my rules by asking for grace to help me to change them into principles, so I do not block my success. I choose to communicate, rather than use the demands and defensiveness of rules.

HEALING EXERCISE

Make a list of the rules that you have for relationships, love, and sex, for both you and your partner. Your list will be much longer than the space provided, but this is a start. If you are upset by something, it means that a rule was broken, and this leads to heartbreak. Examples might be:

For yourself

    I must be cheerful

    I must not go too deep

    I must not show anger

For your partner

    You must be on time

    You must be faithful

    You must be considerate

Rules for Relationships

For yourself

_____

_____

_____

For your partner

_____

_____

_____

Rules for Love

For yourself

_____

_____

_____

For your partner

_____

_____

_____

Rules for Sex

For yourself

_____

_____

_____

For your partner

_____

_____

_____

You may find hundreds of these rules, many of them contradictory, and all of them hiding old pain. For instance, you may have a rule to be heroic. As a rule and a role, the hero is supposed to be and act heroic. It may be compensation for feelings of hurt, rejection, guilt, or unworthiness. Compensations prevent you from receiving the rewards when you give. A heroic rule, which is reactive, unaware, and clumsy, may even have you trying to be "heroic" when it is not called for. Any rule is a block to giving and receiving, to being flexible and responsive. Recognizing our rules is another route to healing our fractures and, ultimately to regaining our wholeheartedness.

2.

MANIPULATION—THE PATH TO HEARTBREAK

Manipulation is a defensive position that comes from old heartbreaks and stems from our feelings of unworthiness. We do not feel worthy of receiving, so we feel that we have to be calculating in an attempt to have our needs met. We may become sneaky and even use others if it helps us toward our goal.

But manipulation is often so clumsy that it leaves our "victims" feeling bad, used, or taken advantage of, and made into "objects." They feel that they have lost and we have won. This is a poor strategy to use on lovers, friends, family, and business partners, because it leads to fights over needs and constant competition. It can lead to revenge and withdrawal as it escalates back and forth, until there is heartbreak and war. Manipulation is offensive to those around us—it belittles them, insults their intelligence, and puts them in the position of being a perpetual loser. Imagine the havoc this creates in a sexual relationship! When we manipulate to get sex, our partners feel railroaded into complying. If this approach continues, sex is not going to be a very attractive proposition.

The main problem with manipulation is the fact that whatever we get, we get through trickery and not through any sense of personal value or reward. We may have won, but we are all too aware that we have used trickery to get there. Manipulation lowers our self-worth the more we employ it. But until we can heal our heartbreak, we will continue to employ it because we can't see another way of meeting the great hunger of our needs. The path of manipulation effectively leads to heartbreaks, because those involved either want to push us away or stop giving to us. Manipulation leads to resentment. We may win the battle, but we will lose the war.

HEARTBREAK PRINCIPLE

Manipulation is a behavior that alienates people. The more we employ it, the more we hurt others and ourselves. It comes from old heartbreak and, if unresolved, leads to more heartbreak.

HEALING PRINCIPLE

Having the courage to communicate about what we want, and letting go of our need to have it, sets up a situation where we are more likely to succeed, both in the long and short term.

HEALING SUGGESTION

As you commit to allowing everyone to win in every situation, you prevent manipulation, power struggles, and competition.

HEALING CHOICE

I commit to treating everyone as an equal partner, rather than turning them into objects to meet my needs.

HEALING EXERCISE

Review some of your heartbreaks and painful situations. Examine them to see if you were manipulating, because you didn't feel worthy. If so, you didn't receive what you tried to take and, through your taking, you alienated those around you.

Heartbreak or painful situation

_____

_____

_____

What was I trying to get?

_____

_____

_____

_____   _____

_____   _____

Now ask yourself if you received what you were trying to get—it's another way
to tell if you were manipulating because if the other people involved were alienated from you, they recognized your manipulation and moved away. Be willing to forgive yourself and all others involved in those situations.

===

3.
GIVING TO GET

We feel hurt when we are trying to take or get something. We
often mask our taking under the guise of giving. This is not
true giving, but a place where we are seeking to put others in
our debt, so they will "owe us." This usually causes the other
person to resist our giving, or to receive what we are giving,
while rejecting or shying away from what we want to take in
return. At one level, sacrifice is an attempt to force others to
be loyal to us, so that they feel obliged to give back to us, or to
sacrifice themselves for us when we want or need it. Sacrifice
makes others feel they have to do something for us because we
have done something for them. It is love by contract, which is
not true love.

When we demand reciprocity, we are not really giving, but
giving to take. This sets up role-playing and can lead to deadness if it carries on for very long. In many cases, however, it
doesn't even get that far before we suffer a heartbreak. We
may have only one little area where we need caring, and we
feel outraged when our small demands are not met, or when
our partners appear to be unavailable or uninterested—clearly

not keeping their side of the bargain. This obviously leads to hurt feelings, rejection, and, sometimes, depression. If we feel hurt, we need to examine the reasons why. In almost every case we find that no matter how well we covered our tracks, the real reason why we were giving was to get something in return.

We are irresistible when we give without wanting or needing a certain response or result in return. When we are giving ourselves fully without expectation, we become irresistible because it doesn't matter how the other person responds. We feel full just because we are giving.

When we are taking, they soon "need their space." When we are trying to take, we are very resistible and very "rejectable."

Our feelings of hurt show us where we have surreptitiously been trying to take. When we learn to give rather than take we will be successful and we will find love waiting for us. In any situation where we are trying to take, we will find only defeat and heartbreak. If we don't recognize that our pain indicates the lessons we need to learn, and then use that as an opportunity to heal, we will continue getting hurt, blaming others, and backing away from life. Needless to say, everyone loses when that occurs.

We cannot be rejected unless we are trying to take something. If we only want to give, we can't be pushed away. If we only want to give, we become irresistible. If we only want to give, their response doesn't matter or, at least, it doesn't disappoint us. When we need people to respond in a certain way, our giving is a form of taking; therefore, we create our own resistance and others will act it out. When we want something, people want to pull away from us.

The acid test for whether our giving is true giving or a form of taking is the following: *If we feel good and receive in what we give, just by the art of our giving, it is true giving. If we somehow feel hurt, or rejected, we are trying to take.*

HEARTBREAK PRINCIPLE

We can only be hurt when we are trying to take, and we will suffer heartbreak because of it.

HEALING PRINCIPLE

Giving opens the door to receiving, and it is irresistible to those to whom we are giving.

HEALING SUGGESTION

If you feel hurt, examine where you have been trying to take. As you let go of this taking, you will become attractive once again. If you have become dependent, your attitude has become one of taking and, as a result, your partner will need his or her space. When you notice your partner moving away from you, use it as a signal that you are trying to take. Recognize that the energy of taking pushes your partner away. Let go of these attachments if you want your partner to move toward you again. As soon as you do, they will automatically come toward you. If your partner does not join you, you haven't let go, in spite of what you have told yourself. This principle is one of the key principles for success in relationships. As Confucius said, "The smart horse moves at the shadow of the whip."

HEALING CHOICE

I choose to be aware and to honor my partner's signals. If they move away from me, I will let go of my dependence so that they will have the opportunity to move closer. I choose to give freely and generously.

HEALING EXERCISE

Review your life for times when you felt hurt in a relationship. Then, examine situations in your relationship when you felt your partner move away from you.

Hurt in relationship	What I was trying to take
1. _____	_____
2. _____	_____
3. _____	_____

When my partner moved away	What I was trying to take
1. _____	_____
2. _____	_____
3. _____	_____

Choose to learn this lesson and let go of anything that is left over from these incidents.

4.

CONTROL—IF YOU LOVE ME, YOU WILL DO IT MY WAY

If you love me you will do it my way! These are dangerous words that stem from a dangerous attitude. It is only a matter of time before we will end up suffering a heartbreak by using—or even thinking—these words. They are a form of emotional manipulation and blackmail that suggest we will do anything to get our needs met. The number one mistake that we make in relationships is to think that our partners have been put on earth to take care of our needs—our way. We will not feel hurt, rejected, or heartbroken in this situation unless somebody is refusing to play by the script that we wrote for them, or unless someone refuses to do what we had planned for them. Of course, many times, we never even gave them the script or let them know what they would need to do to keep us happy. We mistakenly think that if they really loved us, they would be able to read our minds, and we shouldn't have to tell them what we want or need. This is a recipe for disaster.

Control is a way of trying to get others to do it our way. When we control others, we attempt to keep ourselves and others from getting hurt. We use coercive methods to get our way and to keep us and our relationships secure. It is a covert form of bullying, although it is not as alienating as manipulation. Our attempts to get others to do it our way typically backfires, because control breeds resentment and triggers power struggles. Control is a mistaken form of dealing with our fear. It is the opposite of trust and confidence and when we control we close the doors to communication, which is a fundamental feature of any good, happy relationship. The extent to which we control is the extent to which we still have heartbreaks buried inside us. Control is compensation that attempts to prevent future heartbreak. Unfortunately, it typically brings heartbreak by bringing a power struggle. In a relationship where control succeeds in keeping heartbreak from occurring right away, it brings boredom. When this occurs, we either settle for the situation or back away from the relationship, because we are bored. Change may occur in our relationship as a result of control, but it will be counterfeit. We have not changed the dynamic within ourselves or the relationship. When we settle for the situation, we don't bring about the underlying transformation to have our relationship reach new levels of trust and healing, and both of us feel as if we've lost.

When we back away from a relationship, it can bring up the old heartbreaks unless we stay so independent that we are not emotionally involved. If, however, we are not emotionally involved, we limit the meaning and possibility of our relationship.

Many people are so sensitive to any type of manipulation and control that when someone tries to make us do things their way, we react independently just to show we won't be ruled. Unfortunately, it is this independent behavior—which comes from heartbreaks—that leads to further heartbreaks.

HEARTBREAK PRINCIPLE

Using our power, independence, or emotional blackmail to control others is self-defeating and only leads to power struggles.

HEALING PRINCIPLE

With a healing attitude, every painful situation and our ensuing emotional reaction to it can be used as an opportunity to realize a new level of bonding. Returning to the place where the separation occurred and re-establishing the lost connection heals the problem.

HEALING SUGGESTION

Whenever someone around you is emotionally reacting, recognize that it is a call for help. There is a wounded child within them that is begging for love, in spite of their behavior. Whenever your own pain comes up, communicate about it in a mature fashion to enlist your partner's support, rather than bullying them or using your emotions as a weapon.

HEALING CHOICE

I will ask Heaven's help in any situation where I am, or others around me are, in pain. I commit to being open to the inspiration that comes to me.

HEALING EXERCISE

Think of a time that you over-reacted to a situation. What were you feeling? What old pattern in your life did it reflect? What self-concepts were you supporting? Who were you trying to control? What did you want from them? What purpose do these negative self-concepts hold for you? What excuse do they give you? What situation was probably at the root of this?

Imagine yourself back in the original situation that came to your mind. Re-establish the bonding in that scene by imagining lines of light connecting you with that person or persons. See the lines of light reconnecting your center with theirs. Now, review the scene as it unfolds with bonding, while you exchange the gifts you have to offer. Each time we re-establish bonding we reclaim a part of our heart that was broken and move toward a healed and completely giving heart.

5.

EMOTIONAL BLACKMAIL

It is apparent that some emotions can be used as a form of attack. Anger, for instance, is quite obviously an attack. We have all felt pressured when somebody tried to exert their control over us by laying guilt trips. Unfortunately, when we use guilt as a means to control others, we may win a number of battles, but we will eventually lose the war. All forms of emotional blackmail involve using negative emotions and the guilt they inspire to try to control someone so that they will do things our way, or to punish them when they don't. But emotional blackmail and control build resentment, which then works against us. Emotional blackmail includes all forms of pouting and tantrums as a way to get what we want.

Depression, hurt, rejection, over-sensitivity, heartbreak, or suffering of any kind can be used as weapons. When we are suffering, we often don't realize that we are using these as weapons or as forms of control. And if our emotions don't work to influence significant others to do things our way, we use our heartbreaks as a form of revenge. We bleed all over their doorsteps announcing to the world, "Look at what this terrible person has done to me! Look what they have done to me!" Think of someone who is depressed, suffering, or dragging their long face day after day. This long face says, "I am this way because of what you have done or failed to do."

Heartbreaks and failures in our adult lives send a message to the world that we have been failed by our partners when we needed them most, and, ultimately by our parents. We blame our parents for our present because we believe they are ultimately responsible for our well-being.

Yet, underneath all forms of emotional control, the primordial call for love and help is still there. If we respond to this call for help, we will be helped when we need it in return. If we respond angrily to someone's manipulation, control, or blackmail, it is only because we do the same thing ourselves. As we choose to respond to another's call for help, we are released from our hidden guilt about employing emotional blackmail for our own needs.

HEARTBREAK PRINCIPLE

When we attempt to control others through our emotions, we place our needs ahead of theirs and of our relationship. This form of control can quickly turn from blackmail into emotional abuse. We do this at the cost of our relationship. As our partners resist this behavior, a power struggle can turn into another heartbreak.

HEALING PRINCIPLE

If we express our negative emotions in a mature way with the intention of healing, they cannot become weapons used to bring unhappy outcomes for ourselves and others.

HEALING SUGGESTION

As you become aware of your own emotional indulgence and blackmail, talk about it and apologize to your partner for the fear or pain that has caused you to act in such a way. Take responsibility for your feelings by realizing that they stem from the past. Without blaming, share the pain that you are going through with those around you so that you will enlist your partner's help. This allows you to heal your pain, layer by layer, through communication.

HEALING CHOICE

I choose to be aware of how I use my negative emotions and to be neither indulgent nor abusive with them. I choose, instead, to use them as an opportunity for healing.

HEALING EXERCISE

Think of three situations where you were using your emotions as a form of attack. Forgive others and yourself. Write or call them to apologize for your immaturity. Ask for their forgiveness. You may find this experience so satisfying and helpful that you may want to do it with many more people. Caution: do not try to call someone who has broken up with you. Write to them instead. Be aware that calling will always lower your "stock" with this person and writing, unless done with complete integrity, can just be used as another ploy to hold on to them. If you do it with any kind of holding on, even energetically, you will defeat yourself and extend your suffering.

6.

THE WIN-LOSE ATTITUDE

The win–lose attitude is completely destructive to relationships. In this situation our needs come first, which puts our partner in a losing position. Unfortunately, this is the level at which we always begin first relationships—underneath the first blush of love, we definitely want things our way. If we see that this attitude cannot succeed, we will begin to learn the way out of win–lose situations and into partnership. In a win–lose scenario, winning becomes the most important thing for us in the relationship, for this is the way we get our needs met. We want our way to be the only or the most important way. We want our thinking, our plans, and our views to determine the relationship. We see the world according to our needs, and this is how we assess what is right and wrong. We are not above manipulating or seducing to get our way but, when we have succeeded, our partners feel as if they have lost. They will only allow this to happen so many times before they want to quit the relationship, because they feel as if they've been diminished or belittled.

In this stage, for example, sex, romance, or getting presents can become a way of proving to ourselves that we are loved. But for our partners these demands can lead to an overwhelming sense of defeat. As our partners begin pulling away, a power struggle ensues. If we don't fight it out, boredom and deadness can set in as a result of both parties pulling away in order to avoid defeat. The win–lose attitude means we're going to have to lose at least half of the time to keep the game going. It may not be right away—or even in the same relationship—but we will have to pay the piper for dancing to the tune of win–lose. This attitude, which is based on scarcity and fear, is the belief that someone has to lose for us to be able to win. It leads to competition and power struggles that distract us from the way forward. Competition and power struggles are actually forms of delaying the inevitable, and they are favored by the ego in order to cause us to spend time in the loser category, thus reinforcing the "fight to win" belief.

When we take an attitude of mutuality and cooperation, we can find a way for both of us to win. Compromise, where both parties feel like they have lost, is not the answer. We have to communicate in order to find a mutual path on which we are both equally happy to continue. When we do find that path there will be success for each of us, as well as for our relationship. It is crucial to change our attitude to win–win if we want to live without heartbreak.

HEARTBREAK PRINCIPLE

With a win-lose attitude, it is only a matter of time before our attitudes lead us into heartbreak and defeat.

HEALING PRINCIPLE

It is crucial to change our win-lose attitude, and to heal any vestige left over from heartbroken parts that foster a win-lose attitude.

HEALING SUGGESTION

Examine your life for evidence of the win-lose attitude. It may be in just one area of your life; it may pervade your way of dealing with the world; or there may only be a few remnants left over. You can find this in any area where you have felt that you have "got one over on someone," or when you experience the glee of having beaten someone. On the other hand, you may find evidence of this pattern by someone acting this way toward you. When you have been in a losing situation it reflects a hidden or repressed self within that still preys on others. It is important to forgive the person who did this, as well as yourself, and integrate the victimizer-victim with you.

HEALING CHOICE

I commit to change every bit of the win-lose attitude in my life into a win-win attitude.

HEALING EXERCISE

Examine your heartbreaks for the win-lose attitude that was present, and determine how you were playing win-lose. Choose three situations where you felt like you were taken advantage of so that you can discover the hidden self that you have within that preys on others.

Heartbreaks I have had   **How I was playing win-lose**

1. _____   _____

2. _____   _____

3. _____   _____

Situations where I was taken advantage of **Hidden selves**

1. _____   _____

2. _____   _____

3. _____   _____

Now, choose to forgive yourself and everyone involved in all of the situations. Invite any hidden self that you brought up to your awareness, for a respite from all the hiding. Any self within us wants to be known and recognized. Ask this self what its purpose is. Recognize that you may have to ask a few times to find its root purpose. For example, if the hidden self says its purpose is to kill you, then ask what the purpose of that is. You will always get down to its root purpose. It might be something like, "To take you out of pain" or "To finally bring you peace." Once you get to the deepest root, you can begin to address the bad strategy that this self has been using.

7.

BETRAYAL

Betrayal is one of the worst and deepest dynamics of heartbreak and it pervades all human relationships. The root of betrayal is almost always in childhood. We believe that we have betrayed a parent, a sibling, or a friend and suffer guilt. Guilt and betrayal go hand in hand, so we set up betrayals for ourselves in our later relationships in order to pay off our guilt. This, however, just reinforces the treachery, and it can cause some nasty heartbreaks in our relationships, our careers and our families. Guilt for what we perceived to be a betrayal earlier in our lives is almost always the cause of later heartbreak. We can pinpoint this situation in our own lives if we have been the victim of a series of betrayals by friends, families, or lovers.

Like many other things, we betray others when we make our own needs paramount. We have set up situations where we rely only on ourselves and focus only on our plans to get our needs met—at whatever cost. We are betrayed because we set up a situation in order to absolve our guilt. All betrayal is indicative of self-betrayal or of an attempt to defeat ourselves. No one could ever succeed in betraying us unless we are betraying ourselves or feeling badly about betraying others.

It is crucial, in every instance, to behave in a way that does not lead to the betrayal of others. If we do succeed in betraying someone, we will enter a cycle of attempting to pay for it through sacrifice or with deadness and heartbreak. We may also betray others in the mistaken belief that we are somehow "bad" or unworthy. Most important, perhaps, our egos will tempt us to betray others because it prevents both us and our relationships from moving forward in love and happiness. At a fundamental level, we may begin to betray others because we feel betrayed by God. We may feel guilty about not "living our purpose," or giving the gifts we have come to give in our lives, and we feel that we have betrayed God. We then go on to set up situations in which we ourselves are betrayed in order to make ourselves feel better about not fulfilling our promise. When we are betrayed, we feel betrayed by God and cannot see that it was often us who started the cycle of betrayal and guilt in the first place.

Rather than taking from others or a situation in order to get our needs met, we can ask our higher mind to show us a way for everyone to win. We can ask for a miracle to allow everyone to succeed. Betrayal is entirely based on misunderstanding and, therefore, it can be healed by becoming aware of why we believed we were betrayed in the past and seeing how we have set up a similar, repeating pattern in our own lives.

HEARTBREAK PRINCIPLE

Betrayal, which is one of the major causes of heartbreak, stems from our original betrayal–guilt pattern. Unless our family is truly bonded, there will be major elements of betrayal, treachery, and heartbreak.

HEALING PRINCIPLE

A temptation is the last-ditch attempt of the ego to stop a major gift or opportunity. To avoid falling for the temptation to betray others, we can ask for the help of our higher mind. It will show us the way through and into a much higher level of love, partnership, and success, which the temptation hides.

HEALING SUGGESTION

Your integrity allows you to receive. Betrayal blocks receiving because of the guilt. At the deepest level of the mind you feel guilty, because you believe that you have betrayed God by not fulfilling your purpose or giving your gifts. As a result of your attempted betrayal, the ego then has you believe that God is your enemy and is out to punish you. This, of course, is only your projection of your vengeful self. It's crucial to understand that God cannot actually betray or even be betrayed. This deepest relationship that you have with God sets the pattern for your betrayal pattern with yourself, your family, and your relationships.

HEALING CHOICE

I commit to healing all betrayal patterns in my life by forgiving God, the world, my family, my relationships—both past and present—and, most important, myself.

HEALING EXERCISE

Complete the following exercises to discover your betrayal-guilt pattern:

My heartbreak involved	The betrayal	Guilt I was paying off
1. _____	_____	_____
2. _____	_____	_____
3. _____	_____	_____

People I betrayed	Guilt I felt	How I punished myself
1. _____	_____	_____
2. _____	_____	_____
3. _____	_____	_____

Now, forgive everyone involved in all of those situations.

8.

COMPETITION

Competition is one of the root dynamics of any problem and it is the essence of our ego; it makes us feel that we need to have more than anyone else does in a certain area, even if it is in a negative way. It encourages us to use comparison to prove we are the best, but comparison always leads to pain. Competition is based on a belief in scarcity, and both scarcity and competition are the result of broken bonding, fear, and separation. Once bonding has been lost, we take on an attitude of "every man for himself."

An unhealthy sense of competition is based on the mistaken belief that winning equals success. We think that if we win, by proving our superiority, we also naturally succeed. In all the years that I've worked around the world, I've only met one person who had a bonded family while growing up. This would then mean that, for the most part, all of us have competition to heal. Competition is the root of power struggles, the Oedipus conspiracy, and the deadness that can occur in relationships. Naturally then, if unchecked, competition leads to fights, especially where we are trying to prove that we are the best. I have seen elderly couples who have been together for decades have the most ridiculous fights, because they are still competing. Deadness occurs when we move away or withdraw from our partners so that we cannot be defeated and used.

Competition, like power struggles, hides fear of the next step. We avoid this step to success and our fear of it by acting as if winning over someone is success.

Sometimes we can be so successful that we are unaware of our competitiveness. Our conscious belief is that we are the best. Where there is a problem in a relationship that contains a power struggle or deadness, there is always a dynamic of competition. This is also one of the key factors when one partner seems to fail another. Even when we are victimized by our partner's actions, we are still proving that we are morally or spiritually the better person.

Competition is based on authority conflict, fear, and separation, and these core dynamics are three of the basic elements, along with competition, that generate the ego. It goes back to some of the most hidden elements of our relationship with God, where we are competing to knock Him off His throne and take over. This represents the deepest, most hidden layers of the unconscious mind that I have ever come across, and it is the root of our blaming God for the conditions of the world. Since He's doing such a bad job of everything, doesn't it prove that we should take away his God license and be in charge ourself? I have found that these issues are buried in the deepest layers of the unconscious mind, because the ego set them up as the last, most powerful defenses against us going into Oneness.

HEARTBREAK PRINCIPLE

Competition for needs generates heartbreak. The heartbreak is a way of proving that we're the best by having won, or, if we seem to be at the losing end, proving that we are the morally superior person.

HEALING PRINCIPLE

The willingness to bond in partnerships allows us both to win.

HEALING SUGGESTION

Examine your life for areas of competition. Pay particular attention to places where you feel you're the very best and would never compete, which is actually engaging in hidden competition. If someone around you is failing there is evidence of this.

HEALING CHOICE

I commit to heal all of my competition and to turn it into partnership.

HEALING EXERCISE

Examine the times when you were heartbroken to see who you were competing with, what it was about, and what you were proving.

Heartbreaks	Who was I competing with?	What was I competing about?	What was I proving?
1.	_____	_____	_____
2.	_____	_____	_____
3.	_____	_____	_____
4.	_____	_____	_____
5.	_____	_____	_____

Now, examine the evidence of competition in your family as you were growing up. How did this affect your relationships? Examine your key relationships for evidence of competition. This may show up as competitive behavior in either one or both of the partners. Remember to look for evidence of your competitiveness at work, because this attitude knows no boundaries, and you will bring this into your key relationships and family. Once you see the evidence, make new choices about what you want in relationships, because competition destroys partnership. Ask yourself, "If I were to know, how old was I when the competition began in my family as I was growing up?" Return to that age within, and ask your higher mind to return everyone at that time to their center. Ask to be carried to a deeper center, if necessary, to bring everyone peace. Now, see the lines of light extending out from the light within you and connecting with the light within everyone in your family. Give your whole family the gift that would heal this problem. See the gift and its color passing up the family tree to your ancestors on both your mother's and father's sides of the family.

9.

SPECIALNESS

Specialness prevents joining and relating in relationships. Because relationships are filled with so much healing power, the ego attempts to make something up to defeat its powerful gifts. The ego sets up specialness to try to divert us from joining. It is a form of indulgence that takes, rather than gives, shares, or receives. The ego uses our relationship to build a shrine to itself. It aggrandizes us at the expense of our partner because, if we're the most special, they are clearly not. Our partners feel undervalued and less important which undermines the relationship. It is designed to ensure that our needs are met, that we receive our "due" admiration and love from our partners, and that we are kept separate, or "one step above" them. No matter what form the "specialness" takes, it is an attempt to take from our partners, while maintaining a degree of separation that protects our egos. Relationships should be a path to peace and happiness. Specialness is a way of making the relationship all about ourselves, rather than about both of us, with our own needs becoming more important than the relationships or our partners.

There can be no relationship problem without some degree of specialness, so we must all work through it if we are to succeed. A heartbreak occurs because of an insult to our specialness—when we felt we weren't treated specially enough. All specialness demands attention, and every complaint, at some level, is a complaint about our specialness not being fed.

HEARTBREAK PRINCIPLE

All hurt and heartbreak comes from our wounded sense of specialness.

HEALING PRINCIPLE

By forgiving our own and our partners' specialness, and trusting the unfolding process, we come into partnership in our relationships. When we are angry at our partners' specialness, it is because we still feel that particular specialness in ourselves.

HEALING SUGGESTION

Examine your life for grievances. Notice how they are places where you haven't been treated specially. Be willing to let go of this specialness for success in your relationships.

HEALING CHOICE

I commit to healing my specialness, because I would rather have love and my partner in all of their beauty.

HEALING EXERCISE

Examine your heartbreaks for points in which your specialness wasn't honored, as well as how your heartbreak was a reaction to that insult. Then list all the places that bother you about your present, or past, partner's specialness.

Heartbreaks	Your thwarted specialness	Your reaction
1. _____	_____	_____
2. _____	_____	_____
3. _____	_____	_____
4. _____	_____	_____
5. _____	_____	_____

Partner's	Grievance with	Where this specialness/ partner's specialness shows up for me
1. _____	_____	_____
2. _____	_____	_____
3. _____	_____	_____
4. _____	_____	_____
5. _____	_____	_____

Now commit to wholeheartedness rather than specialness. Specialness will defeat everything you ever truly wanted while wholeheartedness will fulfill your dreams.

━━━━━━━━━━━━━━━━━━━━

10.
TANTRUMS

At one level, many of our heartbreaks are a form of tantrum, because we didn't get things our own way. Through tantrums, we attempt to make others do what we want them to do, which, of course, rarely works. Tantrums can have a deleterious, even devastating effect on our lives. We experience hurt in an obvious way—through tantrums or pouting in order to point out when we are not getting our own way. Yet we continue to pout and stamp our feet in the belief that we will ultimately get our own way when our partners feel guilty enough for how much hurt they have caused us. Every tantrum includes the element of pouting with anger.

A tantrum occurs when we are in such emotional pain that we are blinded and feel "justified" by the emotional and physical abuse we dispense. We feel such a personal sense of torture that we are unaware of the torture we are inflicting on those around us. There is probably no quicker way to lower our stock with those around us than to punish them with our immaturity in a tantrum. When we have a tantrum we are suffering a heartbreak so great that part of ourselves is fractured. When the fracturing or trauma is powerful we may have no idea of what we are doing, and we may have no memory of when it acts out.

For example, I knew a very conservative woman who always spoke her mind whether you wanted to hear it or not. There were times when her sense of self-righteousness became vitriolic. If she was ever confronted about her attack, she had no memory of ever having said or done those things. This is a sign of an old, major heartbreak at work. Although this person was operating at a higher level of maturity and success, there were parts of her operating at a much lower level of awareness. Part of her had never grown up or gotten beyond her heartbreaks. Within her were wounded children trying to get their way, sometimes operating at the emotional maturity level of a two- or three-year-old.

HEARTBREAK PRINCIPLE

A tantrum is a form of emotional explosion that we use to attack others in an attempt to control them to meet our needs. It pushes them away and leads us to heartbreak.

HEALING PRINCIPLE

A commitment to heal our painful emotions, rather than using them to try to get something, is a big step toward maturity and peace.

HEALING SUGGESTION

Examine the patterns of the different tantrums that you have used in your life, such as pouting, anger, and emotional outbursts. Resolve to heal these patterns so that you can maturely communicate your needs.

HEALING CHOICE

I commit to healing all my tantrum patterns so that I might share my love and gifts instead.

HEALING EXERCISE

Choose three of your biggest tantrum patterns. For each one, ask yourself how old the self is that had the tantrum. Imagine taking this child-self and holding it in your arms, loving it until it grows up and melts into you. After each integration, you will feel happy and at peace. If you are not feeling joyful then there is another wounded self from the past that wants recognition. Ask yourself, "If I were to know, how old is this wounded self, and what is it feeling?" Now hold this child-self in your arms, loving it until it reaches your present age and melts into you.

11.
THREATS AND VIOLENCE

When we are in great pain, we feel justified in inflicting pain on those around us. Yet, in spite of our justification, there is no excuse for abusive behavior. When we are abusive we will, at some level, feel guilty about our actions. This can set up a vicious cycle of attack–guilt–attack. Be aware that when a relationship has regressed to threats and violence, it is on its way out. Neither partner, nor the relationship itself, can grow and move forward. Instead, each partner is heading in a self-destructive direction and the relationship is heading toward disintegration. If we do not want this to occur, we must personally take some strong steps to change, whether we are the threatening and abusive party or the one being threatened and abused. Only one of us needs to have the motivation and willingness to save the relationship, because we are all 100 percent responsible for our relationships. In other words, we all have 100 percent of the power necessary to change them.

When we believe that our partners have to meet us halfway, or that they're the ones who have to change first, then our relationships and our families are doomed. If we believe that we have to "win" by making our partners change, we are clearly more interested in the fight, in being right, and in demanding our own way than we are in the truth, in healing our relationships, in taking responsibility, and in being mature. We can step forward in the situation and become leaders.

Whatever we have in our relationships now is exactly what we want. It is also what we think will make us happy. This is not on a conscious level, because we do feel genuine outrage and anger. But we do create problems in a relationship for a reason. Below our level of awareness we set up situations to meet our needs. Every problem has elements of denial and self-deception.

Once we are willing to examine our conflicted wishes, which have never worked to make us happy, we can change. We may be able to get everyone we know to agree with us that we are in the right and that our partner is the problem party, but we are only deceiving ourselves. We are disregarding our hidden agendas, hidden selves, shadows, pay-offs, excuses, and all the other subconscious issues that are always present in any event that is less than happy.

We must now decide what we want. We always have the choices, and we can either choose to heal and rehabilitate ourselves and our partners, or head down a path that will lead to heartbreak. When we choose healing and commit to this path, there is a way that this can happen. First, we must be willing to be wrong, because if we want to be right, we will do everything in our power to ensure that we are. The present situation is a result of both parties trying to be right. We must be willing to commit to the truth, to ask for a miracle, and to give up any judgments we hold, because they only hide our own hidden guilt. We must see our partners' and our own behavior as a call for help and respond to it as such. We must forgive both our partners and ourselves. If we are willing to see the wounded children within when our partners act out and choose to pour love into them, their needs are fulfilled and the wounds are healed. When we love our partners, these wounded children will grow up and mature. As they melt back into or integrate with our partners, the wires that had been cut in their minds and hearts are reconnected. In the same way, if we are beginning to act in an ugly way, it is time to look within ourselves for the wounded children and to love them so that they can mature, grow to our present age, and melt into us. By communicating with our partners about these wounded children, we can enlist their support, which also helps to heal them and our relationships.

It is important to respect ourselves, because if *we* don't, no one will. It is a mistake to let someone abuse us. It increases our guilt and it increases their guilt, which only leads to more bad behavior. If this situation seems to be one where we are being punished, we must also return to the point where we began to believe we needed to be punished so that we can heal the separation at its origin. Our self-punishment is a mistake and it never works to pay off our guilt—it only increases it. There will always be a strategy involved in this dire situation, and, whatever it is, whatever its reason, we can find it, let it go as a mistake, and make a new choice for what we want. We can even ask heaven to give us a new strategy in its place—perhaps the time has come to resign as our own strategist. To go back to the root situation with our intuition and center ourselves, bond with the others in the situation, and give the gift that is needed, creates healing not only for ourselves, but for everyone, which then changes the pattern of our present situation.

Totally committing to our partners is one of the most powerful methods of healing, because it has the paradoxical effect of having them get better, as well as encouraging our relationships to take a step forward. Every time we join our partners—not necessarily agreeing with them, but truly joining with them—we move forward together. Every time we refuse to blame them or hold a grudge about what they seem to be doing against us, we set ourselves and our partners free. We see their behavior as a call for help rather than an attack on us. Every time we forgive, we move forward. If letting go seems difficult, we can choose again and ask for help from God or from somewhere within ourselves to assist us with letting go and also healing the situation.

HEARTBREAK PRINCIPLE

This is a time of crisis when threats and violence occur in a relationship.

HEALING PRINCIPLE

We can choose whether or not we will allow our relationships to disintegrate in this emergency, or we can use this situation as a chance to emerge to a new level, by healing the fractures and mistakes.

HEALING SUGGESTION

Be willing to commit to healing all of your fractures, which allows you to learn all of the lessons it was set up to teach. Choose to forgive yourself and your partner.

HEALING CHOICE

I commit to my partner, myself, and the healing of this situation. I commit to asking for and receiving miracles to change this experience.

HEALING EXERCISE

Do you want to be part of the solution or part of the problem? Do you want to help or condemn? If you condemn, you will be condemning yourself first, and then anyone else you love, because that is the nature of judgment. If you want to help, you will choose to help all the way to the complete healing of this situation.

If you recognize that you are choosing not to help, it is because you are "using" this situation as a conspiracy against yourself. It is preventing you from fulfilling your true purpose and from moving forward in life. In other words, this situation was planned somewhere in your subconscious, and it is unfolding exactly as you thought you wished. If you are unwilling to change, it is because you are just afraid to let go. What are you afraid to let go of? What do you think you will lose? What control are you afraid to lose if this situation is resolved? Why are you afraid to grow? What complaints are you making that keep you unwilling to change?

Complaint	To whom?	About what?
1.		
2.		
3		

You can choose now to stay in this situation as a form of revenge or as a message of complaint to someone. You can also choose to change. Remember the old adage: "He who contemplates revenge had best dig two graves." It's up to you. When you choose to find your way out, you will find a way. Who and what are you seeking to revenge to cause this situation?

Revenge	Against whom?	About what?
1. _____	_____	_____
2. _____	_____	_____
3. _____	_____	_____

What soul-level gift did you bring into this life to redeem your partner? Would you open up your heart and mind and give this gift? What gift does Heaven have for both of you right now to get you past this crisis? Would you see and feel yourself receiving this gift and help your partner also receive Heaven's gift? Every time you think of your partner, give them the gift that comes to your mind. It is a simple way to get closer to each other.

12.
ACTS AND ATTITUDES OF REVENGE

Revenge is not only an act but an attitude that doesn't work. It can take the form of a direct attack, or it can take the form of attacking others by playing the victim. For example, we may systematically plot revenge on someone who we perceive has wronged us, or we can attack ourselves, or encourage others to attack us, as a more subconscious form of revenge. What better revenge can we get on someone than to make them feel guilty or unhappy? Revenge is destructive; there is no truer adage than the words: "if we live by the sword, we die by the sword."

I once took a young man back through his life and he realized that he had experienced a major trauma about every two years. We traced this further back to an incident that occurred when he was three years old, and his father had been taken away to prison. As a result of that experience, he had decided to get revenge on the world and, because of this, his life had taken on an attitude of revenge that became a series of spectacular traumas. Underneath this trauma, there was a heartbreak at his birth, which came from his feelings of rejection. This set up a heartbreak–victim pattern and encouraged him to continue to hurt himself to get back at his parents.

Our desire to get back at others, especially our parents, sets up other victim, revenge, and heartbreak patterns. Common criminals are often people who get stuck at the win–lose revenge stage. They have often suffered traumas that have caused character disorders so severe that they can only see their own needs and everyone and anything else becomes the focus for their "revenge on the world." They are the ultimate heartbreak victims who become victimizers.

HEARTBREAK PRINCIPLE

Every heartbreak is an act of revenge on our partners, our parents, and even our past partners.

HEALING PRINCIPLE

It is necessary to let go of revenge to heal our broken hearts and our biggest problems.

HEALING SUGGESTION

To assess how much revenge you have in your life, examine where you have consciously tried to get back at others. Think also of times that you've been victimized by heartbreaks or anything else. These all point to hidden or not-so-hidden victim patterns.

HEALING CHOICE

I commit to my happiness by letting go of every revenge pattern that I have.

HEALING EXERCISE

Complete the following exercise to discover your revenge-heartbreak pattern so that you can become aware of it and let it go.

People I've actively sought revenge on	Did it work?	Did the pain stop?	Did it make me happy?
1. _____	_____	_____	_____
2. _____	_____	_____	_____
3 _____	_____	_____	_____

Heartbreaks

Major problems and traumas	Who was I getting revenge on?	Why?	Did the revenge make me happy?
1. _____	_____	_____	_____
2. _____	_____	_____	_____
3. _____	_____	_____	_____

If you see that these patterns didn't work, you might choose to let go of them or to place each pattern in the hands of God. To end this pattern of revenge, forgive yourself, the others in the situation, and God.

13.

NOT LISTENING

Not listening to our partners can occur at many different levels, and it leads to heartbreak and unhappy situations. A failure to listen sets up denial and power struggle. It occurs when we are either afraid to learn and change—because we don't know how to change—or when we are stubborn and refuse to change. But before we can successfully listen to our partners and anyone else with whom we have a relationship, we need to listen to ourselves. Most of us ignore our own intuition or guidance. Many people claim that they were intuitively warned about certain people or situations, and yet they went ahead anyway, with disastrous results.

We also fail to listen to what our partners are expressing verbally. Think how frustrating it is when we *know* we have not been heard—we are not sure whether we have really not been heard, whether others are simply being stubborn, or whether we are not expressing ourselves clearly. When this occurs, we repeat ourselves, and even nag and harangue until we get some sort of response. This issue usually comes up again and again, and we push more and more to get a response. Or we may simply give up and go away.

Turning the tables, we can obviously see that when we have heard what our partners have said, it is essential that we respond. Even if we don't have an answer to a problem or anything useful to say, it's important that we acknowledge their thoughts and appreciate them for sharing. This opens a line of communication and lets our partners know that we care. If we show our willingness to hear what they are saying, even if we disagree, it will be helpful to our relationship. If our partner feels we aren't listening to them, they will feel unappreciated, which shifts the balance of the relationship. Our partners may even begin to despair or to give up on the relationship as a result. Even if we disagree, we can share how we feel and why, because in a good relationship there is no question of right or wrong; we need to join with our partners. This joining helps us to work toward a new resolution. When we disagree, we need to share what we feel and why, and then explain why we feel that way—because of an earlier experience we've had in life, for example. This opens the lines of communication needed to heal the original fracture.

If our partners talk to us about what is wrong in our relationships, they're typically the negative partner in the positive–negative step (see page 41). They probably feel helpless about changing, especially if they continually complain. If we enlist the negative's help in the change, they will give up the complaints and join us in support. If we are the positive, we have the ability to effect a transformation. If we set a goal, ask for grace and for others' help, let go, use the power of choice, join, communicate, forgive, integrate, commit, ask for the truth, and give our willingness, we will move forward. If we don't listen and respond, there'll be either deadness or full-scale rivalry.

There are signs in all of our situations. They are evident in how our partners are acting, what others are saying to us, and in the unfolding process of the situation itself. If we are aware, we can learn the easy way by just the hints and signals that occur, but we need to listen in order to do that. For instance, if our partner is moving away from us, it's important that we let go of our attachments to them in order to win back our attractiveness. If we see anything negative happening in or around our relationship, it is a sign to build the relationship through joining and bonding, because when we see a problem, it is our problem and we *can* do something about it. The more we ignore a problem, the more it grows. A problem just represents fear and an unintegrated, or fractured part of our mind—a conflict within us projected onto the outside environment. We can cut through this fear by our willingness and commitment to change and to truth.

When anyone, including our partners, gives us feedback, we need to listen and to integrate the feedback, even if it seems categorically wrong. It's easy to integrate—we can choose it, or we can ask our higher minds to do it for us. This gives us the energy of their feedback, and applies any bit of the truth they have to our perspective. When we listen to all the signals, respond to them, and use them to guide our course, we have a much greater chance for happiness.

HEARTBREAK PRINCIPLE

To ignore the signals and communication of our partners and everyone and everything around us leads to heartbreak situations that could have been averted.

HEALING PRINCIPLE

The commitment to become more and more aware of our partners and those that surround us helps us to respond and succeed in our relationships by communicating, bridging, and integrating in a way that leads to partnership.

HEALING SUGGESTION

How good are you at listening to your partner? Do you invite their communication or attack them? If you see communication as a chance to indulge and complain, then you will see your partner retreat. Can you avert arguments by sharing your sincere feelings, without stooping to argue back? Do you listen to what your partner is saying and what they are not saying? Can you pick up on others' thoughts using your intuition and closeness? Can you pick up on the unfolding process and what's coming as a result? One thing you can do to help understand the process, and what your partner is saying to you at deeper levels, is to consider that all their communication about anything is symbolic of a message of their feelings about you.

HEALING CHOICE

I choose to listen to my partner and to all the signals in my environment. I also choose to hear the message that is being given to me for my own healing.

HEALING EXERCISE

Listen to everything today as if it is a message from God or a crucial instruction from a mentor. Listen closely to all the messages coming to you through what happens, what others say to you, and what you read. Everything sends you a message for your own healing.

14.
"GOTCHA"

This is a nasty little game we play to get one over on the people around us. We use it to find a place of great sensitivity in others and then we tease or rile them unmercifully about it. We are being competitive, as a form of one-upmanship, to prove we're just a little bit better. "Gotcha" uses put-downs in an effort to build ourselves up. And we celebrate winning in a way that rubs it in, because we feel so threatened and insecure that we need to keep proving that we are superior. Unfortunately, and all too often, this happens between parents and their children, setting up patterns for life. It is hurtful, even heartbreaking, to be at the other end of a "gotcha," and it often brings back childhood hurts and heartbreaks that have formed a pattern in our lives.

People who play "gotcha" are often unaware and insensitive to those around them; they are even surprised when someone makes such a big deal of it. They say, "It was just a little joke!" but they don't realize that their "joke" was an attack against someone. Their insensitivity is, in fact, a defense over their own heartbreak, which leads them to play this vicious game.

I worked with one young man who played "gotcha" with his sister-in-law, and was quite taken aback when she seemed emotionally wounded by a "small joke," which was actually a put-down about her family. He didn't realize that this joke had triggered her old heartbreak feelings. He apologized for hurting her, but he felt intense rage rather than genuine concern. Her woundedness had triggered off one of his own earlier heartbreaks. His feelings of anger and fury masked his own deep wounds. He was also unaware of how his old heartbreak had caused him to use "gotcha" to defend himself against his own pain. He was able to locate the root of his heartbreak in an incident that occurred when he was five, and by healing that, he was able to escape from this pattern of "gotcha."

We can heal a "gotcha" problem and its ensuing aggression—which would also heal our need to win over others in such an obnoxious way—by discovering the original situation in our past, or even in our ancestors' pasts, that led us to feel shamed, criticized, and undervalued. If we feel appreciated, treated with fairness and justice, and accepted, we learn to like ourselves and feel no need to be right. We can reach this state by healing the fractures and perceiving the initial incidents in a different way. And by giving the gifts of acceptance, love, encouragement, and praise to those around us, we will receive them back and open ourselves to wholeheartedness.

HEARTBREAK PRINCIPLE

Our "gotcha" behavior comes from unresolved heartbreaks. It leads back to hurt and heartbreaks for ourselves and others, unless the roots are healed.

HEALING PRINCIPLE

Becoming aware of the subtle belief in our superiority that leads to behavior where we put others down can be the beginning of new choices for partnership, and the healing of the old heartbreaks.

HEALING SUGGESTION

Take a look at your love, family, and friend relationships for this subtle, or not-too-subtle, behavior. You may notice that your "humor" is aggressive or has a way of putting others down. If you use these signs to find and heal your hidden heartbreaks, you will regain both confidence and success.

HEALING CHOICE

I vow to find all areas of "gotcha" in my life, heal the heartbreak involved, and integrate the "gotcha" victim parts of me.

HEALING EXERCISE

Use your intuition to complete the following statements so that you can heal your "gotcha" and "victim of gotcha" personalities.

If you were to know how many "gotcha" personalities you have inside,

it's probably_____

If you were to know how many related victim personalities you have inside,

it's probably_____

If you were to know how many heartbreaks you would have to clear to heal the
roots of the "gotcha" and victim personalities,
it's probably_____

If you were to know how old you were for each heartbreak, you were probably
_____/_____/_____ and so on.

If you were to know what was going on here to set up the pain,
it was probably_____

Now, ask that you and everyone be returned to their center, and bond with the
people in these situations. Give the gifts you have for them and receive the gifts that
they have for you. Finally, choose that all of your "gotcha" and victim personalities
be integrated into one self and then back into you.

15.

POSSESSIVENESS AND JEALOUSY

Both possessiveness and jealousy are counter-productive
behaviors that go hand in hand. Possessiveness and jealousy are
attempts to keep our partners close in the name of love, but
they are, in fact, born from insecurity. We use our partners to
get our needs met, as a way of "owning" them in order to
enhance or ornament ourselves. This can be a complete turn-
off, and the more we do it, the more our partners want to get
away from us. The more jealous and possessive we become, the
more independent our partners become as they attempt to
avoid being stifled. As our possessiveness and jealousy grow and
our partners move away from us, there are typically two possibilities that occur: we can become even more insecure, threatening, and abusive to our partners, or we can choose to heal

ourselves. One leads to disaster and destroyed relationships; the other leads to change.

A couple of years ago I was working with a very jealous and possessive man. We worked to clear out a few layers, just enough for him to feel some relief and to stop acting so belligerently and aggressively toward his wife. The next time I saw him, six months later, he was having an affair, which is something I have often seen happen with jealous and possessive people. The extent to which someone is jealous is the extent to which they are fickle, despite protestations to the contrary. Jealousy and possessiveness have nothing to do with love, and everything to do with thwarted sense of specialness, needs, insecurity, demands, and past heartbreaks trying their best to create new ones. Interestingly, many people claim complete devotion to a partner, but, in fact, any person would have sufficed, as long as their needs were continually met. And when we are jealous, what we see is our own lack of commitment that we have projected on our partners. We confuse urgency and dependency with love.

Jealousy and possessiveness are very destructive to relationships. We abuse and push our partners away while we are trying to make them love us, give us attention, and treat us as the most special person in the world. If our jealousy and possessiveness are great and painful, it reflects places where we are sitting on old massive heartbreaks. These are such painful feelings that if we don't commit to heal them, we pollute our surroundings with our anger, our emotional abuse, and our pain.

HEARTBREAK PRINCIPLE

Jealousy and possessiveness are the fast track to hurt and heartbreak.

HEALING PRINCIPLE

Only healing and communication are effective means of healing possessiveness and jealousy.

HEALING SUGGESTION

Assess the level of your possessiveness and jealousy on a scale of 100. Now assess the level of your partner's, or last partner's, jealousy and possessiveness on a scale of 100. The highest number for either of you is the amount of your jealousy. Your jealousy comes from the insecurity of broken bonding and heartbreaks. If you don't heal it, you will typically become an emotional basket case, an abuser, or very independent, thereby making all of your partners jealous.

HEALING CHOICE

I commit to healing all of my jealousy so that I might feel safe and free, loved and loving.

HEALING EXERCISE

Ask yourself how many jealous and possessive selves you have within you. Now, melt them all together into one big, jealous, possessive figure. It's a hologram that your ego uses to cover a gateway in your mind. Step into the hologram of the jealous, possessive figure, and through the gateway. What's there? This is a part of your mind that you had lost, and the ego covered over to hide the gateway. You have now reclaimed this piece of your mind. How much have you reclaimed? Enjoy and embrace this area of your mind. In rare cases, the other side of the gateway is dark or negative. In these situations, just ask your higher mind to bring the light here and heal it. Now, ask yourself "If I were to know, how many old incidents do I have to clear to heal my jealousy and possessiveness?" Use the intuitive method (see "Gotcha," page 98) to go back to each of these incidents for centering, bonding, and gift-giving. What is the soul gift that you brought in and promised to give to your partner, or any ex-partner, to save them? Now, give each gift heart-to-heart.

16.

HEALING THE HELL OF HEARTBREAK

We have all had experiences in our lives that felt like a living hell. We remember the incidents, but, for the most part, we have suppressed the feelings so that we do not constantly re-experience the intense agony. Yet, the suppression of feelings does not stop them—somewhere within us that torture goes on, but we just don't feel it. The torture of this "hell" ultimately comes from guilt and the belief that self-punishment will eventually bring peace. Our "hell" is our attempt to pay off the guilt and we compensate for this pain by using huge amounts of our vital energy in order to contain it. It is our attempt to live a normal life. The time has come, however, to win back all the energy we have used to defend against this incident. It is time to transform the incident, rather than leaving it as one of the running wounds of our minds and hearts.

All heartbreaks after this event were part of the original pattern of heartbreak, and all the pain we experienced after the first heartbreak was tinged with its pain. Our beliefs about ourselves and life were all affected by the beliefs that were formed and compounded by the original event. Our defenses are still geared toward the event and in attempting to contain the emotional disaster it was for us. Keeping such events unhealed inside us is a recipe for disaster. They eat away at us, which erodes our confidence, courage, willingness, worthiness, and health. It is of the utmost importance that we return to these events and transform them. By correcting the mistakes that led to this event, we can turn back toward life. In place of this heartbreak, we now have strength, compassion, and wisdom, as well as a healing gift to help others out of their hell, with both the authority and the tenderness necessary to bring it about.

If we had cancer we would go to a doctor and seek treatment to be healed. Yet, we tend to shy away from seeking help to heal what are, essentially, emotional cancers. If we don't heal them, they can spread inside us, coloring everything we do and even leading us to choose death. Thirty years ago I knew a woman who had had a hard life full of heartbreaks that had led to divorce. She had just fallen in love with someone new and, once again, felt hope for a partnership. When I saw her again about a year later, her lover was gone and so were her hopes. She was devastated. Three months later, she still had not emotionally recovered and had just been diagnosed with cancer from which she died within six weeks. She had given up. Research shows that in many cases a trauma occurs with a significant partner between six and eighteen months before the onset of cancer.

When these heartbreaks are healed, they give us meaning and sustain us in the face of adversity. Every heartbreak we heal opens us to receive more grace for ourselves and for the world. Heartbreak is a personal war zone that infects our consciousness until it is healed. As our consciousness is raised, so is the consciousness of the world around us.

HEARTBREAK PRINCIPLE

Past heartbreaks and their destructive effects eat away at us until they are healed.

HEALING PRINCIPLE

It is crucial that we heal our heartbreaks, or they will remain as emotional cancers within us, affecting everything we do.

HEALING SUGGESTION

It is time to assess your life to find the scenes that still contain the feelings of shattering events of your life and to commit to their healing so that the self-destructive effects are transformed.

HEALING CHOICE

I commit to healing all the experiences of hell and heartbreak within me.

HEALING EXERCISE

List on a separate piece of paper, the scenes of past, emotional hell that you have within you. Commit to healing these scenes. For each scene, use the intuitive method and complete the following statements:

If I were to know what I began to believe about myself as a result of this heartbreak, it was probably_____

If I were to know what I began to believe about life as a result of this, it was probably_____

If I were to know what I began to believe about love and relationships as a result of this, it was probably_____

If I were to know what I began to believe about men as a result of this, it was probably_____

If I were to know what I began to believe about women as a result of this, it was probably_____

If I were to know what I began to believe about success as a result of this, it was probably_____

Let go of each of these beliefs as a mistake. Now, choose what you would like to believe instead about yourself, life, love, relationships, men, women, and success. Then use the movie of your mind retake method. (See "When we are upset," page 200.) Do the retake twenty times. This sets up a place of partnership in your mind where once there was a sense of war. Now, with each of the scenes on your list, go back and give the gifts that are still within you to give that will heal and transform the scene. After you have given your gifts, if you do not feel totally better, then there is another gift that you have for everyone. Give it. Then, receive the gifts that the people in each scene have for you, and also receive the gift that Heaven has for you, while helping those around you receive the gifts that Heaven has for them all.

17.

SELF-ATTACK

Self-attack is a root cause of every bad thing that has ever happened to us, and it is undertaken both to punish ourselves and to prevent us from fully living our lives. The heartbreak and other forms of attack that we experience on the outside are reflections of how we attack ourselves on the inside. When we attack ourselves we create distractions in order to avoid our true path and purpose.

Self-attack is one of the main ways in which the ego builds its strength and ensures its continuity. We attack ourselves for our disappointments and losses. We attack ourselves by creating losses. We attack ourselves for any guilt we experience and any separation we feel with others. We hide these attacks in great pockets within us. If they are not healed, the self-attack is increased and we then use these incidents against ourselves again and again, rather than using them as opportunities for healing.

When we are dependent, we often set up the greatest self-attacks using things such as heartbreak. Self-attack is a form of obsessive self-judgment that the ego uses to distract us from the calls for help around us. It blocks our potential for leadership, service, and friendship for others, because we are so busy, self-involved, or self-conscious that we don't hear the calls for help. The ego does not want us to hear and respond to calls for help around us. If we reach out to others, the joining that takes place melts away part of the ego and starts a flow in us—until the next bit of self-attack comes up to distract and disengage us from the sweet unfolding of life.

Similarly, a death temptation is the ego's best way of distracting us from an invitation for the birth of a whole new level in our lives. The most dire events of our lives offer the biggest opportunities for breakthroughs and healing, but the ego naturally wants to hide this possibility from us. When we learn to look at all events as healing opportunities, no matter what the ego throws at us, we can use them as a springboard forward. If we forget this, we will suffer, just trying to get through to survive the painful events.

As we are about to step forward in our lives, the ego can encourage even more vicious self-attack both before and after the event. I have seen this quite a bit in workshops when someone is assigned a "stretch," which is the dramatic acting-out of a problem or its healing resolution. Before the event there can be a great deal of doubt, self-attack, and fear, and then after, the ego attempts to abort the celebration of the breakthrough with self-consciousness, embarrassment, or shame. When those individuals are shown the ego's intent, they are able to regain their feelings of victory and joy.

HEARTBREAK PRINCIPLE

All heartbreaks and any problems are forms of self-attack.

HEALING PRINCIPLE

When we realize that the ego uses self-attack to stop us from responding to friends in need, we are motivated to let it go, so we can be of service to them.

HEALING SUGGESTION

It is the ego's intent to keep you self-conscious and self-involved. Examine your life, looking at all of the worst times as a form of self attack to stop your flow of gifts. Recognize how they prevented you from helping those around you and from fulfilling your purpose and your destiny. Use your awareness to keep you from further self-attack and let it inspire you to know there is someone around you who needs your help. When you respond to those around you, you open yourself up to healing and to love and are carried into a new flow in your life.

HEALING CHOICE

I commit to letting go of all my self-attack and to choosing instead to respond to the calls for help around me.

HEALING EXERCISE

After many years of studying the problem of self-consciousness, shame, and self-attack, I found that the ego's purpose was to distract or blind us to the calls for help around us. If we responded to them as being more important than ourselves and our self-torture, we would effectively be healed and able to move on to a new level. In this case, the ego would be defeated and its protective and defensive mechanisms destroyed.

List the eleven worst scenes of your life. With each scene imagine yourself back in it, but this time instead of being caught up in the pain and self-attack, ask yourself, "What is this pain and self-attack trying to distract me from? Who needs my help?" You will find that as you give to that person, both of you are freed from the pattern and from any old feelings. If the scene is not totally resolved for you, then ask the question again and give. When a person comes to mind, see yourself stepping through and beyond the self-torture to reach out and support them.

Worst scene	Why I was attacking myself	Who needed my help?	Gift
1. _____	_____	_____	_____
2. _____	_____	_____	_____
3. _____	_____	_____	_____
4. _____	_____	_____	_____
5. _____	_____	_____	_____
6. _____	_____	_____	_____
7. _____	_____	_____	_____
8. _____	_____	_____	_____
9. _____	_____	_____	_____
10. _____	_____	_____	_____
11. _____	_____	_____	_____

18.
BEING RIGHT

This is a core dynamic that can wreak havoc with our lives. If we are making ourselves right, it's obvious that we are making someone else wrong. When we are making someone wrong, it means we are in a battle, and we have just declared ourselves the victors, even though we may be the victims. Nobody ever really wins a battle, because we ultimately defeat ourselves. When we battle to prove that we are right we don't learn, grow, or join. The fight is a defense. If we are acting righteous, it is because we feel wrong about something within us; our inflexibility forces both us and others to live by rules in an attempt to cover feelings of pain and failure. Our righteousness stops us from being happy.

Every negative situation that has ever occurred in our lives is an attempt to prove that we are right about something. By feeling that we must always be right, we fight battles that we don't really even care about; we may even argue a point that goes against our beliefs or principles, all in the name of winning. Sometimes, we are being right about negative or destructive self-concepts as an excuse to not have to "show up" in our life, in our purpose, in our destiny. Being right is an attempt to prevent pain, but it somehow always leads us right back into it. It is an attempt to prove dark beliefs about ourselves or the world, which gives us an excuse to do whatever it is that we want, even though none of it makes us happy. When I am facing a negative situation, I remind myself to recognize that I am wrong about things or the situation would be peaceful and successful. If I'm right, I'm stuck with the way things are as I have judged them. If I'm right, I can't learn, grow, and change, nor can anyone else in the situation.

A situation is just a combination of many relationships, past and present, that have led to the current experience. If we are willing to be wrong, we can make another choice. If we are willing to be wrong, we can ask for help with the situation. In every negative situation we are locked into a prison made by our own judgments, which always cover guilt. Innocent people do not judge nor do they project guilt. When we ask for help from Heaven, it allows us to see others asking for our help, which opens us and allows us to be flexible, to seek a common solution, and to respond to these calls for help in such a way that the conflict quickly unfolds.

HEARTBREAK PRINCIPLE

Being right places us on the fast track for arguments and battles, and leads to broken hearts.

HEALING PRINCIPLE

When we give up being defensively righteous, we receive the answer that will allow us to help others, and be helped by our higher mind.

HEALING SUGGESTION

Whenever you are in a negative situation, remember to say to yourself: "This is not the truth. This is not what I want. I want the truth. If I'm right this is what I get. I made a mistake in my choice. Let me recognize I'm wrong, so I can know the truth. I need help to see the way. I want happiness instead of this."

HEALING CHOICE

I commit to letting go and healing every place of righteousness, judgment, and hidden guilt so that I can learn my lessons and be happy.

HEALING EXERCISE

Examine your three worst heartbreaks and three of your present situations that are less than happy.

Heartbreaks	What I was being right about	What I was feeling righteous about
1. _____	_____	_____
2. _____	_____	_____
3. _____	_____	_____

Present unhappy situation	What I am being righteous about	What I am feeling wrong or guilty about
1. _____	_____	_____
2. _____	_____	_____
3. _____	_____	_____

Now, for each situation, make another choice. Forgive yourself and your past so you won't imprison others with it now. Ask to be inspired to find the truth. Ask for happiness for everyone concerned. It is what you and they deserve.

THE LESSONS
OF HEARTBREAK

❧

19.
THE ELEMENTS OF HEARTBREAK

The elements of heartbreak are principles, characteristics, or dynamics necessary for a heartbreak to occur. These are characteristics that show up time and time again in heartbreak situations. Some of these aspects are common sense; many are kept below the level of normal awareness. They appear here to remind us and to teach us the lessons of heartbreak.

1. Every heartbreak represents a place where we are victimized. This serves a certain purpose for us.
2. In heartbreak, there is an experience of fracturing, lost bonding, and separation.
3. In heartbreak, there is a level of inner conflict that the outer conflict reflects.
4. In heartbreak, there is resistance, non-acceptance, or

rejection on our part. The extent of this is the extent to which it hurts.

5. In heartbreak, there is an aspect of judgment, interpretation, and grievance. The interpretation is mistaken, and the judgment and grievance hide our own guilt.

6. In heartbreak, there is an aspect of self-deception and denial.

7. In heartbreak, there is a level of emotional blackmail and control. Heartbreak is a form of fighting—we use it to try to defeat someone. (This person may not necessarily be the person in our present heartbreak situation.)

8. Heartbreaks are part of a pattern that contains pain from the past.

9. Heartbreaks represent a form of subconscious communication.

10. Heartbreaks represent a choice that serves a purpose for us.

11. Heartbreaks give us excuses.

12. Heartbreaks are a form of self-punishment.

13. Heartbreaks are a form of revenge.

14. Heartbreaks prove a certain self-concept about ourselves in which we invest, and it represents a fear of change.

15. Heartbreaks come from a place of competition, manipulation, and a win–lose attitude.

16. Heartbreaks support a negative life story that we hold and in which we invest. Without healing this story, chapter after chapter of heartbreak can occur.

17. Heartbreaks represent a fear of intimacy and a fear of the next step. Both represent a lack of confidence.

18. Heartbreaks represent a mistaken strategy.

19. Heartbreaks represent the wounded children within us.

20. Heartbreaks represent an attempt to get past needs met

in the present.

21. Heartbreaks represent a form of illusion, in collusion with our partner.

22. Heartbreaks represent a refusal of our purpose—personally and as a couple.

23. Heartbreaks represent an attempt to get something.

24. Heartbreaks are a refusal to give something that would heal the situation.

25. Heartbreaks are unlearned lessons.

26. Heartbreaks are refusals to be responsible and accountable.

27. Heartbreaks are traps that we set up to hold ourselves back.

28. Heartbreaks may be part of a conspiracy against ourselves and our purpose.

29. Heartbreaks always give a double message.

30. Heartbreaks represent insults to our "specialness," which is our belief that we should be treated as the most important person in the relationship and the situation.

31. Heartbreaks are shattered dreams.

32. Heartbreaks come from the disillusionment and disappointment of thwarted emotional addictions, which we made into idols because we thought they would make us happy.

33. Heartbreaks represent frustrated needs and expectations.

34. Heartbreaks feel like they are deserved because of beliefs in our unworthiness.

35. Heartbreaks represent a form of failing to commit.

36. Heartbreaks represent a place where we give only to receive rewards.

37. Heartbreaks show a place of attachment.

38. On the surface, heartbreaks represent a place where

someone didn't take our script; at a subconscious level, the person acted exactly as we'd planned it.

39. A heartbreak partner or situation mirrors our mind.

40. Heartbreaks fit our family role or roles.

41. Heartbreak is a form of self-attack and self-destructiveness.

42. Heartbreak is a feeling of being unwanted.

43. In any heartbreak situation, both partners have an equal amount of pain and heartbreak inside them.

44. Every heartbreak represents a place where we are fighting God.

Remember these elements, and when you find yourself in a period of trauma or heartbreak, call back on them. Awareness is the key to healing, and by understanding the elements that make up your pain, you can uncover the reasons for it and go on to healing and wholeheartedness.

20.

RELATIONSHIPS AND LOVE

Speaking heart-to-heart, there is nothing more important than relationships. Underneath everything, relationships are based on love. Love is our best chance, our only chance, because it is the essential gift of our purpose. In life, love generates creativity by helping us go beyond the norm to express our genius and beauty. Love is the heart of all fulfillment. Love heals us, blesses us, rescues us, and redeems us; it gives us meaning in the desert of meaninglessness. Love is the answer we seek to move us beyond the fear, and to heal the separation, both of which are at the root of every problem in our lives. Love is the beginning, the end, and the way in between. In love, the path and the goal are the same. Love awakens and refreshes us. Love comes to us laughing as we remember what is sacred. Our innocence, our lovableness, our worthiness, and our wholeness are all love's children.

Relationships can either be a living heaven or a living hell. They can fill our lives with joy and meaning, or they can fill them with emptiness and desolation. When we know love, we know our purpose. Our soul *is* love, and when we allow it to shine, we have fulfilled its purpose. Our relationships and our purpose are the areas that build our happiness; therefore, how successful we are in each of these is the measure of our fulfillment. Without love in our lives, it is difficult to be happy—the colors fade, and the world becomes lonely and dark. With love, the air is filled with fragrance and the brightness of vivid colors as friendships bless our way.

Our relationships create the possibility for love. At school, at our workplace, at home, with our associates, acquaintances, and friends, with our beloved, our family, and even those we pass by or meet seemingly by accident, present opportunities for love to be born again. These relationships are the opportunities for us to show our true meaning, to express our creativity, to regain our bonds, to answer calls for help, and to fill angels with happiness. Our relationships are the bridge home, the bridge to heaven; through them we truly know ourselves, others, and spiritual peace.

Everything is balanced within a relationship, and when it breaks down, or there is trouble within it, all sorts of problems can arise in our lives that appear to have nothing to do with the relationship. But, at a deeper level, all problems are relationship problems, and the rest, such as financial loss or illness, are just symptoms. After several years of working in the subconscious minds of hundreds of people and with many hundreds of symptoms, it became evident—especially as I began to work with people with catastrophic illness—that the relationship issue is really all there is. Relationships are the central facet of our lives, so whether past or present, all problems come down to relationship problems.

HEARTBREAK PRINCIPLE

At the root of any problem is a relationship problem. At the root of our heartbreaks are mistaken, painful patterns from past relationships that have been brought into present relationships.

HEALING PRINCIPLE

To heal ourselves and our relationships with others and God, is to bring back love, joy, and purpose to our lives.

HEALING SUGGESTION

Relationships have primacy in your life, and it is through them that you measure your fulfillment. It is important to learn the principles of healing and transformation, so your relationships can be filled with ease and grace and you can be happy!

HEALING CHOICE

I choose to learn the truth about relationships so that I can be successful in them.

HEALING EXERCISE

Choose three problem areas in your life, such as money, career, or sex. Examine these problems—whether they are from the present or the past—with the recognition that all problems are relationship problems. In this light, you will be able to see that the problem actually began with a grievance held for another person.

Problem	Who was the grievance with?	What was the grievance about?
1.	_____	_____
2.	_____	_____
3.	_____	_____

If you are now willing to forgive everyone and everything related to each problem, you can be free. Be aware that grievances may not necessarily involve a person (for example, a woman I once worked with, who was in a motor vehicle accident, also had to forgive autos). To let go of a problem you may need to forgive God, the world, sex, a place, a group, and even things.

21.

RELATIONSHIPS, EVOLUTION, AND SPIRITUALITY

In my personal experience, and from what I have seen around the world, a relationship is the best means of enjoying ourselves, experiencing love, and being happy. A relationship can make the world bright with color because it allows and invites us to go beyond ourselves in joining with others. This brings the world alive with excitement, adventure, and love. Levels of learning, healing, and joining can occur in a relationship. As our commitment progresses, there is the possibility of communication becoming communion, which opens us to the mystical. The celebrated Canadian author, teacher, and speaker Henri Nouwen (1932–96) said that we can love others to the extent that we love God. The extent to which we love another—truly love another—is the extent to which we open ourselves to loving our God. As we join with another, we are opened to the love and grace of spiritual peace; therefore, a relationship represents a three-way affair—ourselves, others, and Heaven.

When we hold grievances toward someone from the past, there is no way that we can avoid taking it out on those in the present. To forgive anyone is to forgive everyone—including ourselves. Forgiveness moves us closer to all those around us, deepening the bonding, and allowing success in any area of our lives with ease. Everything we hold against another, we hold against our God and ourselves. So, everything that has not been forgiven is in fact held against everyone and against our God. This may sound preposterous yet, time and again, I have discovered that a problem or an issue with a relationship or a person is, in fact, a grievance that they held against their God. When we have been victimized, we blame our God for what we chose and then hid from ourselves. We shift the blame for our actions onto our God, or fate, or whatever we believe in. We can, however, choose to *forgive* our God, which opens us once again to grace. Learning to forgive our God opens us to that part of our mind that is already directly connected to our God—in other words, our spirituality or fundamental peace. Separation can never give us what we want, so as we integrate and heal the fractures in our mind and heal the separation, we move closer to everyone and to spiritual peace.

The earth as a whole is moving toward union, or "Oneness." The more that separation is healed on the Earth, the more abundance and success there is for everyone. The more this healing occurs, the more we will see each other as brothers and sisters of the same happy family. But there is much healing to be done before the illusions and the fractures, along with the pain and suffering they cause, are destroyed. Each time we forgive, the walls of separation that cause competition, guilt, fear, and failure are melted away. Forgiveness allows us to be happy. Every time we have the realization that we are, in truth, all spiritual siblings and, therefore, all spiritually the same, there is a new level of partnership and success in all areas for ourselves, and for the whole world.

The ego is fond of frightening us with the fact that we would lose our independence if we were to join another. Of course, we would lose some of our independence, but the ego uses this idea to deceive us into thinking that we would become virtual slaves with no free will. In reality, we would be progressing and escaping a trap. We move on to interdependence, which is about partnership and commitment. One of the vital principles of relationship—which only committed people know—is that it is our commitment that brings us ease and freedom; it is the total giving of ourselves, withholding nothing, that is the birth of love, creativity, and meaning in our lives. Love with no limitations opens the world to miracles and to the kind of peace we all yearn for.

A relationship can be the fastest way to open ourselves to the bounty of spiritual peace. Relationships continuously show us what is between love and ourselves, and they shed light on areas where we are not totally giving ourselves. To give ourselves totally is to know the beauty of another and to recognize it as a reflection of ourselves. When we negatively judge others, we see them as the mirror of our own self-judgment. It demonstrates where we are neither giving to them nor to ourselves. Where we feel guilty we see others as deserving punishment. This is just another ploy the ego uses to hide the fact that we are all children of God and deserving of all good things.

A relationship is the closest that we can come to experiencing heaven or a type of nirvana on earth. As we join with others—as we give to and share with them—both meaning and direction grow in our life. Our relationships are the means by which we can experience continuous love and inspiration, which overlooks mistakes and finds true meaning in life.

Meaninglessness is the battleground between our ego and the higher mind, and it is the basis of our modern world. We can't stand the experience of meaninglessness, and the death temptation that is endemic to it, so we manufacture our own meaning—something that we believe gives us value in life. We usually value something we attempt to get, such as pleasure, success, or money, or something we do (our job, parenthood, or a sport, for example). Most of our lives are, therefore, based around acquisitiveness or the roles we play in order to hide the meaninglessness. This is the only way we knew how to deal with it. Then there is the concept of compensation, which means that we try to compensate or make up for shortfalls in our lives by filling them with other activities and diversions. Ultimately, compensation leads to disappointment, because it is something we take or do to try to prove our value, rather than accepting that it is who we are that has value. This fabricated or counterfeit meaning can only lead toward shattered dreams, disillusionment, and death because of the disappointment and burn-out that comes from taking and compensating. Love and creativity, the gifts that love brings, and living our purpose, provide the only real meaning in our lives. Every time we truly forgive and join another person, love, meaning, and spirituality grow in our life. All of our relationships—not just our romantic relationships—can help us evolve. When we grow through our relationships, we join into a cycle of love and peace that leads us all back to love, joy, and wholeness.

When there is joy, love, forgiveness, and joining in our relationship, it heals us, comforts us, nurtures us, and brings us happiness. We realize our wholeness, and we remember that we are one with everyone around us, and at peace with our spirit. This is a path of the heart—one which takes courage, given the amount of pain that even the healthiest human being has buried within. There are many millions of personal fractures that stand between us and spiritual peace, but as we heal each fracture between ourselves and our partners, we join at a greater level of understanding and intimacy. When we join with our romantic partner, we begin a new honeymoon period. There are big challenges ahead, but the answer is always to end the separation—to join with our partner at a new level.

HEARTBREAK PRINCIPLE

Every fracture or separation between us and another, or between us and God, will come up in our relationship.

HEALING PRINCIPLE

As we heal any fracture, we heal the separation, and we get closer to everyone, including God.

HEALING SUGGESTION

Your commitment to a healing path leads you to greater wholeness and brings about ease and freedom. It is important that you undertake to heal every fracture, give up every judgment, and end every separation so that your heart, your relationship, and your life unfold.

HEALING CHOICE

I commit to heal the separation with those around me so that I am only and always feeling love. I choose to heal the fractures in my own mind so that my sense of wholeness will be restored.

HEALING EXERCISE

Every relationship in your life is an opportunity for growth and evolution; each time you join with another, separation is healed, and you are more open to God. Choose someone in your life to join with. It can be anyone—someone you love the most or it might be someone that needs your help. Now, today, and for the rest of the week, every time you think of them, send love to them. Imagine that the light within you is connecting to the light within them. There is nothing you need to do, and they don't even need to know. Just send them love. At the end of the day, assess how you feel, how you feel about them, and if you can, assess how they seem to be feeling as a result of your love. As you begin to feel more whole and open, you can send others love, too. You can send love to as many people as you choose!

22.

RELATIONSHIPS AS A TRAP

Whenever there is an opportunity to evolve, transform, and heal, the ego will set up a temptation to trick us. It will appear similar to the healing concept, but it is counterfeit—it is a trap. Since relationships can be the fastest way to grow and have the greatest potential to transform, the ego naturally sets up its best defense against love. Consider these examples:

- Instead of *giving* (of ourselves and our gifts) the ego suggests sacrifice (where we give, but can't receive).
- Instead of *bonding* (connecting with another in love) the ego offers fusion (not knowing our true boundaries—where we end and another begins, which is always a place of sacrifice).

- Instead of *letting go* (having no expectation of an outcome) the ego recommends throwing away (kicking others out of our lives) and independence (not caring about others).
- Instead of *relatedness* (our connection and mutuality) the ego proposes attachment (emotionally holding on to another).
- Instead of *love*, the ego puts forth specialness and self-centered behavior (where we are the most important one).

The ego is always trying to frighten us away from love, because when we truly join with another in love, a certain boundary melts away, a sharing takes place, and bonding is realized. In truth, bonding is rediscovered, because the Oneness that exists between all and everything is always there. We need only to clear the debris over it through forgiveness and love to find it again. We all have millions of fractures, and each fracture is a place of conflict that hides our fear of bonding. We are afraid we will lose ourselves. Yet, we can never lose anything that is essential, and we can only gain by bonding. As each fracture is healed there is more confidence, success, and intimacy. With each healing, we evolve toward greater wholeness and enjoy the gifts that surface because of it.

The ego is always trying to supplant the power that relationships have to transform our lives; the ego changes the purpose of a relationship from giving to getting. The ego attempts to change our relationships into something other than a playground of love, joy, or healing. We try to use others to meet *our* needs, and when these are not met, we feel hurt. But we cannot feel hurt in a relationship, unless we feel frustrated in what we were trying to take. If we take an honest look at all of the upsets and pain in our relationship, we will recognize that they are all related to instances where we were trying to get something from our partner. The number one mistake we make in relationships is to think that our partner was put on earth to make us happy. We translate this to mean that they were put on earth to take care of our needs and to treat us like we were the most special person in the world.

A Course in Miracles analyzes the destructiveness of "special-ness." As children we felt the need to be the most "special" child, and we wanted our parents to recognize us as such. The trauma we felt when they failed to do so manifests itself in our present relationships, and we demand that our partners recognize our "specialness" and treat us accordingly. When they fail to do so, we punish them emotionally and try to control them in order to ensure that our needs are met.

Our hurts come when our needs are not met, and our upsets come from people not acting in the way we want them to. When our happiness is dependent upon the behavior of others, it is emotionally devastating to us, and then potentially dangerous to them. Love, on the other hand, gives, recognizes, and attends, but it takes no prisoners. It holds no one hostage, because love doesn't punish others for their failing to take care of us. It understands and responds to calls for help; love doesn't demand its own way, it seeks for a joining to complete everyone. When we enter a relationship with no demands or expectations, when we consider our partners and not ourselves, we cannot be hurt.

The ego uses the heartbreak of relationships, and their corresponding disappointments to encourage us to give up on life, and turn toward death. Self-centeredness, or "specialness" is a common illusion that is built into every relationship, so unless we transform it into true love and true giving, it will only be a matter of time before we suffer heartbreak. The only way to get beyond such a trap is to recognize the ego's trick, and to commit to love, rather than to being independent. When a conflict emerges, it is just one more thing to heal in a relationship on the way to wholeness.

Without the goal of dedicating a relationship to something greater than worldly love—in other words, spirit—any conflict (fighting or deadness) that comes up can turn us away from our partner, from love, and ultimately from life. Dr. Joyce Brothers had a newspaper column for over twenty years in the United States where people would write in with questions and comments about relationships and she would respond to them. She once stated, "In my experience, single people want to be married and married people want to be dead." This is a common experience. It is time to change our attitude toward relationships. Rather than seeing them as a trap, value them as an opportunity for us to mature emotionally, and evolve—to bond or join with others—and continuously to experience more love and joy.

HEARTBREAK PRINCIPLE

All heartbreak comes from an insult to our specialness (the self-centered belief that we are all that matters).

HEALING PRINCIPLE

Specialness is how our ego demands that its needs be met. As healing and maturity replace our belief that we are what matters most, we evolve, growing in love and wholeness.

HEALING SUGGESTION

How many happy relationships are you aware of? If you see none, then maybe you are being called upon to bring it about and lead the way. How many relationships around you inspire you with the possibility of love and partnership? If you don't see true love, then maybe you are the one being called to transform special love and to have a relationship where you can bring Heaven to earth. It just might be you and your partner who will make the difference, and it just might be your relationship that is a beacon of love, inspiration, and direction to everyone around you.

HEALING CHOICE

I commit to healing at every point where my specialness interferes with my relationship. Instead I choose forgiveness, transformation, and love.

HEALING EXERCISE

Choose three of your major heartbreaks. Examine them from the angle of specialness, and fill in your response to the question.

Major heartbreak	How was your specialness insulted?
1. _____	_____
2. _____	_____
3. _____	_____

With this awareness, what would you now be willing to let go and forgive in each of the three heartbreaks?

I now let go of	I now forgive
1. _____	_____
2. _____	_____
3. _____	_____

Would you now be willing to join your partner, rather than carry on this drama based around your wounds and your insulted specialness?

23.

RELINQUISHING THE PAIN OF HEARTBREAK

Heartbreaks shatter not only our hearts but also our dreams. We feel like we have been stopped cold and that we might never recover from this experience. Time seems to be suspended or to drag on inexorably as the color goes out of our life. We feel like our lives have ended and all hope has fled. There is a sense of loss and a feeling of not wanting to go on.

Life seems too hard to deal with because our horizons have collapsed inward, while our lives revolve like a broken record around the painful incident. The outside world demands attention, but we may not be able to give anything, because the pain can be so strong that it is difficult to relate to anything—work, others, or life. We want it all to be a big mistake—a dream from which we will wake up to find everything has returned to normal. If we go forward, it seems we will bear the scars of this incident for life. If we don't go forward, it may be the final disappointment that sets us on a path toward death.

When we are heartbroken in childhood, the self that we are at that time can "die," and be buried within. Sometimes, an experience is so overwhelming that a number of these selves die and with each of them, a major gift also seems to die. The trauma may be so painful that it is repressed. It may be remembered at a healthier time when we feel more ready and willing to deal with it, or it will come up disguised as present pain. Even as children, we can actually lose heart as a result of the fracture. We are then untouched by what surrounds us and, consequently, we become depressed and dispirited. What most of us do with heartbreak is bury the pain; we push the hell back inside us so we can go on. This is not a good strategy because it compounds the old heartbreak, which has the effect of tying up a great deal of our energy and, as a result, our lives. It demands more energy to keep all this buried, as the heartbreak itself is made up of a lot of misused energy. This misdirected use of energy can make us tired and older. We eventually regain some of our energy on the surface, but inside, the heartbreak is carried around as over-sensitivity or blindness to life. This is an invitation to future heartbreak.

HEARTBREAK PRINCIPLE

The breaking of our hearts can cause us to suffer torture. It can be so painful that we want to die or to act destructively.

HEALING PRINCIPLE

It is important to use heartbreak as an opportunity to heal the pain and all its roots in the past.

HEALING SUGGESTION

All of life is about relationships. They are the central factor of all problems and the root of all our joy. Relationships can be heaven, or they can be hell. Since, for the most part, true understanding of relationships is not taught in school, it is your responsibility to learn about and understand relationships, because they typically determine your happiness. The information and the principles of healing and transformation are available to you if you choose to find them. There are only two directions to move in—one is toward ignorance and heartbreak, the other is toward healing, learning, and love. I highly recommend the latter, because it moves you toward life and happiness, while the former moves you toward death.

HEALING CHOICE

I will use this opportunity to heal myself of all pain and patterns surrounding this heartbreak.

HEALING EXERCISE

Imagine that your pain is like a wall of fire around you. Ask yourself, "Who needs my help? Who is in greater need than I am?" Someone will pop into your mind. Imagine yourself stepping through the wall of fire to help them. Write to them, call them, or send them love from inside you to them. Repeat this exercise until you feel peace and joy. Continue with each layer of bad feeling—it may be only one—until you turn what seems like hell into a birth of love, creativity, and vision. Vision-level gifts such as art, healing ability, psychic gifts, or a new level of sexuality may emerge from stepping through this wall of pain.

24.

HEARTBREAK AND CONFLICT

Heartbreaks represent and come from fractures in our minds. Fractures are parts of our minds that we have "cut off" because they were too painful to cope with. They represent areas of conflict or parts of us that have a different "agenda" or idea of what we want from life. In order to establish a sort of peace, however simulated, we subconsciously hide away these areas and keep them suppressed. We are not normally aware that these parts exist within us, and it is only by going back through our lives that we can establish when and why they were fractured away from our minds and persuaded to lie dormant.

We repress the sides of ourselves that we favor the least— the parts that may have caused unhappiness or been the victim of some trauma. For example, if we experienced an episode in childhood where we were rejected by our parents for behaving independently, we may have decided that independence was a characteristic that would not work for us. Our independent side might, therefore, have been fractured off and hidden.

What happens, however, is that we tend to project our fractured sides onto our partners or situations. Unless we choose to heal, the heartbreaks that ensue can further fracture and divide us, which causes even deeper conflict. In any situation where we are in conflict with another person, we are seeing a hidden part of our own minds. We may even be seeing a shadow figure (see page 229), which represents dark and incredibly painful beliefs about ourselves. The solution is to uncover the parts that have been fractured and to reintegrate them.

When our minds are in conflict, each part wants to go in a different direction, has different goals, and has different beliefs about what would make us happy. For instance, we may appear cool and independent on the outside, and have a more painful, needy side within. This fracture or split is a conflict within us, but it will also show itself as a conflict outside us—in our relationships. Typically, in this instance, we might act out the independent side and project our painful, needy side onto our partner, who, in turn, is projecting their independent side onto us. What we are actually doing is acting out their hidden or subconscious side. They are acting out our hidden or subconscious "independent" side.

Both the hidden and obvious levels of a conflict with our partner are contained in every heartbreak, which is usually the end result of a long line of power struggles. The struggle may be hidden or denied, but it is no less lethal. There is some kind of fight going on that is affecting both partners. One may be attacking while the other is withdrawing, or both may be alternately attacking and withdrawing. In every battle there is a fear of intimacy, a fear of success, and a fear of moving forward, for both partners. On one level, we are using the other person to distract us from the fight that is going on within us. But choosing to respond to them, forgive them, join them, and bridge the differences, allows us to help both the other person and ourselves. It ends the conflict and leads us to peace, confidence, and success. With communication, trust, integration, joining, and forgiveness, we not only succeed interpersonally, but also within our own minds, because we win back our projected parts and resolve the conflict.

HEARTBREAK PRINCIPLE

Every heartbreak is the result of a conflict inside both partners, which also shows up as a conflict in the relationship. Each partner in a heartbreak situation reflects the inner situation of both partners' minds.

HEALING PRINCIPLE

If a conflict is not healed within ourselves, the events of the outside world will sooner or later embody the conflict within. This can prove costly and painful.

HEALING SUGGESTION

In any conflict, commit to both of you winning 100 percent. You can both move to a new level of success emotionally, sexually, or in the area of conflict, whatever that may be. Don't stop communicating until each of you feels like you have both won. A helpful bonding technique is to imagine lines of light joining you together. Each time you join, it increases your connection to your partner. There may be dozens of layers of pain, but with each joining, another layer heals. This gradually improves and progresses the situation toward healing.

HEALING CHOICE

I will not blame, fight, or attack. I will see every opponent as a reflection of the hidden part of my own mind. I will forgive the other person and, thus, forgive myself.

HEALING EXERCISE

If you want to integrate, make a choice to do so. Integration is the joining of two opposite parts into one. As the energies join, what is positive becomes more positive, while what was negative provides a vaccination against future negativity. There is now trust, confidence, and a single goal where there once was conflict. If you would like to experience the integration more vividly, you can actually act out the conflict in your mind in a healing way. Begin by seeing those who oppose you in a conflict situation as representatives of your mind. They will be the main characters in your enactment, and they represent the part of your mind that you are projecting. Now, imagine that the conflict within is placed outside you in a room. The room represents your mind. Name the two (or more, as the case may be) different parts of your mind, and place each part in its corresponding spot in the room. The physical distance between each part represents the distance that separates the parts in your mind. Start the integration by standing in the place you have chosen to represent the part that you "least" identify with. As you begin to identify with it, allow it to speak its mind until it has finished saying what it wants to say. Then, have it take a step forward toward the center of the room. Mark this spot, because you will be returning to it. Now go to the other part (if there are more than two, go to the next part that is least identified with) and speak this part's mind. Take a step toward the center, and mark this spot. (If there are three or more parts, continue moving to the next part that you least identify with until all parts have spoken and stepped forward.) Now, return to the marked spot of the first part. Speak its mind from this place, step toward the center, mark the spot, and move back to the other part (or the next spot). Continue this communication until both parts (or all parts) have stepped forward and joined at the center of the room. Then imagine the parts melting together into one. There may be more levels to heal, but this takes us to the next levels of peace, integration, and confidence. Repeat the exercise until all that remains is healed.

25.

HEALING AND HEARTBREAKS

Love, understanding, acceptance, forgiveness, letting go, trust, commitment, giving, and receiving must find a way into and through the hell of heartbreaks to bring new life. This usually comes in the form of a person—a friend or new love who brings a message of hope. They reach into our hell and connect with us in such a way that we are reeled back in. Being lured back to life and wanting to live again, we once more remember hope and the possibility that we might be lovable, because we see it in their eyes.

These "angels without wings" reach out to us and pull us in from the torrent of pain that was pulling us down. They have enough love and friendship to go beyond any façade, to reach out to us and into us, and to pull us back from the edge.

If we choose to go on after heartbreak and once more open our hearts to love, we will look at life with new eyes. We can be the one with heart, the one who reaches out at just the right time to pull a friend back to life again. As we are saved, so shall we save.

HEARTBREAK PRINCIPLE

What was broken can be healed. Healing will bring more understanding, acceptance, and love.

HEALING PRINCIPLE

The heartbreaks we heal become places of compassion and wisdom in us. After healing our hells, we can march with authority into someone else's hell and pull them out. Every step in our own healing helps heal the world. As we are healed we become a source of strength and inspiration to others.

HEALING SUGGESTION

Healing involves valuing love more than pain. If you are willing, you will see, even through your pain, those to whom you can be an "angel without wings."

HEALING CHOICE

I elect to heal the pain I face today, and all pain inside me, for the sake of all those I love.

HEALING EXERCISE

See your pain or problem as a wall that surrounds you. Someone you know is in need of help. Who is it? Would you be willing to step through this wall to help them? Can you hear their cries for help? In spite of their brave front, can you see and feel how they need you? Would you step through this wall and toward them now? As you reach them, imagine yourself embracing and supporting them. Each time you step through the wall, and toward another, you collapse your problem or a layer of it. When this occurs both you and the other person are back in the flow of life, and you are able to move forward.

26.
EMOTIONS AND HEARTBREAK

When we were young, we learned to respect fire because we burned ourselves. We learned from our mistakes. But we have not been so quick to apply this lesson to our emotions and, time after time, we have stuck our emotional appendages into the proverbial fire. All negative emotions are built on unfulfilled needs. Healing, giving, sharing, and love are the only ways to deal successfully with needs and, emotionally, keep our hands out of the fire.

A negative emotion, such as hurt, simply indicates that a mistake has occurred, and that there is a lesson to be learned. It is an excellent indicator that we can use to motivate us around healing and learning. If we can first, learn to be responsible for our emotions and, second, take the pain as a signal for healing, we can move forward maturely, attractively, and effectively. When a yellow plastic bubble is floating on the surface, it indicates that there is a diver below. In the same way, pain is an indicator—just like the plastic bubble—that there is something underneath. Our willingness to move below the surface will show us what needs to be transformed. When we transform these areas, we reach a new level of bonding and wholeness. If we don't use these negative emotions as signals and motivation for healing, then they become forms of blackmail, attempts to control, and areas of attack. Negative emotions are always calls for help and can be opportunities for stepping forward and growing in our relationships.

As we become responsible for our emotions, we can use the pain as a signal that this area wants to be healed and respond to negative emotions as calls for help. We allow ourself to grow up emotionally, and we learn the lesson, so we stop getting burned. We can begin to fulfill our needs in a mature, responsible way.

HEARTBREAK PRINCIPLE
A negative emotion or upset is a signal that something needs to be healed.

HEALING PRINCIPLE

If we are upset, we can use this as an indicator to heal both what is apparent and what is hidden.

HEALING SUGGESTION

Experiencing your feelings will never harm you; suppressing your feelings may eventually kill you when you have suppressed your feelings too many times. At the very least, the scar tissue grows, gradually removing you from life.

HEALING CHOICE

I commit to take on a new attitude toward pain. I choose to not run from pain but to use it as an indicator of what needs healing.

HEALING EXERCISE

Any negative emotion can be healed by feeling it fully, until it dissolves. As negative emotions emerge, don't turn away from pain. Experience it fully. Experience every nuance of it. Feel every sensation of it; even exaggerate it, aggressively leaning into the feeling. Be mature! Don't act it out in a way that would infringe on others. It is important to remember that the feeling of anger is a defense that hides a deeper feeling. You can shorten the time of feeling anger by intuitively asking yourself what the feeling underneath the anger is and then experiencing that. If you have been resistant to anger, then it is important to feel it until it melts away, and you can move into the next emotion. In this way you can melt away the negative emotion until it becomes positive. It may take many layers of healing before you reach the positive, especially if you hit an unconscious pocket. Don't give up. Experience all your feelings fully until you come to a positive feeling within. You can be doing almost anything else, and still be giving free rein to your feelings. You can ask the angels to be with you and to help you speed up the process. The reason you haven't recovered from painful events from the past, and why they have become patterns, is because you gave up feeling the feelings before you reached the point where there was only peace. As you experience your feelings, you regain lost, impacted energy, and re-associate with your heart. You stop being frightened of your feelings and you heal yourself. Experiencing your feelings in a mature, positive way is the simplest form of healing and getting over all painful events.

27.

HEARTBREAK AND FEAR

Fear is always a key dynamic in heartbreak, and it is the result of past separations, fractures, judgments, and self-attack, as well as the fundamental fear of losing something. It will be present if we are trying to live in the future or when we are projecting the bad feelings of the past on to the emerging future. Where there is fear, it is a sure sign that we are trying to control events ourselves rather than relying on grace or inspiration.

The nature of fear is this: whatever it is that we are afraid of, we are already experiencing it. For example, if we are afraid of heartbreak, we are aware that we are afraid, but we are also feeling the heartbreak at some level. When we fear something, we attract it to us. Whatever we think, believe, or imagine, we begin to manifest in our lives. It's known as a self-fulfilling prophecy. Many times our fear in its defensiveness causes us to bring about the situation we fear the most. In this case, it is heartbreak, but whatever our fear—because fear always has a focus—we will be feeling it and living it, even if it is imaginative.

The mind is always attempting to rid itself of its fears, which are obstacles to moving on. If it has to make our fear real for us to finally attempt to work through it and let it go, then it will do so. The ego is built on fear, although it appears to be helping us, by attempting to keep the fear under control. In other words, most of us spend a great deal of time and energy compensating—doing whatever we can to keep our fears buried or under control. When we compensate we spend a great deal of energy being good or working hard, which both paralyzes us and makes it impossible for us to receive. We may be doing all the right things but we never move forward. Most important, perhaps, this attempt to keep some of the fear under control can never fully resolve the fear, because that would be tantamount to dissolving the ego.

On this side of "Oneness," or total peace, we experience fear. Feelings of separation from our beloved, each other, and our God make us fearful, but, in fact, our fear comes from a deeper, core fear of intimacy. Underlying this is the fear of inadequacy, which is one of the main catalysts to heartbreak. We are afraid that we won't be able to handle the relationship as it progresses, so we make a hidden choice to end it now. When we judge our partner, we resist them or reject their behavior, and this in turn gives us feelings of rejection and fear. If we realize that fear is an illusion, and that it comes from our own misperceptions and mistaken responses, we can stop the fear that generates a self-defeating pattern of fight or flight. Fear can be healed because it is a misperception based on painful beliefs and patterns of the past remade in the present. Once fear is gone, we can see the way through any problem, even in the most dire circumstances.

Every problem has fear as one of its roots, so when the fear is dissolved, the problem collapses. All heartbreaks result from the fear of the next step, because we somehow imagine that the next step will be worse than what we have now. Actually, as we give up the fear and control that prevents us from moving forward, we see that the next step is always better, because the confidence to handle the new level of success comes with it. Fear shrinks us, or it is used to justify our attack on others. It's important to remember that in relationships, we are moving back toward heartbreak when we are not moving toward love. Without continual breakthrough or rebirth, we are stuck in power struggle or deadness, within the relationship.

Fear, as a core element of heartbreak, can be healed with love, joining, forgiveness, and understanding, which bring new romance and honeymoon, or growth and regeneration, to our relationships. Our willingness to heal our fear allows both of us to move forward and to succeed in our lives.

HEARTBREAK PRINCIPLE

In every heartbreak there is a place where we'd rather have the control of heartbreak, instead of the fear of moving forward with this partner to the next step.

HEALING PRINCIPLE

Every problem hides fear of, and resistance to, the future. This can be healed with love, trust, forgiveness, and letting go.

HEALING SUGGESTION

You can easily move through fear if you put the future in heaven's hands. If any fear remains, you can also put that in heaven's hands.

HEALING CHOICE

I choose to end the separation that generates fear by joining others heart-to-heart, even in a conflict.

HEALING EXERCISE

Imagine that someone you feel distant from is standing across the room from you. (This can be virtually anyone as we judge everyone.) The physical distance across the room to where you imagine them to be symbolizes the metaphoric distance between you. Ask yourself, "What judgment holds me away from them?" Then ask yourself, "What fear does this grievance hide?" If you are willing to let go of the judgment and the grievance to step forward and end this layer of fear, do so now. If the fear holds you back at any stage along the way, be willing to put this fear in heaven's hands so you can let it go and step forward. Keep stepping forward until you have reached the place where you imagined the other person to be. Finally, when you reach it, imagine yourself embracing them and feel the confidence in your ability to handle this new level of success.

28.
THE HEARTBREAK DYNAMIC

Heartbreak is a shattering experience that involves an over-whelming and painful feeling of rejection. It fractures a certain wholeness that is in our minds, hearts, and sometimes our sexuality. It pushes us away from the world as we have known it, and we often become confused about our identities and even our purpose in life.

Every heartbreak is actually part of a series of heartbreaks. It reflects a pattern that comes up again and again, until it is healed. Adult heartbreaks are replays of earlier heartbreaks that have their roots in childhood. These patterns are, in turn, replays of heartbreaks passed down through our parents' families. They also reflect challenges that our souls need to heal and to learn from. An unhealed heartbreak causes us to withdraw from the world—it removes us from close contact with people and life. This contact is a symbol of confidence as well as a necessary factor in love and success.

Having experienced a heartbreak, we long to throw ourselves away. As children we experienced heartbreak and were unable to see the world in quite the same way again. As adults, heartbreak can turn our world into ashes. Our heartbreaks become excuses for us to stay withdrawn, defensive, and in control. We become independent because we fear the needs and feelings that led to our former heartbreaks. Yet it is this fear of our own feelings and of being used and hurt once more, that keeps us from opening up to, and joining in, a successful partnership.

Terrible as it may be, heartbreak is not something that is easily righted. Unless the mourning is complete—all the negative feelings are let go—the resulting effects and patterns indelibly mark and scar us. Sometimes we even keep the wound open, which makes us continually run away from relationships. Without healing, understanding, and new decisions, the pattern rules us. It's like a program in our bio-computer that keeps turning out heartbreaks time and again. The heartbreaks that we haven't healed are still going on inside us. They may be buried and compensated for by independence so that there are no ostensible signs, or alternatively, they may keep us in a needy, dependent state in relationships. This, of course, leads right back to possessiveness, jealousy, and more heartbreak. There is no time that our stock is lower in a relationship than when we are needy or dependent.

If hurt occurs (and heartbreak is just a much bigger expression of hurt), and it is not healed, then a revenge pattern begins. Hurt and revenge go hand in hand. We avenge ourselves through overt attack, withdrawal, passive aggression (under the

guise of being nice we are actually attacking), or hurting ourselves. This whole pattern leads to victimization. If we set out to
attack, having been heartbroken once, it is only a matter of time
before we are hurt again—living and dying by the sword.

HEARTBREAK PRINCIPLE

Heartbreaks are patterns of pain that will continue fracturing and shrinking our lives
unless they are healed.

HEALING PRINCIPLE

The pain of heartbreak has a great deal to do with both old heartbreaks and how
we are thinking and acting in the present. This can all be healed.

HEALING SUGGESTION

Commit to healing all experiences that are still upsetting you, so they will no longer
hold you back. Include all forms of loss, hurt, and guilt that still affect you. Choose
to learn and unlearn, to forgive yourself and others, and to take responsibility so that
you can once again have the confidence for love, success, and freedom.

HEALING CHOICE

With heaven's help, I choose to heal all that is holding me back in my life.

HEALING EXERCISE

Bring to your mind the most painful situations in your life. Imagine that God, Jesus,
Buddha, Quan Yin, Mohammed, or your Higher Self is there to help you. Ask for
their assistance in changing this experience to one of peace and joy. Sacrifice your
suffering, so you can let in the love and grace.

29.

AWARENESS AND HEARTBREAK

Awareness creates flow. There is a natural pleasure that comes from awareness as we discover what we have hidden from ourselves. As we learn about and understand ourselves and the world around us we are able to make changes. Since the greater part of what is happening in a heartbreak situation is below the level of our awareness, this new information allows us to respond accordingly, thereby correcting it. Awareness is a leadership principle that allows us to move forward and to help others in a similar fashion.

Without awareness, and because of fear, we don't allow ourselves to recognize the hidden dynamics or patterns that are going on. A heartbreak pattern is much like a reef; during the low tides of life it is visible, and is either suffered or dealt with. During the high tide of life it is submerged and not evident to the unaware. Without awareness, it is the in-between times, as we are approaching the shore of another partner, when these shoals have the ability to rip the very heart out of our relationship.

Awareness empowers us. By giving us better and more educated choices, it opens our life to new possibilities. All of us have been victimized, and we have all made mistakes in our choices. Some of our choices were made by fractured parts of our mind that were emotionally arrested at very early ages, which typically led to further emotional fracturing. These choices were hidden away with the parts of our minds that made them. It is time to choose awareness. Only by discovering what we have hidden from ourselves can we change it.

We don't have to fall for the ego's trick of blaming ourselves when we're not blaming others, because this only clouds awareness. Choosing to be aware at all times will allow both the hidden elements and the new possibilities to be shown to us. If we are curious about the missing pieces we can be inspired by the answer that is within us, rather than planning and making strategies, which ultimately lead to failure and to more heartbreak. With awareness, we can even go back to past incidents and create flow where we were fractured.

HEARTBREAK PRINCIPLE

Whenever we feel pain in a situation, we can be sure that our partner or other person in the situation feels the same pain, even if they are acting differently.

HEALING PRINCIPLE

Awareness creates flow where we have been stuck and shows us new possibilities.

HEALING SUGGESTION

What you don't see can hurt you. It is not only a good idea to know that there is a snake in the grass, it is also good to know where it is and if it has any friends.

HEALING CHOICE

In this incident (present and/or past), I now ask to be made aware of the hidden elements. I ask to have the awareness to know exactly what to do in a situation and exactly how to clear it.

HEALING EXERCISE

List ten painful situations where you don't understand why someone acted in a way that caused you pain. Realize that the pain you experienced was exactly what they were feeling inside.

Incident	Pain I experienced	Pain they had inside
1. _____	_____	_____
2. _____	_____	_____
3. _____	_____	_____
4. _____	_____	_____
5. _____	_____	_____
6. _____	_____	_____
7. _____	_____	_____

Incident	Pain I experienced	Pain they had inside
8. _____	_____	_____
9. _____	_____	_____
10. _____	_____	_____

Now look at how that pain within (both yours and theirs) caused you to act in a way that may have had a negative effect on others. You now know how it feels to act in a way that is harmful or hurtful to others, so are you willing to forgive the person(s) in the incident(s)? Are you now willing to forgive yourself or would you rather keep the pattern and the pain? You have the power to end the pattern right now! For your sake, and the sake of those you love, do this now.

30.

FRACTURING AND THE HUMAN MIND

The human mind is a magnificent apparatus. It contains vast intelligence, wisdom, and genius. It extends to the realms of spirit, which contain the light and love with which our God created us. This is where we can experience "Oneness," being part of all that is. Between "Oneness" and the levels of our mind of which we are conscious, there are millions upon millions of fractures.

Each one of these fractures is a conflict, containing different beliefs, and different parts of us competing for different things. Each of these parts compares itself to the others as the most special, the most deserving of love and attention—even negative attention. Each of these fractures, which are self-defeating patterns inside us, generates conflicts outside of us, because they represent unhealed pain and suffering within. Each fracture we heal brings more confidence, which leads to more success, and a greater ability to receive and to enjoy ourselves.

The world is a reflection of the millions of fractures in our mind. It is made up of dualism, where we see ourselves in the here and now and we see the world juxtaposed upon us. At the higher stages of evolution, we move beyond this duality; we recognize there is no difference between ourselves and others, and between ourselves and the world. This creates levels of bonding, and the joining allows higher levels of grace, love, and joy. We are all moving toward this but until we get there, we must heal the separation—the myriad fractures and conflicts within ourselves. These internal fractures lay at the heart of every problem we have with others. As we bridge the fractures in our own mind, we naturally find ourselves bridging the gap between ourselves and others.

I have seen people experience light, love, or Oneness—even sheer joy and ecstasy—when they were able to go deep inside the mind during the healing process. From what I've seen, it appears to me that we are evolving our way back to that Oneness. Every fracture we heal not only accelerates this evolution in our mind, but also quickens it in the whole world.

HEARTBREAK PRINCIPLE

Every heartbreak, which is the result of a fracture within, creates a new fracture and, along with it, conflicts and self-defeating patterns.

HEALING PRINCIPLE

Addressing our heartbreaks heals the fractures that cause conflict; it bridges the gap within our own minds, and between ourselves and others. Healing our heartbreaks accelerates the journey back to Oneness.

HEALING SUGGESTION

When you are in a conflict, see everyone as representing lost or hidden parts of your mind that want to be joined with you and reintegrated.

HEALING CHOICE

I commit to heal the fractures that led to this situation. I commit to realize my wholeness.

HEALING EXERCISE

Bring someone to mind that you are, or have been, in conflict with. Move back in time to before the conflict began, and imagine a bridge of light going from you to this person. Now that the differences are bridged, begin exchanging gifts with them (for example, you might give them the gift of trust and receive the gift of openness from them), until there is peace and partnership between you. If there is a chronic problem between you, then there may be a number of layers remaining. Repeat the exercise at each deeper level until the whole conflict falls away.

31.
DENIAL AND HEARTBREAK

Denial is a key element in heartbreak. Denial causes us to be blind and defeated. There are signs and signals that we refuse to read, or naïvely interpret to fit our rose-colored world when we are in denial. But all of these elements are crucial aspects that could lead us to an understanding or acceptance of the situation around us. Denial is an inappropriate defense against fear and loss; it blinds us, so we miss what is really needed in a situation.

Successfully meeting a challenge involves knowing all of the elements of a situation. It is important to read the signs and signals to make choices effectively and to seek the truth in a situation. It is important to clarify the confusion or ambiguity about, for example, where a partner might stand regarding certain issues, such as fidelity, or how they view the relationship. Some of us who have had a lot of heartbreaks reach a place where we hate surprises—even good ones. Communication and clarification can readily help. Communication, if it is carried out until there is resolution, will build a bridge to the other person in such a way that there will be forgiveness and joining.

In places where the pain of heartbreak has already occurred, denial continues to play a part. The extent to which there is denial is the extent to which there will be misunderstanding and, therefore, pain about the situation. All of us have a great need for understanding; it is one of our primordial needs. It helps resolve fear and instill confidence and bonding. It heals the illusion that keeps us mis-stepping and making painful mistakes, the illusion that comes from wish fulfillment. At the deepest level, understanding shows us how and why our lives are unfolding. It also encourages us to take responsibility for the choices we have made, even if we hid them from ourselves after we made them. When all the hidden elements are uncovered and understanding has freed us from the situation, the feelings of loss, fear, neediness, hurt, rejection, heartbreak, revenge, guilt, failure, unworthiness, expectation, sacrifice, and independence will disappear. We will be able to see every-one else's innocence and responsibility, including that of our parents, which is where the patterns typically began. Our own responsibility also becomes clear. We are not free of a situation until the pain is gone—the lesson learned, the gift given on our part, and we are once again reintegrated on the inside and bonded on the outside.

We may believe that there is no longer a heartbreak prob-lem if we can't feel it anymore. Unfortunately, we continue a pattern of denial long after heartbreak has occurred. This is where the compensatory roles of dependence, independence, or sacrifice come in. All three of these behaviors show us that we still have unfinished mourning—we haven't allowed our-selves to know all of the elements and emotion involved. Similarly, attack demonstrates denial, whether we are the one attacking or the victim. When we are attacking we attempt to equalize the situation, which we justify because of our needs. When we are attacked, we bury guilt within, and old, similar unresolved situations from the past rear their heads or deepen the fractures. When we are attacking or abusing ourselves mentally (even subconsciously) it is easy to find someone on the outside to help us do it.

Power struggles and conflicts also demonstrate denial, because each of these reflects a conflict within ourselves. When we repress something, we necessarily project it onto the outside world, because we can't stand the feeling of conflict. We project the side with which we least identify. At the deep-est level of reality, therapeutic change occurs as we take responsibility not only for ourselves, but also for those around us and for what is going on, because this is what is happening within us. Change can take place because we remove the denial and heal the fractures within. If there is something to deny, there is no question that we have judged and resisted something. Denial is our attempt to hide it from ourselves and from others.

When we imagine there to be no problem because we don't feel one, we continue projecting our judgments and conflicts outside us, not realizing that all problems around us are, in truth, our own subconscious patterns and mirrors of our own mind. With this awareness, we can learn our lessons with grace. Instead, however, out of fear and judgment we refuse to acknowledge them as ours. The extent to which we do not acknowledge the lessons and situations around us as our own, is the extent to which we become victims. Consider this situation: there is a knock on the door and someone on the other side says, "Lesson delivery for you." We could open the door and accept the lesson, no problem. But if we refuse the lesson, the knock gets louder and louder. Pretty soon the doorbell is ringing, and there is kicking at the door. We have moved the dresser in front of the locked and barred door. In spite of this, the lesson *will be* delivered. Attempts are made to break down the door, but we ignore even this. When the lesson is finally delivered, we are frightened or wary because our door was broken by the delivery. How much easier it would have been to open the door in the first place!

Even now, in our present situation, there are hidden elements of which we could become aware if we were willing to see. All it takes is willingness and openness to read signals. When we ignore a problem or deny it, we aren't making it go away. It will finally become so big that it breaks into our awareness. By then, it is usually quite painful.

Naïvete, which is a form of denial typically parading as youth, presents a gullibility that begs to be taken advantage of. The effects of naïvete create dark lessons for us all. The opposite of this is a willingness to learn our lessons easily. We can ask for clarity as well as clarification from those around us. We can ask to see what we have been unwilling to see and finally to be shown the way out. Our higher mind has all the answers which come through intuition, inspiration, and vision. It will show us all the hidden elements and the way through.

HEARTBREAK PRINCIPLE

All pain and problems have an element of denial and self-deception.

HEALING PRINCIPLE

Awareness and truth bring healing, with an ability to act effectively by knowing and responding to what's hidden. We have already judged something and ourselves. If we know enough to hide it, we actually know what it is. Self-forgiveness helps us to see what we have hidden.

HEALING SUGGESTION

Ask to see the truth periodically in your relationship—to be aware of the hidden elements and to free yourself from fear. Take a moment to quiet your mind. Ask yourself which situation in your life carries the most denial—otherwise known as potential for future pain. From your heart ask that what you have hidden from yourself is shown to you. Be as specific as possible, but most of all ask this from your heart. Ask that the answers come easily and smoothly, and that what you discover can be resolved with grace. Begin asking questions and communicating with your partner to discover what you have been naïvely assuming. Allow clarification to come to the situation and be as unattached as possible to what the answers may be. Communication can save you a lot of time and a lot of pain so communicate until each of you has succeeded in clarifying your position.

HEALING CHOICE

Today, I ask for the truth about both my present situation and the past.

HEALING EXERCISE

Review three situations in which you failed or one that was heartbreaking. Examine all the elements that you hid from yourself, which led to pain, problems, or failure.

Pain/problem/failure	What I hid from myself	Why?
1. _____	_____	_____
2. _____	_____	_____
3. _____	_____	_____

Now, forgive yourself for hiding things from yourself or for being too frightened to clarify the issue. Review at least two more situations, and forgive yourself for these, so you can learn the lesson and heal at least a layer of the pattern.

Pain/problem/failure	What I hid from myself	Why?
1. _____	_____	_____
2. _____	_____	_____

32.
DENIAL, DISSOCIATION,
AND CHARACTER DISORDERS

There is a vicious cycle that begins with denial and ends in heartbreak, which in turn leads to more denial and then to more heartbreak. We back away from our feelings and from life, and we become insensitive to others' feelings. If there is enough heartbreak, we turn ourselves and others into objects. Life becomes survival of the fittest. A great deal of emotional shattering and old heartbreaks can lead us to become "sheep," "wolves," or "watchdogs."

If our courage has been sapped, we will usually lead a life of cultural conformity, becoming a "sheep," or someone who doesn't want to rock the boat or stand out in a crowd. More than anything we want to fit in. We follow the status quo and look to the norms for our behavior to avoid any trouble. This kind of living is meant to protect us from fear but, unfortunately, "wolves" prey on "sheep," and we often become victims.

Some of us who have had our hearts broken become "watchdogs"—someone who protects the "sheep" from the "wolves." We can be policemen, soldiers, or just natural protectors, who stand up to bullies in spite of our size. We can be quite heroic in our defense of others, but we cannot receive the rewards for these heroic actions. We are acting not from our hearts but because it is a role we have chosen to play. It's an act to cover over the buried pain within. Unfortunately, there is no real difference between the "sheep" and the "wolves."

Sometimes heartbreaks can lead some of us to become a "predator" or "wolf"—someone who believes that manipulation and taking are the norm. We take what we can get, using any means possible. We are often bullies who are unconcerned for others' welfare, needs, or feelings. There can be a potential for criminal behavior if we are left unchecked. Sometimes another broken heart wakes us up; sometimes it leads us to further dissociation and to victimizing others in the hope of not becoming a victim.

The "wolves" are those of us who were so heartbroken that we developed character disorders. We often resort to violence as a way to feel excitement, because we have withdrawn from pain and emotion. We have set up a hard, even criminal, attitude as a form of personality to deal with the world so we will not be heartbroken or victimized again. This leads us to seek to win at all costs—even to the point of victimizing others.

Individuals with character disorders don't believe that they have a problem; they believe the problem is always caused by someone or something else. They are never responsible; they think it is never their fault. The negative things done to them are excuses for their behavior—using, abusing, victimizing, taking; it is always justified, at least in their own eyes.

All of us must pass through the heartbreak stage where our own needs are central and paramount. Although we don't necessarily wish to abuse in any way, we are highly competitive, tribal, and nationalistic at this stage, and our manipulation, jealousy, possessiveness, using, begging, borrowing, and stealing can be justified in this period of pain and need. We can be unaware of how our behavior leads to pain or distance in others and in eventual disaster for ourself.

When I worked as a therapist in drug rehabilitation with the U.S. Navy and the U.S. Marine Corps, many of the men who had signed exemptions for rehabilitation were individuals with character disorders; they signed up for an easy discharge. At first, they claimed that their problems were caused by the Navy or Marine Corps, their officers, the system, and, finally, all authority figures, of which I was one. Most would move beyond this stance as their rehabilitation progressed, and they began to take more responsibility for their own lives. Some of those who were locked into this stage as manipulators, people-pleasers, ring-leaders, or thugs, had to be confronted time and again on the issues—their victimizing of others, blindness, victim mentality, insensitivity, manipulation, and their need constantly to take. I eventually learned that all of these behaviors were compensation for major childhood heartbreaks. When people began to move through these heartbreaks, they would move forward and make changes quickly.

When we imitate Cleopatra, the Queen of Denial, life has

a way of breaking down our doors, breaking through our defenses, defeating us completely, and bringing out the soft underbelly of our worst pain. As we discern some of the key but hidden elements surrounding heartbreak, and heal the past in the present, we can see with new eyes. Awareness carries with it a level of confidence, and always brings inspiration. If we want to understand, we will. If we allow for awareness, it will show us the problems and how to evolve and move through them.

HEARTBREAK PRINCIPLE

Denying and defending against pain by running away from it, or inflicting it on others, are strategies that do not work. The pain will not only be greater, but it will also painfully surprise us. The less we succeed in any area of our lives, the more we have hidden things from ourselves.

HEALING PRINCIPLE

Any painful or problematic situation—past or present, and no matter how ingrained the behavior—can be healed by realizing the truth, so there can be ease, freedom, and resolution.

HEALING SUGGESTION

To realize the truth and to begin healing a painful situation, simply state from your heart, "This is not the truth. This is not what I want. This is not God's will for me. I want the truth. Show it to me now."

HEALING CHOICES

I choose to be aware of elements I have hidden from myself in relationships, health, money, sex, success, etc. I commit to learn the lesson and to become aware of hidden factors in my present relationships as well as in my old heartbreaks.

HEALING EXERCISE

In the tables below, fill in the response to the headings for three hurtful or problem situations in your life. Use your intuition to assist you so that you can become aware of the hidden patterns surrounding your heartbreak. If nothing comes to mind, let yourself guess the response.

When were you hurt by another?	What did you deny?	Previous heartbreak situation where the other person cut off their feelings	Your own heartbreak that led to the event	Previous heartbreak for them that led to the event
1.				
2.				
3.				

When did you hurt someone by your behavior?	What you were not aware of?	Previous painful situation where you experienced the same hurt as the person now hurt by your present behavior
1.		
1.		
1.		

33.

THE VICTIM OF HEARTBREAK

All victims need to be treated with love and compassion. It is the only true stance to someone in such pain and need. We have all been victimized, and we will all continue to be victimized until we finally graduate from the victim–victimizer cycle, which brings enlightenment. We are frightened to the extent that we fail to take responsibility for ourselves, our worlds, and everything happening around us. Frightened people attack! We try to equalize a situation with our anger or we withdraw in self-attack. We feel we are always justified in our anger until guilt sets in. These behaviors can cause others to feel victimized by our aggression or withdrawal. When we regain our power and confidence, we are able to move into bonding and partnership.

We are either heading toward victimization or toward responsibility. It's a continuum of choice:

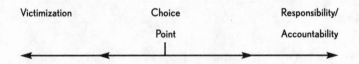

If we choose to head toward accountability and responsibility in a number of situations we can change the choice point.

No matter how much or how often we choose responsibility and accountability, we will continually have the choice about which direction we will head in, until we reach enlightenment. As every fracture inside us reaches the surface with its denial and defense there will be a major temptation to victimize or be victimized. By choosing to move toward responsibility and accountability, we will not fall prey to that temptation.

When as a victim we are ready to regain our power, we change our attitude and decide to step forward in our life; we desire to learn fully the lesson of the event. When we learn the lesson, our natural wisdom, compassion, and love can change the world around us. With this choice we begin to discover the elements that we hid from ourselves—the other choices that we have made and buried. This is just the beginning, because all the dynamics, hidden issues, and mistaken strategies will also be brought to the surface for healing and for making new choices.

There are always hidden agendas in being a victim, and they include calls for love and help, as well as trying to defeat and control someone. Being a victim is our attempt to get old needs met in the present, our desire to punish ourselves for old guilt, and our attempt to protect ourselves from fear. It is a way to get revenge on others, as well as providing us with an excuse to do whatever we want to avoid moving forward in life.

The victim stance is the weakest stance in life, because we have given up our power so that we don't have to be responsible. But victims become victimizers! When we compensate, rather than heal, we are inadvertently victimizing others, because compensation is just "acting" in the opposite way. There is no truth or love here, and as a matter of course we begin to act out the victim behavior on others. When we are blind to where we felt victimized, we go out to blindly victimize others. Our continued victim stance keeps us unavailable—in a place where we cannot give ourselves to others around us when they need it. What was done to us, we do to others, unless we are healed. We then pass the victim stance onto those closest to us. The only hope of breaking this cycle is to heal ourselves. As we do, we can then extend ourselves and our healing to those around us.

HEARTBREAK PRINCIPLE

Our choice to be a victim weakens and puts us in a victim cycle, where there is even greater temptation to be a victim. It carries a hidden agenda which may work, but will never make us happy.

HEALING PRINCIPLE

Forgiving others and ourselves for the times when we were victimized allows us to heal. We can then extend ourselves and our healing to others.

HEALING SUGGESTION

All victim situations have a purpose although it may be hidden. Choose three situations where you were victimized in the past, and for each one complete the following statement: "If I were to know what purpose this situation served for me, it was..." When you see what purpose you attempted to have it serve for you, you can now see that it did not succeed in making you happy. You can now make the choice to let those mistakes be corrected and replaced by what will truly work.

HEALING CHOICE

I commit to becoming part of the solution by healing myself, rather than remaining part of the problem.

HEALING EXERCISE

Victim situations   **Accountability principles**

_____   _____

Three situations where I was   **What it allowed me to do**   **What I didn't have to do**
victimized in the past were   **as a result**

1. _____   _____   _____

2. _____   _____   _____

3. _____   _____   _____

When you see what purpose you attempted to have each situation serve for you, you can see that it did not succeed in making you happy. You can now make the choice to let those mistakes be corrected and replaced by what will truly work.

34.
VICTIM PATTERNS

Every time that we have unhealed hurt, a victim pattern is set into motion, in which we take no responsibility and have no power. We now have an excuse not to face our fear or our lives, which also helps us to avoid our purpose. As a victim we are typically in our greatest need—calling out for love and help, but we are unaware of the pattern controlling our life. The victim pattern (all forms of victimization) is filled with buried elements, old pain, and hidden agendas. At some level, we are all seeking revenge for old wounds.

Some of the people upon whom we are getting revenge by hurting ourselves have no idea that this is what is occurring. In a similar fashion, all our adult heartbreaks are based on an attempt to avenge ourselves on our parents for how poorly we believe they treated us as children. Every heartbreak we experience as an adult states: "Because you hurt me as a child, because you didn't love me enough, because you didn't teach me about love, this is the result. It is your fault."

Being a victim has hidden elements of aggression and even violence. For the most part this aggression is turned against ourselves to wound someone else, but it can be just as violent. For example, we may become depressed, suicidal, ill, or reckless and invite dire things to happen to us because "then they'd be sorry." We set up a form of self-attack as emotional blackmail to let them know how badly they hurt us or how they did-n't take care of us. In any victim situation there is as much aggression in the victim as there is in the victimizer.

HEARTBREAK PRINCIPLE

As victims we are calling for love and asking for help. This is a place of primordial need and also a place of attack, self-attack, and excuses about our lives and purpose.

HEALING PRINCIPLE

The key to moving beyond every victim situation is forgiveness—both of others and of ourselves.

HEALING SUGGESTION

In every situation where you were victimized, imagine that things had happened exactly as you wanted them to. Why? How would that serve you? What did it allow you to do? What was it you didn't have to do as a result of this happening?

HEALING CHOICE

I commit to giving up every victim situation in my life. I will no longer use them to hide from myself, my promise, and my purpose. I choose to let my victim choices go and let them be replaced by inspiration and love.

HEALING EXERCISE

Choose five situations where you felt like a victim. Use the following questions to assist you in becoming aware of these hidden elements, and letting go of the victim pattern.

Victim situations	Who was I asking for love from?	Who was I getting revenge on?
1. _____	_____	_____
2. _____	_____	_____

3. _____ _____ _____
4. _____ _____ _____
5. _____ _____ _____

35.
RESPONSIBILITY AS EMPOWERMENT

When we choose to stop blaming others, and begin to discover the buried elements of our minds—becoming accountable for our lives and what happens—the ego's next ploy to keep us from moving forward is to try to make us blame ourselves. There is no sense in blaming ourselves instead of someone else, because either way we become stuck. Until we realize that, in every situation, everyone is totally responsible, accountable, and innocent, we still have some issues to work out. Responsibility is the willingness to acknowledge that, ultimately, we have power to determine how our lives turn out. Our happiness in life is up to us. Our lives unfold as a result of our choices, even though some of these choices happen in a split second and are then immediately repressed. In all life situations, we are always able to choose our attitude toward our lives and what has happened, which ultimately determines our experience in them.

The ego is always trying to delay, distract, and keep us from moving forward to the point at which it would lose some of its hold on us. It is always taking the sign for heaven and putting it over the door to hell, and taking the sign for hell and putting it over the door to heaven. Wherever there is a healing principle, the ego will attempt to put in a trap, a counterfeit principle that resembles the healing principle. For instance, in terms of responsibility, the ego will attempt to have you take everything on your shoulders which is a role or a job. It is false leadership that blocks teamwork, because it is a place of sacrifice built on a grievance so that there is no possibility of reward. That increases our dissatisfaction and feelings of being hard done by. It completely limits our success while increasing our off-the-ledger costs. Responsibility is really our ability to respond which allows us to claim our natural authority and power.

HEARTBREAK PRINCIPLE

The extent to which we fail to take responsibility is the extent to which we are liable to heartbreak.

HEALING PRINCIPLE

The extent to which we take responsibility increases our maturity and "response-ability," thus empowering us.

HEALING SUGGESTION

Assume as much responsibility for your life as you can. Sacrifice—or carrying everything on your shoulders—is a form of counterfeit responsibility.

HEALING CHOICE

I take responsibility for everything about my life. I will not blame others or myself as this stops me from changing for the better. I am the only one who can change my life. I choose to change it now. I want my power back and I will ask for heaven's guidance to make better choices.

HEALING EXERCISE

The following exercise will help you to assume responsibility for your life and to make new choices about what you don't like. Remember a previous situation of victimization. Examine it in terms of it being no one's fault, including your own. Judge no one but imagine everyone is equally responsible. Notice the feeling of release and freedom that is yours when you accomplish this. As your understanding increases, so does your responsibility. It becomes a natural response of bonding and maturity. Do this with all situations where there was victimization. Every problem you have is a place of complaint. What are you complaining about and to whom? When you complain, you are making yourself a victim in the situation while expecting others to change or do the work for you. Now, instead of complaining, assume 100 percent responsibility for the problem situation with a no-fault, no-blame attitude. When you assume responsibility, you can make new choices, choose a different attitude, and change a situation.

36.
ACCOUNTABILITY AND HEARTBREAK

Accountability is taking responsibility for our lives and for everything that has ever happened to us. The more accountable we are, the more effective we are in our lives. Accountability is the recognition that we made all the choices that designed our lives. We are all in different stages of realization about our accountability. The extent to which we are responsible and accountable is the extent to which we are mature and to which we experience freedom and power. We hide most of the reasons that go into our decisions and, therefore, bring about events in our lives that seem just to happen to us. When we take responsibility through our accountability, we are freed.

We are purposeful beings; everything that has ever happened to us has served our purpose. We always have some reason or purpose behind an event, but our thinking mind is defended against knowing this. Our intuition, on the other hand, would provide us with the reason or the purpose for any event, should we really want to know. Accountability is a principle of empowerment; it neither judges, blames, nor attacks anyone, including ourselves. When we understand accountability, we are freed from pain and the past, because it heals the vicious cycle that occurs when we do not heal our victim experiences. Victims become victimizers unless we heal the areas in which we were victimized.

Accountability recognizes that all of us are 100 percent responsible for our own lives and for the world around us. The ego, however, is always trying to change accountability and responsibility into guilt and sacrifice. When we stop blaming others, there is a tendency to blame ourselves. But blame of any nature is a trap that prevents communication and change. If we believe someone is guilty, we feel justified in blaming and attacking, which begins a power struggle. If we believe that we are guilty, we will punish ourselves by withdrawing from life, which punishes others, even if we love them. Being a victim is the most powerless, and the most ineffective stance, because it keeps us caught in the vicious cycle of victim/victimizer.

Being responsible means that we have the ability to change our feelings, our attitudes, and even our situations. Being accountable means that we have the ability and the power to know that everything that occurs happens through choice. We have all made some bad choices, but these can be corrected. When we begin exploring our minds for accountability, it is important to maintain an attitude of lightness and self-humor because it allows us easily to correct the mistakes we have made. As we bring out the hidden side of our minds, through understanding and self-forgiveness, we free ourselves; as we let go of where we have been victimized in the past, we are empowered.

When a person is sharing a victim experience, and we begin to explore the hidden subconscious elements together, I often ask them to *pretend they wanted this situation to happen.* I know that they didn't want it to happen, but just to humor me, I have them pretend that they did. Why? Why would they have wanted it to be that way? How would it serve them? What purpose would it serve? For example, we may think that we did not want to separate from a partner, but if we look at the hidden elements we find unexpected reasons, such as having to choose between a job and that partner, or a parent and that partner. It is a good time to explore the ego and what it has kept from their awareness. It is amazing what comes to light when we do this, and it typically goes right to the heart of the issue.

HEARTBREAK PRINCIPLE

Every heartbreak is a place where we assume no accountability. We believe it was something done to us against our wishes. This belief locks us into the pain and the victim stance.

HEALING PRINCIPLE

To be accountable is to realize the hidden elements in a situation, and to correct them through the power of understanding, choice, and forgiveness, thus freeing ourselves.

HEALING SUGGESTION

Commit to understanding all the hidden elements in your heartbreak situations. When you have come to full understanding, there will be no need to forgive anyone.

HEALING CHOICE

I am now ready to be fully accountable for my life and for everything that happened in it. I choose to be innocent and free.

HEALING EXERCISES

Answering the following questions, or filling in the blanks where applicable, will help you to understand the hidden elements in heartbreak and victim situations. It is best to answer with the first response that jumps into your mind. This bypasses the ego and its defenses. Choose a past heartbreak to start with, and then you can repeat the exercise with any heartbreak or victim situation.

If I were to know, what does this heartbreak allow me to do?

_____

What is it I don't have to do by having this heartbreak occur?

_____

What does this heartbreak give me the excuse to do (or not to do) now?

_____

Having this heartbreak justifies my decision to _____

_____

Having this heartbreak justifies my position of _____

_____

Having this heartbreak makes me right about _____

_____

The guilt I am attempting to pay off by having this heartbreak is _____

_____

This heartbreak reflects a power struggle that I am having with

_____ and _____

and _____

This heartbreak reflects a grievance that I have with _____ in the

present, and also _____ and _____

from the past.

The fear I am trying to protect myself from by having this heartbreak is _____

_____

The need I am trying to have met by having the heartbreak occur is _____

_____

The need from the past that I never received, and I was trying to get in this present situation is _____

The next step that I was afraid to take, which this heartbreak protected me from, was _____

What was I afraid to lose if I didn't have this heartbreak? _____

_____

I felt I was unworthy of the next level of success in this relationship because _____

_____

The beliefs I hold about myself that I am trying to reinforce by this event are

_____ about life _____ about relationships _____

about significant others _____ about emotions _____

about sex _____ about abundance _____

about love_____

The reason I am reinforcing these ideas is so that I could _____

_____

The reason for this belief is that it allows me to _____

_____

I wanted this relationship to end here and now because _____

_____

The need that was not being met in the relationship that caused me to end it was

_____

I was afraid to receive _____ which caused me to end the relationship.

37.
HEARTBREAK AND PAST PAIN

All heartbreaks are part of a pattern and, at some level, the present heartbreak is our attempt to heal the whole pattern. Heartbreaks are replays of past pain, earlier heartbreaks in relationships, and earlier heartbreaks in our childhood. These childhood heartbreaks reflect heartbreaks our parents had in their life. One of my greatest surprises as a therapist was to find that all pain had an antecedent; all pain is from the past.

Any pain from the past will cause us to act in some type of defensive manner or behavior. Typically, these defensive postures show themselves as: trying too hard, being too cool, or always playing the helper. They are, of course, recipes for future heartbreak because when we try too hard, the other person will want some space; when we're too cool, our partner will think we don't care enough to really engage in a serious relationship; or when we are the helper, we're trying to make ourselves indispensable. This role seems to create safety but it also creates deadness, because we are doing something because we feel we are supposed to do it rather than choosing to do so. We are actually afraid to be equal to our partners and risk intimacy, so these defensive behaviors, like all defenses, bring about what they were trying to prevent.

All the pain we experience is unfinished business from the past or fractures in the mind that we carry from the past into the present. These fractures will be pushed to the surface so we can heal them but, unfortunately, past pain is disguised as present pain. We don't realize that this present pain is actually the baggage or past pain that we carried into the situation. Subconsciously, we tend to make people from the present represent significant people from the past to focus the past pain in present disguise, which is called "transference" in classic therapy. We relive our heartbreaks time and again until we learn the lesson of transference, and recognize that all present pain is a real opportunity to clear out the past and begin anew.

As a young man, pacing my small cottage helped to heal one of my significant heartbreaks. I remember that for days I would wake up at 4:00 A.M. and begin pacing, which allowed the great pain inside me to surface—pain so great that it took my breath away at times. This pain would be replaced by depression when I went to work, but as soon as I was able to feel the pain again, the depression would ebb.

"Walking the pain off" was a method prescribed to me by a fellow therapist, a war vet who had, for four days, walked out of the hills of Vietnam back to base camp after an ambush that had left him the only man alive from his company. When he saw the pain I was in, he suggested I "walk it off," as he had done while recovering in hospital. As he walked, his pain and "survivor's guilt" continually lessened until it finally melted away.

By following his method I was able to move through the heaviness and pain that filled me. On the third day after my heartbreak, as I was wandering through my cottage in the pre-dawn hours and crying out the pain, I had a flashback of me as a baby, standing in my crib and crying for my mother. I re-experienced this pain and, as I let it go, I reached a whole new level of healing and freedom. It was this experience that helped me to recognize that all pain was unfinished business from the past.

Unfortunately, we hold our present partners hostage to our past pain, in that we make our present partners pay for the pain we suffered as children. When we are aware of this, we can take more responsibility for our emotional reactions by adopting a healing attitude toward them. Without this awareness and healing attitude, we are forced to repeat the mistakes of the past in the present, which only compounds the fractures we suffered as children.

HEARTBREAK PRINCIPLE

All pain is from the past. Every heartbreak compounds a heartbreak pattern.

HEALING PRINCIPLE

In an upset or heartbreak, we have the opportunity to clear the whole pattern.

HEALING SUGGESTION

Examine where you are using defensive postures in your life, which are setting you up for heartbreak. Are you trying too hard? Are you being too cool? Are you always playing the helper?

HEALING CHOICE

Whenever I am upset, I choose that both the present and the past be healed.

HEALING EXERCISE

Choose an upset or problem that you are presently experiencing and complete the following statements with your first most intuitive responses. Using "If I were to know" bypasses the defense "I can't remember." Often we cannot remember precise incidents but we remember the sense and energy of a situation. Revisiting the feeling and reconstructing the script helps us to rewrite the past and heal the pain.

If I were to know when the root of this present situation began, _____

_____

 I was probably at the age of _____

If I were to know who I had the problem with, it was with me and _____

_____

If I were to know what was going on, it was probably _____

_____

Imagine the scene was a script that you had written. Now, rewrite it. Keep rewriting it until everyone looks and feels great in the scene. It may take several rewrites, so do as many as are needed to have a scene that feels complete. If a scene won't be rewritten, there is an even deeper root at an earlier age that you must go back to.

Once again, choose a present problem, but this time, feel the feeling of upset. Exaggerate it; feel it more strongly. When you do this, you keep yourself from being overwhelmed or out of control by the emotion because, now, you are directing it. Allow yourself to feel every nuance of the pain or upset. Remember that anger always hides a deeper emotion such as need, loss, abandonment, hurt, rejection, guilt, expectation, burn-out, etc., so if you try to experience the feeling the anger hides, you save a lot of effort. As you continue to experience your feelings, you will move to earlier situations. Should this happen, experience the feelings until you go to an even earlier situation, or until you feel joy. With chronic problems, you might feel bad for a couple of days, but if you pay attention to this process, and set the goal of healing, you can win back portions of your heart and mind that have been caught in pain. You can do this feeling and healing process while you are doing most anything else, even while you are sleeping, by just setting the intention.

38.
INNOCENCE AND HEARTBREAK

We are not free until we are innocent, which means that not only do we feel fully innocent, we recognize that everyone around us is also innocent. Blaming others will not make us innocent; it is only our hidden guilt projected on to them that appears as their guilt. If we are not innocent we do not feel lovable, and we will punish ourselves and others for it. Heartbreak is a form of self-punishment and self-attack where we are attempting to pay off the guilt of the past by attacking ourselves with heartbreak. Whenever we punish ourselves, we end up hurting those around us through our pain or withdrawal. Attacking ourselves never works to get rid of the guilt; it only compounds it, because we now feel bad or guilty about the new heartbreak. Our hidden guilt typically stems from our families and feelings of failure. This is compounded by all of us feeling at the deepest level of our mind that we caused their problems, or that we stole one of our parent's love from the other, and caused them heartbreaks and break-ups. There might be guilt about being born, or winning competition with siblings, or parents, and then having them fail. Typically, these kinds of guilt are buried, yet we punish ourselves or get others to punish us for them. Guilt is layered in our minds. As we release each layer, we feel better about ourselves and, therefore, treat ourselves and have others treat us better. Be prepared, however, for the next layer that arises as unworthiness, self-attack, sacrifice, regret, compensation, loss, failure, and valuelessness. The ego builds its walls through guilt, but innocence melts them away, and where we were once split or fractured, we are joined.

HEARTBREAK PRINCIPLE

Heartbreak is a form of self-punishment and self-attack to pay off guilt. In any victim situation we also feel guilty for having been victimized, because guilt and feeling bad are basically the same thing. The extent to which we carry any pain or bad feelings from the past is the extent to which we feel guilt.

HEALING PRINCIPLE

Our accountability and self-forgiveness free us and open the doors we have slammed on life and love.

HEALING SUGGESTION

As best you can, be willing to forgive yourself for any situation where you feel guilty. Everyone feels guilty to some extent but, ultimately, it is not the reality. Guilt is only a trap that you are using to hide your fear and to turn away from your power and freedom. If there is guilt it means that there is something that you don't yet understand about a situation. Any attempt to hide your guilt with grievance, blame, or judgment is ineffective, but it does show you that there are still layers of guilt within you to be resolved. So, until you forgive yourself and others, you will be trapped and held hostage to the past. You are a victim.

HEALING CHOICE

I choose my innocence. I choose to forgive myself. I choose to forgive everyone else in this situation and to see their innocence as well.

HEALING EXERCISE

Choose three victim or heartbreak situations. Your responses will bring awareness to your hidden guilt around these situations. You can now choose your innocence instead.

Victim or heartbreak situation	What was I punishing myself for?
1. _____	_____
2. _____	_____
3. _____	_____

Now, would you be willing to forgive yourself for the sake of the truth, for yourself, and for everyone you love?

39.

ONLY YOU CAN BREAK YOUR HEART

Everyone has had broken hearts and, seemingly, in every broken heart, there is someone or some situation that has gone against us.

One of the very first empowering things I learned as a therapist was that we are the only ones who can break our hearts. It is a choice. To believe that someone else can break our hearts is tantamount to believing that they could somehow unscrew the top off our head, crawl down inside us, get our heart, then crawl back outside us, and smash it on the floor. This is illogical. Only we have access to our feelings. Although our emotions seem to spring up from inside us in response or reaction to the outside world, in truth we make a choice about how we will respond to a certain situation. Since denial is one of the key aspects of any heartbreak, we obviously hide this from ourselves. The choices we make in judgment, and how we choose to respond to a situation, determines our experience of it.

As our maturity grows, we become more aware that we can choose how we perceive someone or something and that we can choose how we respond. The more pain that we have locked up inside us, the more we react or overreact to the situation at hand. Because of this, we feel we have little control of our responses. It is important to know that we always have a choice; even now, in response to the pain of old heartbreaks coming to the surface, we have the choice. We can either choose to keep seeing things in the same way, or we can learn the lessons that will show us a truer way of perceiving them. We can pray that love comes into the situation, and this will occur—unless, of course, we have other hidden agendas. As a therapist I discovered that pain dissolves when truth or understanding is realized. So, bringing the situation to full understanding is a most important factor in healing.

HEARTBREAK PRINCIPLE

We are the only ones who can break our own hearts. There is a choice.

HEALING PRINCIPLE

The choices we make, the judgments we have, and our responses to a situation determine our experiences.

HEALING SUGGESTION

As you acknowledge that you are the only one who has access to your feelings, you can choose how you will respond to any situation.

HEALING CHOICE

I have the ability to choose how I will respond to situations that trigger me, as well as the pain that is triggered. I now choose that they be used for healing purposes.

HEALING EXERCISE

Choose three heartbreak situations and then list at least three responses for the choices and judgments that you made in each.

Heartbreak situations   **Choices and judgments I made**

1. _____   _____

2. _____   _____

3. _____   _____

Now that you have become aware of your hidden or not-so-hidden choices and judgments, ask yourself:

If I were to know, what was the pay-off for this situation? _____

_____

The answer demonstrates the motivation behind the situation. Discovering the hidden elements allows for new choices. If you got an answer that did not feel complete, ask yourself, "How did this serve me?" Keep asking this question until your answer does feel complete.

40.
HEARTBREAK AS A CHOICE

In 1975, when I was working at the Naval Drug Rehabilitation Center, I met a young sailor who came to the rehabilitation center after only ten months of being in the Navy, six of which were in boot camp. As soon as he finished boot camp, he was given orders to spend six months on a ship. While he was at sea, he received a "Dear John" letter from his girlfriend, which caused him to spiral into depression and drugs. He entered rehabilitation, but during the course of his therapy all he talked about was his heartbreak.

During one session, after he had, once again, spoken in glowing terms of his ex-girlfriend, and how devastated he was by her letter, I said, "But you didn't want her anymore. Why didn't you want her?" He got a startled look in his eyes as if he had just suddenly woken up and replied that she wasn't educated enough. She wasn't interested in education, and he wanted to go on to higher education. When I asked him again why he didn't want her, he recognized at an even deeper level that he believed that they seemed to want and value different things in their lives. I asked him when he had decided to break up with her, and he immediately responded that he had decided to break up with her about two months before he'd left, but decided to just wait and let it slide until he got back. So, when she wrote and ended their relationship, he forgot that he had wanted to end things with her. He could not believe that he had completely forgotten. From that day forward he began letting go of his ex-girlfriend and his life spiralled upward.

I began to realize that in spite of how things appear in a relationship, everything that occurs within it, is through collusion. I realized that no relationship breaks up unless we choose it to break up. We often hide and deny this from ourselves yet, secretly, at least one part of our mind directly and distinctly wanted the relationship to end. It was this part that was in control at the time just before the break-up occurred.

When a relationship ends, each partner chooses the best side to take, in order to move through and out of the relationship. One person typically chooses to be independent—the one who instigates or initiates the break-up. This person often takes the role of the scapegoat or the bad guy. The other person chooses the dependent position. He or she comes away with all of the heartbreak, pain, suffering, dependency, and holding on. Understanding that we made a choice for a heartbreak can free us from feeling like a victim in the situation. We would never have chosen this or, indeed, broken up, if it were the perfect relationship for us. If we were fully satisfied, if our desire and our love for them was stronger than our need to protect ourselves from our fear of being hurt again, we would still be in that relationship. As we realize that we somehow believed that they weren't the right one for us, we can let go of our heartbreak and begin changing our heartbreak pattern.

HEARTBREAK PRINCIPLE

Every heartbreak comes as a result of a choice that we made. No one leaves us unless we choose for them to go.

HEALING PRINCIPLE

Becoming aware of our choices, even the ones made and repressed in a split second, allows us to become aware of our accountability and our power.

HEALING SUGGESTION

As you become aware of your choices, remake any you don't like. Decide that the hidden feelings and choices will join together with the feelings and thoughts of which you were aware. This will help you to move forward.

HEALING CHOICE

I commit to becoming aware of all my hidden choices. I choose accountability and power.

HEALING EXERCISE

Make a list of all of your heartbreaks. With each one, pretend that you wanted it to occur, and ask yourself, "What was the pay-off for this heartbreak?"

_____

For each heartbreak that you lost someone, imagine that there was some reason that you didn't want them as your partner. Why? _____

_____

Remember that you have a split mind in these situations. The heartbroken part still wanted and loved the ex-partner. Now, with the help of your higher mind, see both of these parts melting down to their pure energy. Then see that energy melting back into you.

41.
ACCEPTANCE AND REJECTION

We only feel hurt or heartbreak when we resist or reject something that happened. It is only by rejecting someone, their behavior or the situation at hand that there can be heartbreak; without our rejection, there is no pain. What we resist, we push or tear away from ourselves; when we refuse to accept, we break our hearts. Sometimes, we do this to such an extent that a part of us dies inside. But be assured, it is waiting to be resurrected and re-integrated. We think that these parts of us were killed by others or by life but, in truth, they were suicides. We felt life or the situation was so painful that we could not stand it, so we quit. But now, with this present heartbreak, we can once again choose our attitude toward both it and the past heartbreak. In effect, our choice will affect how we stride into the future and even how we view that future. When we reject or resist something, it persists in our life, until we finally accept it. We may not like it, or we may not believe that it is the ultimate truth because there is pain involved, but as we accept something in our life, we can move forward. Acceptance becomes a core healing principle in heartbreak situations.

What we do not accept, we fight or defend ourselves against and through denial, power struggle, compensation, or control, we seek to contain and minimize the damage. This never works, because what we do not accept remains broken and holds us back. We may try to press on in our lives but, in truth, we can only limp forward. For instance, let's pretend that we have been friends since we were children. Somehow we get into a big argument and your attitude toward me becomes something like: "Spezzano this is for you" (obscene gesture) "...and that's for the horse you rode in on. . ." (further obscene gesture). My attitude, after about twenty-four hours, is "Boy, what a stupid fight. This is my best friend. What a mistake that was." Now all I'm feeling is all the wonderful friendship feelings I've ever felt for you. I'm apologetic and you are rejecting me. The one that rejects feels rejected. I may be feeling a bit sheepish, but I'm feeling the friendship. You, however, feel rejection, because it is you who are rejecting me. This may be covered over by anger, righteousness, or independence, but you will still be the one suffering.

In the late 1970s, I was in a workshop conducted by a friend of mine, Bob Trask, who provided an excellent metaphor for acceptance. Imagine that we are at the feast of life. We are eating our favorite food, and it's just delightful. In this feast, as soon as we have finished our dish, we move one seat to the right, and eat what is served, which is porridge. It is not our favorite, but we can still eat it. Then, as we accept that and finish that portion, we move to the next seat, and here we find okra. We don't like vegetables, and okra is beyond us—green, slimy okra, just like somebody blew his nose in our dish. We can't accept this. We refuse to accept this but, until we do, we cannot move on. We have to stay in our seat until we decide to eat our okra. Then, and only then, can we move on in the feast of life.

HEARTBREAK PRINCIPLE

Unless we are the one resisting or rejecting we cannot feel hurt or heartbreak.

HEALING PRINCIPLE

Accepting a situation allows us to move beyond it in our lives. If we can't, it will continue to affect us, and we will be tied to the past in a painful, self-defeating way.

HEALING SUGGESTION

If you refuse to accept what's put in front of you, you can stay there, as no one is going to force you to move on. Even if part of you moves forward, you will feel the loss of that part that remains stuck.

HEALING CHOICE

I now choose to accept what I resisted and rejected, so my life can move forward. I will use grace to show me how to accept everything that happens to me in my life today.

HEALING EXERCISE

With the following hurtful or heartbreak situations give at least three responses to each question. With each response, be willing to let go of the defense or fight against your pain, and accept what you resisted or rejected so that you can move forward.

The last situation you felt hurt

1. _____
2. _____
3. _____

What did you resist or reject?

_____

_____

_____

Your biggest heartbreak

1. _____
2. _____
3. _____

Who and what did you reject?

_____

_____

_____

42.

HEARTBREAK AND PERSONALIZING PAIN

Many heartbreaks come about because we personalize someone else's pain and behavior. We think their behavior was an attack on us for something we did or didn't do, rather than recognizing that it was a manifestation of the pain they were experiencing. Personalizing pain is a recipe for disaster. With the awareness that others' painful reactions to us are actually calls for help and love, we can let go of rejection and allow ourselves to give the gift of ourselves, to others and to life. Let me give an example of this from an experience that started out as a "story," but ended up as a profound healing.

Bill hated his father and was, as a result, always getting into trouble with authority figures. Bill worked in the military, and he felt that all of his authority figures were after him. He felt oppressed and victimized just being in the presence of officers. In one session, we traced the root of this back to when he was three years old.

Bill's parents had been having a fight about money and about Bill. His father, because of his own childhood heartbreaks, had not accepted selfish behavior in himself, and compensated for it through sacrifice. In the fight, Bill's mother was accusing his father of caring only about himself, which left his father volcanic and threatening. Bill, because of his fear and anxiety about his parents' fight, and the guilt that the fight was about him, behaved in a way that was certain to get his father's reaction. He reached out and tore the toy his sister was playing with out of her hands, causing her to cry. His father reacted violently, hitting Bill and throwing him onto his bed. Bill hoped that his mother would come to comfort him. He felt heartbroken about his father's attack and heartbroken when his mother never came.

After discussing this scene for a little while, we went back to an even more primordial situation. Using his intuition, Bill "remembered" a situation that occurred when he was a three-month-old fetus in the womb. Bill's parents had just realized that his mother was pregnant and they were feeling ashamed and guilty because they were unmarried. They were frightened because they didn't have the financial resources or the maturity that would help them to deal confidently with this situation. They also felt rejection, knowing that their parents' reaction to this would be negative. It was at this point that Bill began to feel guilty and unwanted.

This belief set up a pattern that was to run throughout Bill's whole life: he couldn't keep up a relationship. Time after time he felt that his partner was not there when he most needed her. He was in a place where authority figures, such as his commanding officers, seemed to single him out for attack. In any group situation he would typically become the scapegoat. As we talked, it became obvious that Bill was using the situation to punish himself for feeling that he had ruined his parents' life. He also felt hurt that they hadn't wanted him. I asked him how he would feel and respond if he were in his parents' predicament. He admitted that he would feel frightened.

Bill was able to see that his parents were not rejecting him, but simply feeling ashamed, guilty, and scared. He realized that his life-long pattern of rejection was based on a mistake.

I then asked him if he would be willing now to open the door that he had slammed on his parents when he felt rejected as a baby and as a young child. While I watched, he closed his eyes. When he opened them, a palpable change had come over him. A level of relaxation, warmth, and openness marked this change.

In a later session he told me that his behavior around officers was no longer reactive, negative, or paranoid. He felt confident, and even able to laugh, rather than feeling intimidated or attacked. Women also seemed to find him much more attractive, and let him know this in no uncertain terms. Bill learned a vital life lesson that day: his heartbreaks were the result of misunderstandings. He had personalized his parents' negative emotions, and rejected them in defense.

HEARTBREAK PRINCIPLE

Most heartbreak comes from personalizing others' pain and behavior. What we personalized was what we thought was done against us, rather than something that actually occurred for someone else. What we interpreted affected our thoughts and feelings (sometimes hidden) toward the other person.

HEALING PRINCIPLE

As we bring understanding to old situations that we personalized and interpreted as rejection, we can open the doors that we closed on our gifts, ourselves, and others.

HEALING SUGGESTION

Examine an experience from the present and one from the past to discover where you personalized others' pain and saw it as a rejection.

HEALING CHOICE

I will not personalize others' pain as a personal rejection. I will see their painful reactions as a call for love and help. I will not interpret others' behavior, as it will say a lot more about me and my motivations than about them. I will see any behavior that is not love as a call for love.

HEALING EXERCISE

Choose one incident from your life that was painful. (If you still put it in that category, there is some residual pain.) Ask that grace and peace be given to you. Imagine that you are there just before the incident occurs, and ask for grace and peace to fill you. Wait until you are full of grace and peace, and then proceed through the incident with acceptance instead of resistance. As you are moving through the situation, realize that the others' painful behavior came from their own pain—it was a call for help. Respond to that call by sharing your peace with them. If there is any feeling other than peace, proceed through the exercise again from the beginning.

43.
EVERY REJECTION IS A SEPARATION

When we experience a strong enough hurt, rejection, or heartbreak, fracturing occurs, which causes a split in our mind. This fracturing is a separation between ourselves, the situation and the people involved. Emotional fractures might take a moment or a lifetime to heal, and our attitude toward this is crucial, because it will determine our experiences in life. It is important to take an attitude of healing, rather than denial and projection. If we don't take care of these old fractures, they take care of us.

When we back away from life and others because of our pain, life becomes more of a burden or sacrifice, and there is more conflict or deadness. These fractures are places of lost bonding. Bonding is a natural love connection that brings about success. Any area where we are not successful is an area where we have lost bonding—there is a fracture, a place of separation.

Every fracture contains fear, guilt, and pain, and maintains the separation and conflict. The old loss or fracture sets up a coping mechanism, which is actually a self-defeating defense, to try to help us deal with this pain. In turn, the pain typically shows itself as dependence, independence, or sacrifice. Dependence only leads to more rejection and heartbreak. Independence (acting as though we don't care) leads us to become the inadvertent victimizer, because of our fear of heartbreak. When we deny our own needs and feelings, we are unaware of anyone else's needs and feelings, and can easily disregard them, thereby causing hurt. Sacrifice is the role of the untrue helper, where we take care of others in order to avoid our own pain. We subconsciously fear that if the other person gets better, we will also have to take a step forward in life. Our sacrifice enables us to hang on to that fear. Even though there may be a real desire to help, we are subconsciously holding the other back. None of these defenses work in the long-term, and ultimately bring about the very hurt that the defense was attempting to prevent.

HEARTBREAK PRINCIPLE

Heartbreak causes us to separate from ourselves, from life and from others.

HEALING PRINCIPLE

Every heartbreak is a place where an internal conflict led to an external conflict and then the fracture of a heartbreak. These are places of lost bonding. When we return to the root of the problem and bring about bonding instead of separation, we heal the whole pattern.

HEALING SUGGESTION

Every conflict is the result of separation. Every time you end the separation with for-giveness, communication, joining, or loving, it helps to heal your split mind.

HEALING CHOICE

I choose to extend myself or reach out to everyone to help heal the separation in myself, others, and the situations around me.

HEALING EXERCISE

Choose a situation in your life where you feel separate. Now, ask yourself, "If I were to know, where did the root of this heartbreak begin?" _____

_____

When you recall an earlier situation, imagine yourself back there, and notice that you are feeling the separation even now. While you imagine yourself in the past, allow yourself to move to your deepest center, the place of the light within yourself. This is the place of your spirit. As you fully experience this wonderful place, imag-ine this light moving out of you as a beam directed toward the other people involved in your memory. Then, see these beams of light connecting to their light. Allow yourself to experience the connection as you re-establish the bonding with those around you.

44.

HEARTBREAK AS COMMUNICATION

Everything is communication. Communication is not just what we say, which is only a very small percentage of commu-nicating, but also how we speak, what we do, and anything that happens to us in our lives. Most of the time, we are unaware of our communication and the message we are attempting to convey, because it is below our level of awareness; it is sub-conscious communication.

A heartbreak is a rather dramatic form of subconscious com-munication meant to emphasize a point. Although we may not be aware that heartbreak is a communication, or of the message that is meant for others, it nonetheless affects us. Without awareness, we will continue with this type of communication until we feel that we have conveyed and others have received our messages; until they do so, we continue having pain or hurt in our lives. Subconscious communication is ineffective because it is not only below our level of awareness, but it is also often below the awareness of those to whom we are trying to convey the message. When we are out of touch with our deeper feelings and choices, we will often experience heartbreaks and other painful events such as accidents, illnesses, and injuries, which are all common types of subconscious communication. Through working with numerous individuals and their heartbreaks I have found that this type of communication is always a subconscious message to significant people in our lives. Subconscious com-munication also sends a message to our mother, our father, our partner or ex-partner, ourselves, our God, and any other person who has played a significant part in our lives.

With the awareness that heartbreak, or any other pain in our lives, is a communication, we can make new decisions. We can choose to become aware of our feelings and communicate effectively, because discovering and understanding these sub-conscious communications gives us the core dynamics of the problem at hand. We can understand the messages that we have for the significant people around us by simply being aware of what we are trying to express.

A profound example of this simple technique occurred in a workshop where I worked with a young woman who was three months' pregnant. Several of her previous pregnancies had ended in miscarriage between the third and fifth months, and she was also in danger of losing this baby. As I began to explore this heart-wrenching issue with her, I recognized that with all these miscarriages she was giving a message to her father, who was an extremely religious man. She recalled that in the few times her father had talked to her as a teenager, he had always told her not to have sex. While this may have been appropriate when she was a single teenager, now that she was married, it was inappropriate and ruining her life. The subconscious message that she was trying to give her father by having these miscarriages was, "I love you." Yet the strength of this past message and her desire to please her father dictated the present conflict and her choice for heartbreaks. A pregnancy meant that, obviously, she'd had sex, and in her teenage mind, loving her father meant obeying him by not having sex. When she became aware of her message and how she was choosing to communicate it, she was able to make new decisions and effectively communicate with her father. He, of course, supported her in her marriage and her pregnancy. Needless to say, the rest of the pregnancy went smoothly, and it was an easy birth with a joyful outcome for everyone.

With this type of communication it is important to discover the messages we are sending to every significant person involved, because each message we are conveying is a reflection of an unmet need within us. Our needs are results of old fractures—lost or unbonded parts that we haven't yet healed. Common forms of subconscious communication are reprimanding, scolding, attacking, or carrying on a fight, with the hidden message that someone (ourselves or the other person) has to sacrifice or lose so that the other might win. Another common message is attempting to hold on to a past love. All subconscious communication is ineffective and painful, but in its most deadly forms we can actually believe that in order to give our message of love, we must sacrifice and hurt ourselves, like the woman who had several miscarriages. It is crucial that these misunderstandings are recognized and changed, otherwise the level of self-destructiveness can become lethal.

HEARTBREAK PRINCIPLE

All of our heartbreaks and hurts are subconscious communications with messages to significant people.

HEALING PRINCIPLE

Our heartbreaks are opportunities to become aware of our deeper feelings and to begin communicating effectively to everyone around us, especially those we love.

HEALING SUGGESTION

Without awareness of what you have hidden from yourself, you will continue experiencing pain, so be willing to bring it to the light where you can make new decisions and heal the mistakes that have led to your pain.

HEALING CHOICE

I choose to become aware of my hidden messages and agendas in all my heartbreaks so that I can effectively communicate the messages I want to give.

HEALING EXERCISE

Choose your most painful heartbreak and examine it in terms of subconscious communication. Where applicable, fill in the person's name, and then the message that you were specifically giving to them through this heartbreak. With each person, use the following statement: "If I were to know, the message that I am giving (person) by having this heartbreak, it is probably...."

Person	Message
Mother	_____
Father	_____
Myself	_____
Sibling(s)	
_____	_____
_____	_____
_____	_____
God	_____
Partner or spouse	_____
Ex-partner	_____
Other significant people	
_____	_____
_____	_____
_____	_____

Now review your messages. How many were about needs? How many were about fights or grievances? How many were about sacrifice? How many were about holding on? (Any attempt to give love, forgiveness, etc. fall in the holding-on category.) How many were asking for forgiveness? With this new awareness, you can begin to communicate openly about the hidden feelings. Along with communication, use the following principles to assist you in healing your heartbreak:

1. Where you were trying to have your needs met, give to those around you what you were trying to get.
2. Where there were fights or grievances, ask Heaven for the grace of forgiveness for everyone involved so that you can heal your judgment, which hides deeper guilt on your part.

3. Where you were sacrificing yourself (or asking others to sacrifice themselves), choose the truth to come in and free you, which brings a new level of success and partnership.

4. Where you were holding on, let them go. Imagine putting them in Heaven's hands, as one of the best gifts you have ever received. What we have received is truly ours to give. You can now give back to them so that you won't use them to hold yourself back.

45.
HEARTBREAK AND POWER STRUGGLES

In any power struggle, we are trying to persuade somebody to do something our way and to meet our needs. We attempt to control, use or conquer them, because we think that our way is the right and only way. Though we might be blind to our stubbornness, we are not open to any other point of view. This kind of attitude only leads to trouble, because not only does the other person feel imposed on, disregarded, neglected, and not cared for, but we will also, at some time, have to face these same feelings. When we are playing a win–lose game, we will make others lose. But to keep the game going we will need to lose at least half of the time. We can win now and lose later, or lose now in an attempt to win later, but whatever is going on, it is a nasty pattern that won't work, because fighting each other to get our needs met is not what is really going on.

Below every fight is the fear of moving forward. A power struggle is a great disguise to cover the fact that we are both frightened of the next step in success and intimacy in our relationship. This step in intimacy would create change and a win for both of us without either having to sacrifice. Another aspect of power struggle—or the win–lose game—is that when we win and they lose, our partner goes into sacrifice. Sacrifice is a place where we cannot fully give ourselves to others or the situation. If our partners are in sacrifice—doing what we want—our relationships will become boring and uninteresting to us. Even if we win and get our own way we actually lose through their withdrawal.

Fights resulting from power struggles usually begin because of a misunderstanding, where we stubbornly hold on to our interpretation of the situation, even though it is this interpretation, not our partners' actions, that actually hurts us. Power struggles create a descending spiral into heartbreak as each person negatively responds to what the other does. Power struggles are an attempt to be right at any cost. A couple will regress as if they were two children fighting, and the conflict can go on for years as they lose all perspective. The fight can easily become more important than anybody else, including any children. At this level the fight becomes an addiction, and both partners count their wounds and blows in a deadly game. This is a game that no one wins, where both partners and significant others in the situation pay the price. Whatever pain is generated from the fight is equally put on to bystanders, including the children; there is nothing that we say or do to our spouse that doesn't affect our children in some way. Physical, verbal, or emotional abuse between parents can scar children for life with heartbreaks of their own. Unfortunately, in this kind of game, when we are obsessed with our own pain or neediness, we become blind to its effect on others.

While hurt is a natural response to things we don't like, it will not be a happy story if we use it as a weapon indirectly to attack others by moving into a victim stance. Our attitude toward hurt or conflict, either within or outside us, decides whether we live a happy or an unhappy life. If we feel righteous in the hurt, anger, or defense, we will try to run away through withdrawal, attack others to equalize the situation or to get revenge. This turns our lives into stories, with chapter after chapter of negativity. Whether we either actively hurt ourselves as our part of the fight, or try to inure ourselves to the hurt so that we can wound another, it will come to a bad ending. Our short-term glee in defeating another can soon become long-term heartbreak. Continual hurt and attack between each other will become an exchange of deeper hurt and bigger attack that creates a negative spiral—an attitude of revenge that cannot succeed.

As we are willing to give up the hurt and heartbreak to see the other person in the situation as a partner and a necessary part of our happiness, and move forward in commitment or bridge-building, there is always a way for everyone to win. Every power struggle hides fear, so when we recognize that the fight is ultimately fear-driven, and join in partnership, it ends the fear. If we have the courage to change, we will find a way, even when we have painted ourselves into a corner, because the answer is within us. There is no problem that is impossible for grace to change, but we must be willing to move forward and to give up our self-righteousness.

HEARTBREAK PRINCIPLE

We go into power struggle when our partner has not met our needs or treated us as special. Therefore, we believe that they must be punished. This power struggle is an attempt to save us from heartbreak, but because it is built on old heartbreaks, it actually compounds them, which effectively hides our fear of intimacy, sexuality, and success.

HEALING PRINCIPLE

Communication about our pain and old heartbreaks, rather than fighting to get our needs met, changes power struggles into partnership and joining. This is where both partners move forward into success and intimacy. Only when both partners win is there true partnership and integrity.

HEALING SUGGESTION

Be willing to be wrong about how you interpreted everything that led up to the power struggle. It is only your thoughts that are hurting you, so change them.

HEALING CHOICE

I commit to give up my hurt and heartbreak. I choose to communicate about my feelings, rather than fight to get my needs met.

HEALING EXERCISE

Rather than continuing the fight with your partner, choose instead to share your upset feelings. If you communicate with integrity, you will heal yourself, move forward, and change not only the situation, but also how you see your partner. Communicate what is upsetting you without blame, and speak of how these upsetting feelings have been a part of your life. These feelings may be occurring now, and might even have occurred at the beginning of the relationship, but they are also something that you had long before you met this person. Experience the feeling as you speak of the past so that as you share you will clear at least one whole layer of the problem at hand. Refuse the temptation to blame, because it stops communication and starts the fight. If you do not communicate with integrity you will be fooling no one but yourself, because blaming or making your partner wrong, is only an attempt to remain in control. It is an attempt to hide your guilt by beating up your partner for what you feel guilty about. If you have shown little integrity in the past by attacking your partner, or blaming them for your feelings, they may have a less than enthusiastic response when you begin truly communicating. Continue with integrity, and they will soon realize that you are genuinely asking for their help, and not using this sharing as a means of attack.

====

46.

WHEN WE ARE UPSET

All of us experience upset or pain, but without maturity an upset can become a weapon that we use against others. When we use upset as a weapon, we tend to withdraw or attack by lashing out at those closest to us. These are both attempts on our part to make us feel better at the other's expense. It can be our children, our partners, or those we work with, who are on the receiving end of our upset. When the pain becomes too great, there is a tendency to become blind, and we react rather than respond to our own feelings and the people around us. We feel righteous and justified in our behavior. Later, this can turn to remorse and regret, or it can turn into a power struggle, with emotional or physical abuse. This is such a self-defeating pattern in our relationships that it deserves closer attention.

To change a power struggle, we first need awareness. It is important to begin examining just how often we get angry, get even, argue, complain, physically or emotionally lash out, how often we are dismissive or belittle those around us, and how often we display painful or depressive emotions. All of these behaviors can be abusive to the people around us, especially when we have no awareness of what others are experiencing as a result of the way we deal with our own pain. Reaction and abuse is a result of emotional cowardice—we are afraid to feel our bad feelings and to go into our own pain, so we spread it around. The answer is to observe aggressively whatever the bad feeling is and still to behave maturely. The feeling might at first get worse because of what we have buried, but it will gradually get better. For instance, if we are experiencing heartbreak, really perceiving our feelings and moving into the pain—feeling every nuance of sensation—gradually eases it. It is the same for feelings such as depression and sadness, but be aware that if we hook into a very deep layer of emotion it may take a couple of days to "burn" through it. Anger also is a defensive feeling so it may take longer to burn through it to the deeper feelings. We can immediately move through the anger if we are willing to feel the deeper feeling underneath that it defends.

Awareness in itself is not enough to change a power struggle. We also need to realize that our behavior and pain will not get better unless we decide that it will, unless we commit to healing. It is our choice whether we live a mature, responsible life, or a reactive, pain-producing one. Our emotional indulgence wounds those around us with the pain that we have inside, so it is important to realize how crucial it is to take the next step in maturity. The key is to make a total commitment to using our upsets as opportunities for healing, rather than as weapons, because anything less will come back to haunt our relationship. There is no excuse for abuse, and with commitment, for the most part, we will never lose control. If we do, we catch ourselves a lot sooner, we apologize, and we immediately undertake to heal and break our cycle of pain and abuse. The good news is, we don't have to do it alone! We can enlist and invite others around us to support us in our healing. We can pray that we will be open to all the grace and unseen support around us. All of us love to help and support others—especially those we love—because it makes us feel good.

HEARTBREAK PRINCIPLE

When we are reactive, we hold other people hostage to our pain and immaturity. We condone and choose that those of us who are wounded have the right to wound or emotionally pollute the situation, rather than take responsibility for our own feelings and change them.

HEALING PRINCIPLE

Our upset or pain will not get better until we decide that it will, which is a step toward emotional maturity.

HEALING SUGGESTION

Choose to have a new attitude toward your pain and upset. Experience every bad feeling you have until all of them melt away like butter in a hot frying pan. Do this until you feel good!

HEALING CHOICE

I commit to healing every upset I have so that I will no longer abuse the people around me.

HEALING EXERCISE

Choose a current situation where you are experiencing upset or pain. Now, feel the bad feelings around this incident. Continue by completing the following statements:

If I were to know when this bad feeling began for me, it was

probably _____

If I were to know who was with me when it happened, it was

probably _____

If I were to know what happened to cause this feeling to begin, it was

probably _____

Now that you have discovered the particulars about this feeling, use the following simple technique to change the pattern. (This is also an effective technique for changing disturbing dreams.) This past scene has been in your mind since it happened, and it is negatively affecting you. So, to change it, imagine that the original scene is a "first take" in a movie production. You are now going to do a "second take" so that it can be a better scene. Imagine the scene changing so that it becomes a better quality movie, and then do a "third take," and a "fourth take." Even though the scene becomes higher quality with each "take," continue on until you have done at least ten retakes, because the number ten symbolizes a new birth. If you continue to thirteen retakes you will remake the chronic soul pattern that you carried into life with you; at twenty there is a whole new level of relationships around your particular pattern.

47.

HEARTBREAKS IN THE HERE AND NOW

To understand heartbreaks, it is important to realize why they are happening in the here and now. Every fracture has been within us for a while, so there is a reason why it is surfacing now in our life. In general, our lessons emerge according to the healing schedule set up for us by our higher mind. But, with understanding, we can move through our lessons easily and gracefully, rather than painfully. To understand the hidden agenda of the ego is to assume responsibility for our lives, which empowers us with the opportunity to choose once again and to regain our hearts. Only with our hearts can we make peace with ourselves and with those around us. As we assume responsibility for our lives—ourselves, others, and the situation—we regain our maturity, which is a highly attractive quality, especially to a partner.

Every heartbreak is a part of a long-standing pattern. It might be worth considering why this heartbreak is happening now. Discovering how it serves us, and why it is happening now rather than later or earlier, allows us to understand the hidden agenda involved around our heartbreak. On the surface, this heartbreak is something that we didn't want to happen but, with awareness of the hidden agendas, it becomes obvious why it *has* happened. As we acknowledge that it is happening for a reason, and become aware of our hidden agenda, we take responsibility for this situation and make a new choice. Rather than the guilt, we now have the ability to respond to ourselves and to others in the situation, which is an important aspect of maturity.

HEARTBREAK PRINCIPLE

There is a hidden agenda in every heartbreak that includes why it is happening in the here and now.

HEALING PRINCIPLE

To uncover the hidden agenda allows us to recover ourselves, to assume responsibility without guilt, and to make better, more empowered choices.

HEALING SUGGESTION

If you become curious about why this heartbreak situation has occurred now, it will allow you to discover your hidden agenda and heal it.

HEALING CHOICE

I choose to uncover all hidden agendas in this situation so that I might make better choices.

HEALING EXERCISE

Choose a past or present heartbreak situation. To discover why it is happening here and now, ask yourself the following questions:

If I were to know, why is this heartbreak happening here? _____

_____

If I were to know, why is this heartbreak situation happening now?

_____

How does it serve me to have this heartbreak happen here and now,
rather than before? _____
Or rather than later? _____

If an answer does not present itself readily to any of the above questions, then dwell on it until an answer emerges. You can work on this in the back of your mind all day.

48.

HEARTBREAKS AND THE WOUNDED CHILD

All of us have wounded parts within, and many of these are wounded children. Whenever we had a heartbreak or trauma, the personalities and self-concepts that were fractured at that time became emotionally arrested, and they have not grown up since then. Even though these selves were stopped at the time of the fracturing, separation, and lost bonding, each one of these wounded children within us, even babies, has a purpose that it is trying to accomplish. We might have an eight-year-old within trying to make peace in the family, or a three-year-old that is in charge of protecting us from pain. Imagine what the strategy of this three-year-old self would be. In a good third of the cases that I have dealt with, where a wounded three-year-old was in charge of keeping their adult person out of pain, the strategy was to kill them so they would no longer suffer. The three-year-old self had no awareness that this strategy was creating a great deal of suffering on the way to getting the person out of their pain.

In childhood situations where the heartbreak or trauma was so extremely painful, the child within us can die or become unconscious. When a child dies within us there is a "death direction" pattern that is set up, and it actively continues within us until it is healed. As the body is a metaphor for the mind, our body is typically at much greater risk health-wise if there is a child buried within us. Our mind is so prolific that when one self dies, a new self will come to take its place and lead the way, but sometimes the pain of the trauma is so great that this new self also dies from the pain. I have dealt with people who had as many as a dozen selves that died as a result of one trauma. With each death of a part of ourselves, we are turned away from life and toward death.

When we discover a dead child, we can take the child in our arms, blow the sacred breath of life back into it, and bring the child back to life. As we pour our love into the child, it begins to grow and mature, and when it finally reaches our present age, it melts or integrates into us. In a similar fashion, when a wounded child is discovered within, we can just hold and love this child so that it will also mature and integrate with us.

Where we kept running into heartbreak in the past, we can now be successful in our life. In many ways these wounded parts or children, reflect hidden parts in our mind that have their own agendas, where all of them are attempting to be helpful in their own way. Even when these attempts to help are self-destructive, it is just a misguided strategy that can be changed with love and integration.

HEARTBREAK PRINCIPLE

When we experience a fracture or some form of lost bonding, the self leading the way becomes emotionally arrested at that age.

HEALING PRINCIPLE

We can find these wounded selves or children, and through our love release them so that they can mature and reintegrate, thereby reconnecting fractured parts of our mind and heart.

HEALING SUGGESTION

Use every problem or upset as an opportunity to find and heal your lost selves. You can't be upset unless part of you "got arrested."

HEALING CHOICE

I choose to find the wounded children within me and to heal them so that I can become whole.

HEALING EXERCISE

Choose a present problem and a past event that was painful. For these two situations, and for any heartbreak situation when you are feeling upset or even feeling anything less than joy, ask yourself, "How old is the wounded self within me:"

at the root of this present problem? _____

at this past event that was so painful? _____

at the bottom of this upset? _____

If the wounded self within is a child that has died, blow the sacred breath of life back into it. Now, love this self. Imagine that you are holding this self in your arms, and pouring love to it while it matures to your present age. Then imagine this self melting into you, reconnecting to your heart, and reconnecting to your mind, which allows it to accomplish its purpose. At the end of this you will feel peace and joy. If you do not feel peace and joy after this integration, it is because there is another wounded self that wants to be acknowledged. Ask how old this wounded self is and repeat the process until you reach a state of joy.

49.

HEARTBREAK AND NEEDS

Heartbreaks come from our needs not being met. It is these needs and their incumbent fears, that encourage us to possess and control our partners in order to make them the safe suppliers of our needs. Our needs and dependency, spoken or unspoken, lowers our attractiveness, which can bring about a negative response from our partners. All of this, of course, creates a power struggle in our relationships, which then leads to heartbreak because we make the fulfillment of our needs the primary goal in our relationships. Our needs make us defensive and generate inequality, which keeps us from loving and joining our partners in intimacy. Paradoxically, if we made joining with our partner the primary goal of our relationship, it would meet and even heal our needs.

Needs are pain and loss with mouths, which is off-putting to others because they are unsuccessful attempts to conceal means in which we are trying to take. Our needs are the result of loss and, therefore, lost bonding in the past. When we are needy, we are fearful and urgent because we are trying to fulfill the past in the present. We get angry at those who haven't acted in the way we need them to in order to satisfy our needs.

So, our grievances are basically the result of our unmet needs and are only replays of past situations where our needs weren't met. We demand and try to take from others, but when we do, what we are not giving, we cannot feel or receive. What we give to others, we are open to receiving and therefore if we give, our needs are satisfied.

When we try to get our needs met, we meet resistance and set the heartbreak pattern in motion. Any heartbreak or victim situation is typically a place of old unmet needs, and although it's heartbreaking that a victim situation occurs, it is also part of a pattern of old heartbreaks. The old heartbreaks and lost bonding keep us fractured within, and conflicted on the outside—hungry, and seeking in the present for someone to fulfill our past needs. It is the power struggle and the resulting fight over who gets whose needs met first and last that leads to our hurt and heartbreaks.

At the level of hidden choices and strategies, our heartbreak represents an attempt to get primordial needs met now. Some of these core needs are the attention, care, and love that we thought we could get from the relationship. Heartbreaks also represent our power struggle with and act of revenge on someone from the past who did not meet our needs. We can heal our needs in our relationships with love and forgiveness, and by giving to, joining with, receiving from, and bonding with our partner. In an ongoing relationship, maturity is reached as needs are successfully communicated, managed, and ultimately healed, because the choice for maturity is the choice to replace needs—which are a lack of love—with love.

HEARTBREAK PRINCIPLE

Our heartbreaks come from others acting in ways that don't meet our needs. It is the fighting over needs that leads to heartbreak.

HEALING PRINCIPLE

Every relationship gives us the opportunity to heal our needs and to communicate successfully, rather than to withdraw and attack. Giving what we need and forgiving others where our needs were not met, allows us to heal, which brings us more confidence, and adds to our attractiveness.

HEALING SUGGESTION

Use every upset as an opportunity to heal your needs and become more whole. It is important to not bully those around you to have things your way, which is only an attempt to get your needs met. So, be willing to accept your needs and to forgive yourself for having them. Healing the original fracture and loss by ending the separation that started it, or forgiving others in the present circumstance of unmet needs, will bring you to greater success, both in your relationship and your life.

HEALING CHOICE

I choose to be aware of my needs and to use every upset as a place for healing and building my life. I commit to heal my needs by giving, instead of trying to take, and to respond to others' needs as a call for help.

HEALING EXERCISE

Choose your three most recent heartbreaks.

Heartbreak	*What needs were frustrated?*
1. _____	_____
2. _____	_____
3. _____	_____

Now, examine your behavior in terms of the needs that led to your heartbreak. Notice how you reacted when your needs were not met by the other person. Did you attack with anger, try to control through blame, or withdraw and pout? Take note of these behaviors so that you can watch for them and if you notice you are acting in the same way, you can stop the fight and start giving. Now ask to become aware of one of your central, core needs—love, sex, recognition, abundance, etc. What is it? Whatever the need is, give it. Give what you need to your partner so that you can heal it.

Now, choose one of your major needs, and ask where it began. Your intuition will give you the answer. Be with this need wherever it began and notice that under it, there is a gift. You have come to give this gift to everyone. What is the gift? Imagine that this gift has a color. Now, see and feel this color generating from deep within you, filling you. When you are completely filled with this healing color, begin radiating or sending it to every person in the original situation where the fracture occurred. As you do, each person will be filled with the gift that this healing color represents and the need will be satisfied for you and for everyone.

═══════════════

50.

IF IT HURTS IT ISN'T LOVE

Many of us are confused about heartbreak because we believe that heartbreak comes from loving someone. Heartbreaks are actually the result of unmet needs. Heartbreaks do not come out of love. Love doesn't demand; with love, we don't need to have things our own way. In love, there is understanding, acceptance and forgiveness. Love allows us to be compassionate and merciful, to let go and communicate. Our love gives and wants only to commune. Conversely, with needs, we indulge, demand, reject, misunderstand, judge, hold on, blame, pout, throw tantrums, and attempt to control, which are all ways of hiding our fear of intimacy.

The extent to which a relationship hurts shows us how needy or fearful we are. Needs are time bombs of pain and conflict. They are our attempts to take, while unable to receive. Only when we try to take something can we get hurt.

How we handle our needs is crucial to our maturity, and depends on whether we consider needs to be weak and fearful, or whether we can see them as a call for love and healing. Every relationship gives us this choice: we can bridge the gap in our relationship that the needs are showing us, or we can try to get them met—which eventually leads to our partners feeling used and resentful. Our partners will withdraw, so as not to be used, and it is this distance that creates deadness in our relationships.

We can replace needs with love, which brings success and wholeness, through forgiveness, letting go, and joining our partner. Where there was taking, now there is giving and receiving. Where once there were demands, there is communication, invitation, and requests. Where there was competition, there is now joining, cooperation, and sharing. Where there was blame and emotional blackmail to get our needs met, there is giving or forgiving, which heals our need.

HEARTBREAK PRINCIPLE

Hurt comes from our needs not being met. In our neediness, we seek to take, but secretly push away what we want, so we can't receive.

HEALING PRINCIPLE

Healing needs, attachments, and pain will allow our relationship to grow and become whole.

HEALING SUGGESTION

If you get hurt from doing things for others out of love, it is not love. You are actually trying to get your needs met, in the disguise of love. Examine your relationships for how your need holds them hostage, and be willing to heal the needs and the fractures they imply, with bonding.

HEALING CHOICE

I commit to heal all the places in myself and my relationship where my needs are disguised as love.

HEALING EXERCISE

Look at your relationships and the instances where you have tried to disguise needs as love. Now, make a new choice for understanding and maturity so that you can let these needs go. Imagine each need as a grain of sand that is causing you pain and hurt. Gather all of these grains of sand into the palm of your hand and be willing to give them to Heaven. As you place these needs into Heaven's hands, what are you given in their place?

51.

HEARTBREAK AND SHATTERED DREAMS

We tend to get over the loss of a person, situation, or thing much faster than we get over the shattered dreams surrounding the event. Several years ago, I was working with a man who was experiencing heartbreak, although he had let go of any need to have that particular partner. As we were exploring his pain, I discovered that what he was still holding on to was his dreams of true love, raising a family, and living happily ever after. Further, his belief that he was equal to any situation, that he was lovable and that women were trustworthy had also shattered. When he finally let go of these dreams, he met a beautiful, mature woman; they were engaged in six months, and married in a year. As we let go of our shattered dreams, we are ready to move forward.

As a result of working with this young man, I began a more in-depth exploration of heartbreaks and discovered that every heartbreak is not just about a specific person—it is also about dreams that have died. The shattering of our dreams can actually have a more destructive effect on us than the loss of a person. Typically, these dreams are really some form of illusion—something that we think can sustain or support us, which really can't. It is only after we let go of the shattered dreams—mourn and release them—that we are able to begin the new chapter in our lives. The same principle applies to heartbreak: we need to discover which dreams were shattered and let them go. If we are unable to do so, we will become trapped in our disappointment. It takes great courage to begin again, rather than just substituting new dreams for lost dreams. It takes even more courage to open the door to our hearts and to ask ourselves what would really make *us* happy.

HEARTBREAK PRINCIPLE

When a heartbreak occurs, the extent to which it occurs is the extent to which our dreams were shattered. If our shattered dreams are not healed, we will not open ourselves to another relationship for life to begin anew.

HEALING PRINCIPLE

It is important to recognize that these shattered dreams were illusions and could never have sustained us. It is crucial to become aware of the dreams that were shattered in our heartbreaks and to let them go. As we do, something that can better sustain us comes to take their place.

HEALING SUGGESTION

Since no situation is finally resolved until your shattered dreams are released, it is crucial to do this, in order to move forward in your life.

HEALING CHOICE

I commit to find all of my shattered dreams and to let them go, so I can learn what really sustains me, and how to be truly successful.

HEALING EXERCISE

Choose three heartbreaks each for your childhood, youth, and adult years and list at least three shattered dreams for each.

Childhood heartbreaks   **Dreams shattered**

1. _____   _____
2. _____   _____
3. _____   _____

Youth heartbreaks   **Dreams shattered**

1. _____   _____
2. _____   _____
3. _____   _____

Adult heartbreaks   **Dreams shattered**

1. _____   _____
2. _____   _____
3. _____   _____

Now write your shattered dreams on a piece of paper. Literally burn the paper as a symbol of letting them go. Now, imagine that you are opening the doors that you closed when your dreams were shattered.

52.
HEARTBREAK AND THE SCRIPT NOT TAKEN

Any instance where we have been hurt is a place where others did not follow the script we assigned to them. Many fights result from competition surrounding the "battle of the scripts," because we become upset when our co-stars don't act according to our plans. The problem is that sometimes, we didn't even let them know that we were giving them a script; we just expected them to follow it. We get upset or hurt because we believe they should have known how to act or behave. Many times we expect our partners to be mind-readers, and we let them know that they have messed up in a big way by the long face we drag into the room, by our suffering sighs, and by our heartbreaks. The issue is further compounded by the fact that we are the co-stars of our partners' scripts and we are not acting according to what they have written for us.

When we learn to be more realistic and to communicate about our needs and feelings, we invite our partners to know us. If we try to force them to do things our way by using emotional blackmail, we lose the opportunity to mature, which will bring success for ourselves, our partners, and our relationships. If we value our relationships and our partners more than our need to get our own way, to be right, and to have every one of our needs met, love will blossom, joining will take priority, and success will be natural.

HEARTBREAK PRINCIPLE
A heartbreak is a place where our scripts weren't followed.

HEALING PRINCIPLE

When we communicate our feelings and our needs directly, we stand a much better chance of success and partnership.

HEALING SUGGESTION

Start thinking of other people as your equal, and treating them as you would like to be treated. Others were not put on earth to be the props in your play, but to co-create with you.

HEALING CHOICE

I choose to be more open, communicative, and empathic with those around me.

HEALING EXERCISE

Choose three people with whom you have a major heartbreak. Examine these situations to see how the script you assigned to those involved was not followed.

Person   **Scripts assigned**

1. _____   _____

2. _____   _____

3. _____   _____

If there is still some pain involved, and there must be or these heartbreaks wouldn't have come to mind, be willing to let go of these scripts, and forgive yourself for expecting others to meet your needs.

53.

HEARTBREAK–THE SCRIPT TAKEN

As we've seen, heartbreak comes from the other person not accepting the script we have assigned to them. Yet, at a deeper level, that person was doing *exactly* what we wanted them to do. They were acting *exactly* how we wanted them to act, because we actually wanted the heartbreak to happen. As strange as it sounds, we often subconsciously believe that a heartbreak will change a situation with which we are unhappy or help us to achieve something. Heartbreak is a choice. We often choose it in a split second and then bury the reasons for our decision in some deep, defended areas of our minds. We need to draw up those reasons, to examine them, before we can understand the root of our pain. When we have let them go, by understanding them, we can move forward.

The reasons why we want others to follow our heartbreak scripts may seem to be sound at the time, but they will never bring us true happiness or fulfillment, because they are all fear-driven. The most common reasons for choosing heartbreak are:

- our need for independence
- our desire for revenge
- the need for a weapon to defeat someone in a power struggle
- our attempt to pay off guilt
- to protect ourselves from fear
- to avoid losing something important to us

- to get something
- to be right about something
- to prove some positive or negative ego concept about ourselves
- to have our needs met
- to gain attention
- to be loved
- our need for an excuse
- as part of an ongoing heartbreak story
- to make us happy—we may have made idols of a person, a relationship, romance, sex, heartbreak, suffering, or crucifixion, thinking it will bring happiness
- to gain control
- to trap ourselves, because we are afraid of: our purpose; love; sex; the next step; our own inadequacy; our gifts; losing control; our lack of worthiness; not having enough value, for ourselves, or the other person, to commit; being ourselves; stepping up to a new level; and failing

HEARTBREAK PRINCIPLE

We chose our heartbreaks for some misguided reason that we usually hide from ourselves.

HEALING PRINCIPLE

We can now choose to become aware of our hidden scripts and to let them go.

HEALING SUGGESTION

It is time to step up and no longer use the past and its pain to hold you back. Just as a broken bone becomes stronger after it heals, your heart will be stronger than it was before the heartbreak.

HEALING CHOICE

I choose to become aware of my mistaken choices in my heartbreak situations. I choose to let them go and to step forward toward true love.

═══════════════

HEALING EXERCISE

Choose a heartbreak situation that was extremely painful for you. Now imagine going back to the split second in which you chose the heartbreak over happiness. Find that moment before you buried your decision and the reasons for it. When you begin to identify those split second decisions in your past, you can catch yourself making these types of decisions as they happen, which can be life-saving.

What was the purpose of your decision? _____

What were you attempting to get from the heartbreak? _____

_____

What did it allow you to do? _____

What could you avoid doing by having the heartbreak? _____

_____

What excuse did it give you? _____

What were the other significant but hidden factors in the heartbreak that are now coming to mind? _____

Although they may have been successful to some degree, recognize that these were all attempts that did not bring you the success you truly wanted. Be willing to put all of these mistaken reasons in Heaven's hands and to receive true love instead.

═══════════════

54.

HEARTBREAK AND OVER-SENSITIVITY

Childhood heartbreaks can lead to over-sensitivity in adults. This condition is the root of much adult heartbreak, and one of the main reasons why we are unable to maintain relationships. When we are over-sensitive, everything irritates us. We feel that nothing is being done the way it should be, and we fairly bristle with antagonism. Relationships cannot survive in this hostile environment, and we normally find that we are constantly single or on the way to being so once again.

What is the cause of this over-sensitivity? Once again, its roots are in childhood. At an early stage in our development, we lost or moved away from our centers. In other words, we were pushed off course by repeated traumas or heartbreaks at influential stages in our lives. We lost our sense of internal balance, and our protective outer skin. *Everything* bothers us because we have no sense of proportion and we have no protective self-confidence or self-love.

We make up for this by becoming emotional bullies or abusers in order to protect ourselves. We demand things on our terms and make others hostage to our emotions. Our partners walk on eggshells to avoid "setting us off," and they eventually give up and leave. Over-sensitivity can cause nothing but heartbreak because we have lost touch with ourselves. We cannot see our own sensitivity because we have fractured it away and suppressed it. We compensate by playing the opposite role—the tough guy who stands for nothing. The problem is that when we take this stand we also put ourselves in the position of being unable to receive anything, because nothing is ever right or good enough. The end result is further heartbreak, a confirmation that we are unworthy, and we become more sensitive still to the perceived slights of others.

We need to stop and assess where and why we were pushed off-center as children. We need to understand why we have lost our outer skins, and why we have locked ourselves in an endlessly self-deprecating pattern. We hide away our sensitive cores to avoid being hurt, but we cause continual hurt by doing so. The answer is to heal the original fractures and to learn to see the value and needs of those around us. When we give ourselves to others and care about their needs, we open ourselves up to love, which is the greatest healer of all. Every time we give instead of condemning, we feel a little better about ourselves and the little things that used to aggravate us to distraction no longer have the power to upset us. Paradoxically, our own needs will be met to the degree that we are able to meet the needs of others. And as we value others, we will be valued for ourselves because it brings both value to ourselves and to others. The love that it engenders both in and around us is food for the spirit, and it brings us back to our center where we are able to see things in balance.

HEARTBREAK PRINCIPLE

Over-sensitivity comes from heartbreak and feelings of emotional abuse in childhood. We are now blind to the emotional abuse that we perpetrate and pass on to those around us, as we use our over-sensitivity as a threat, and come down heavily with emotional punishment when we are thwarted.

HEALING PRINCIPLE

To heal our over-sensitivity, it is necessary to become aware of it and the ways in which we use it. It is crucial to identify where this dynamic began, to forgive whoever broke our hearts as children, and to forgive ourselves for being emotional abusers.

HEALING SUGGESTION

Blindness to others while making your own feelings paramount characterizes your over-sensitivity. It is important for your own emotional balance to integrate these two aspects so that you can return to your center. Returning in your mind to the original heartbreak and asking that everyone, including you, be returned to their centers allows you to bond with your perceived perpetrator, and then you can be joined once again.

HEALING CHOICE

I choose to forgive others for their emotional abuse of me. I choose to be aware of the needs and feelings of others around me, and to forgive myself for emotionally abusing others.

HEALING EXERCISE

Choose a person who you feel has emotionally abused you. Now be willing to forgive them for acting toward you out of their pain and state, "I forgive you [name] so that we can both be free." Now ask that you are intuitively returned to the core heartbreak where your emotional sensitivity began, and ask that your higher mind carry you back to your center—that place of peace, grace, and balance within. As you reach your center, ask that everyone in the situation be brought back to their center. Now, from your center, imagine your light connecting to the light within everyone in the scene and vice versa. When everyone is connected with the light, ask yourself what gift you could give to each person that would heal them of their pain. As the gifts for each person come into your awareness, give this gift to them. Each of the people in the scene also has a gift for you that will help you heal your pain. Receive the gifts that they have for you.

55.

HEARTBREAK–VICIOUS WOMEN, ABUSIVE MEN

Many times our old heartbreaks leave us frightened enough to become control freaks. We dominate our partners and keep them in line by attack or by threats. We are blind to this pattern within us, but whenever we feel threatened we resort to attacks—verbal, emotional, or physical. We have no sense of balance and can easily get lost in a diatribe or harangue at the least provocation, fighting for how, in our mind, things should be. Usually this extremely painful dynamic hides a series of very painful heartbreaks. In turn these heartbreaks hide some very real gifts of which we are frightened, and want to hide or control.

For example, in every problem involving communication, the hidden gift would be superior communication, or perhaps the inspiration to know exactly what to say, or the ability to bridge differences. The easiest way I have found to solve large problems is to find the gift hidden under the trap itself. With every sexual abuse problem I have ever dealt with there was always a precocious gift of sexuality that the person had within them. Given the distortion of sexuality in our world today, it takes great courage to be a leader in this area.

A common example of this type of behavior occurs in men who are not normally abusive, but become so when they lose the control that they experience being the independent partner in a relationship. They are the independent partners, and their partners are the dependent ones until the balance of power shifts in the relationship. When women become the independent partners, and the men dependent, the relationship reaches a crisis point. It throws the independent partner into the pain, neediness, jealousy, and possessiveness of the dependent position. As independent partners they had not been very considerate so their partners are now just as inconsiderate. They feel so out of control that they resort to shouting, and then pushing and shaking. This behavior only lowers their stock further, and their long-term girlfriends or wives soon leave them.

Once when I was out to dinner with another couple, a friend of ours began verbally attacking my wife. On previous occasions this man had tended to be abusive. His wife, my wife, and I all spoke to him about his attack. He was so blind to what he was doing that it took the three of us, individually and collectively, to point out what was occurring so he could see it. He had absolutely no idea that abuse was going on. That night he had an extremely bad case of self-attack to the point where he had trouble breathing and his heart stopped once. He was probably re-living the original heartbreak, which was the root of his abusive behavior.

Another time, I had a friend call for help because his wife was verbally attacking him so badly that he couldn't stand it. When I had been on the phone with them for ten minutes, his wife was so verbally abusive and vicious that finally I stopped talking to him, and confronted her about her maliciousness. She justified it by saying that she needed to be this way to be heard. It kept on without respite. I finally asked her to call back when she was mature enough not to "gun down anyone in sight." She later called and apologized, now willing to get to the heart of the old fracture. People caught at this stage are completely blind to it and to the effect they have on those around them.

I have been witness to adults attacking their children—sometimes even their adult children. When I confronted them later about the attack and why they had said what they had, they would be surprised, totally blind to it, and they would completely deny having said any such thing. This is a sign of heartbreak so big that it creates what is clinically called hysteria—outbreaks of emotion and abuse that are later completely forgotten. Trauma can be so big it even leads to multiple personalities. This is a clinical condition where different selves take over at different times. Sometimes the other or main personalities aren't even aware of these sub-personalities, and the person experiences blackouts or memory loss.

All of us have thousands of personalities that grew out of pain and broken bonding, but there is a difference between these and clinically diagnosed multiple personalities. All of our personalities compete, have different goals, are conflicted, and subtly stop us from receiving. The bigger the trauma, the larger the fractures we have inside, and the more independently these selves will operate.

Everyone in the position of abuser is blind to the effects of their abuse and the emotional and physical rights of others. Their problems all stem from massive heartbreaks they'd suffered as children, but this does not excuse their behavior, or give them the right to abuse others. It is our responsibility to be aware of the effect we have on others, physically, verbally, emotionally, and energetically. It is important for us to be in charge of ourselves and to respect others. Otherwise we are merely recreating the heartbreaks we received.

We are not in abusive situations by accident. We are in them because we are being given an opportunity to heal a subconscious part of ourselves, typically a wounded child. The abusive person is part of our life experience and part of our mind. When we recognize the one abusing us as part of a conflict within us, we can integrate this part. This may open other hidden negative levels, yet this part is simple. It only takes commitment to healing and forgiveness to make changes. When you can see that you are being abusive and how, you are on the road to recovery.

HEARTBREAK PRINCIPLE

There can be a heartbreak pattern so big in people that, in their blindness and pain, they induce heartbreaks around them by attack, complaint, and abuse. This will only cause more heartbreak until it is healed.

HEALING PRINCIPLE

Awareness, respect, and the commitment to heal are crucial in these situations.

HEALING SUGGESTIONS

If you have a toxic person around you, it is important that you don't sacrifice yourself to their abuse. Respect yourself and ensure that everyone respects you on an interpersonal level. The world is often a reflection of your mind, so find the old hidden pain within, and heal it. Use this as an opportunity for healing, rather than just a bad time. Clear the hidden guilt that causes you to punish yourself and heal the hidden heartbreaks inside.

HEALING CHOICE

I commit to healing my hidden heartbreaks so that I don't abuse myself, abuse others, or have others abuse me. I will see an abusive person in my world as an indication that there is some abuse or heartbreak still hiding in me. I commit to healing it.

HEALING EXERCISE

Sometimes abuse hides such big and complicated patterns that these exercises need to be repeated until the abuse completely disappears. This includes healing the abuser, the victims, and anyone else affected. Sometimes one healing exercise is all that's needed to change everything. Sometimes it's layer-by-layer work. Ask for Heaven's help. Ask for a miracle! Good luck!

Choose a situation where you are being or have been abused. This abusive situation indicates that you feel you deserve to be punished. Intuitively respond to and complete the following statements:

If I were to know how old I was when I mistakenly decided that I deserved to be
punished, it was when I was the age of _____

If I were to know who was with me at the time, it was_____

If I were to know what it was that occurred to cause me to make that decision, it
was probably _____

The decision I would like to make now is_____

Now ask your higher mind to carry you and everyone involved back to their
center, that place of peace and grace inside. If you are still not at peace, ask your
higher mind to carry you back to a deeper center. Usually one is enough but sometimes you may need to be carried back to two or three deeper centers. In rare
cases you may need to go back more. When you feel everyone in the situation
experiencing peace, imagine yourself bonding with them. Imagine that lines of light
from your own internal light are connecting you to everyone. Then imagine yourself giving gifts that would save people from their pain. When you have given those
gifts heart-to-heart, receive the gifts that they have for you. Now, receive and help
others receive the gifts that Heaven has for all of you.

Use the following exercise to go to the root of the heartbreak that is generating
this abuse situation. Complete the following statements:

If I were to know where the root of this abuse situation began, it was when I was
at the age of _____

If I were to know who was present, it was_____

If I were to know what was happening, it was probably _____

_____

If I were to know what I decided then that's affecting me now, it's _____

_____

What I choose now instead of that is _____

Now ask your higher mind to carry everyone back to their center once more.
What gift do you have deep within you that would heal and save the person or people present? Imagine that the gift has a color. Fill the recipient with the gift and its

color. Now, see that gift and its color going back along this person's family lines until it has reached and healed the root of that problem. If there is more than one person, do this with each person in this situation.

56.

HEARTBREAK AND SHADOW FIGURES

A shadow figure represents an aspect of self-hatred that we have denied and repressed. It is a fracture, in that it is something that we buried away when it caused us pain or trauma, but it is much more profound than just the pain, fear, and guilt of such fractures because it also carries self-hatred. A shadow figure is a personality that we have buried because we despise it. A shadow figure is an identifiable personality, and normally the opposite of the person we appear to be on the surface.

For example we may have done something as children that we believe caused our parents great pain or loss. We identified ourselves as being the cause which is typical for children. We may have blamed ourselves for their ill-health, relationship problems, divorce, general unhappiness, or even death. Instead of living with the great guilt of being a bad and wicked person, we labelled that part of ourselves as being bad, and repressed it away. But it exists within us as a shadow figure, and it festers there as it is left to wallow in the belief that it is bad. A shadow figure hides a belief that we are bad or wicked. This self-concept may at times cause us to act in such a way but it is not the ultimate truth. Whatever we might have believed at the time to cause us to shut it away, it was just part of a conspiracy to hide our true goodness, power, and purpose. The important thing to realize here is that we simply perceived this part of ourselves to be bad, and it was this mistaken perception that caused the shadows. We need to go back to the original trauma or heartbreak and uncover the reasons why we blamed ourselves, why we felt rejected, or why we believed that we were wicked or evil. With this awareness, we can forgive ourselves and see that we are all truly good no matter what may have gone wrong. Punishing ourselves for guilt and shadow figures is one of the major reasons that bad things happen to good people.

We can recognize the existence of shadow figures by looking for areas of compensation. When we work hard, struggle to be good, and appear, on the surface, to be model citizens, but do not receive anything for our efforts, we are hiding a shadow figure. We are struggling to make up for the guilt and bad feelings by proving to the world around us, and ourselves, that we really are good and that this shadow self does not exist. But everyone has shadows. Shadows also become evident when we do all the right things for what we believe are the right reasons and we hit a brick wall. We never move forward, and we cannot understand why. The fundamental reason for our inability to progress is the fact that we believe, deep within ourselves, that we do not deserve to. Our shadow figures hold us back because they contain the deep-rooted belief that we are bad. We will either punish ourselves for this, or compensate for it, or both. If we feel guilty and we struggle to prove that we are worthy, we do so in a sacrificial way. We can't open ourselves up to the love rewards that will encourage us on our path because we have put up a wall around our core feelings. We may be subconsciously afraid that these selves will be discovered, and we never let anyone close enough to catch a glimpse of what we perceive to be our bad core. This is one of the roots of our fear of intimacy.

A good indication of the size of the shadow figure we are hiding is the intensity of feelings we have for other people. If we actively resent, detest, hate, or vilify someone around us, for no real obvious reason (although it may seem like a good reason at the time), we are projecting our shadow figures onto them. The projection of shadows also relates to transference, where we take some issue from our past (normally, but not always, with our parents) and bring it into our present relationships. But even in this original situation with our parents, siblings, or whatever, we are projecting aspects of pain or self-hatred on to them. Projection relates to the deeper level of relationships where everything that occurs demonstrates our relationships with ourselves. Transference and projection are the causes of most of the conflicts we have with our workmates, our lovers, our partners, and our friends. We are transfering our own unhealed problems and conflicts onto them and onto the present situations in an attempt to heal them. At a deeper level we are projecting aspects we don't like about ourselves. We could not survive with this guilt within ourselves, so we seek to put the blame onto others rather than addressing the root cause of the problem, which is within ourselves. This seems to give us both distance and superiority, but it's important to remember that if we see a problem in someone, it is effectively our own problem.

Some people punish themselves with heartbreak for the guilt of their shadow figures. I have worked with people who broke their hearts at the hands of a shadow figure they projected onto those around them. A number of times over the years, I have heard the poignant heartbreak story of the "black widow." This is the shadow figure that leads us to believe that our sexuality is destructive, and that we will kill our partner with it. With this shadow figure, a woman will push away her beloved so as not to harm him, breaking both their hearts in so doing. Typically I would show these women how these shadow figures were ego traps to hide major gifts of healing, sexuality, and an ability to heal destructive or poisonous energies. We would then go on to integrate the shadows, and win back the gifts, sometimes in time to win back their partners.

The key to unlocking our shadow figures is to change our perceptions. Everything that occurs around us is really only our perception of events. If we choose to look at things, to interpret them differently, we are freed from them. The same holds true for the past. If we locate the trauma or incident that led us to believe we were bad and change our perception of it, we can accept that these shadow parts of ourselves are not evil and we can integrate them back into ourselves. We can free ourselves from the subconscious guilt and negative feelings that are preventing us from moving forward. We can heal our deep-seated fractures and shadows and accept ourselves and the love that others have to give to us.

HEARTBREAK PRINCIPLE

A shadow, or core negative self-concept, is a part of our mind for which we punish ourselves. We sometimes act out the negativity, or project it to have someone else act it out for us in such a way as to bring about the heartbreak that we subconsciously feel we deserve.

HEALING PRINCIPLE

A shadow figure is ultimately untrue but it serves us, especially when we are afraid of our purpose, our true goodness and the power of our own minds. These shadows can be healed through forgiveness, integration, and other methods that heal these mistaken self-concepts.

HEALING SUGGESTION

Since shadow figures are one of the major traps that prevent love and true happiness, it is important for us to find and heal them.

HEALING CHOICE

I commit to find and to heal all of my shadows, thereby reasserting my innocence, my worthiness, and my identity as someone deserving of all good things.

HEALING EXERCISE

Examine your life for shadows that you have either acted out, or that you get or got others to act out for you. Imagine melting all of them into your higher mind. This will give you back the lost energy that has become destructive and self-destructive. Now, examine your life for compensation—roles where you get no reward or nothing seems to come back to you no matter what you do. What is the shadow or shadows that lurk underneath these parts of your life? Imagine taking each shadow and melting it into its compensation. This will create healing and balance. This energy will move forward and finally give you the ability to receive in these areas.

57.

HEARTBREAK AND ANGER

We often become angry, even furious, as a result of our heartbreaks. Anger is an attempt to keep from feeling hurt, and while it may bury the heartbreak feeling for a while, we will usually end up feeling *both* anger and hurt. Our anger is an attempt to control others to meet our needs. It may win the battle but it will lose the war. It never successfully heals the anger inside us, so it tries to change others to make us feel better. This leads to fights. Only changing ourselves will work to make ourselves, the others, and the situations better.

Our anger can take a number of forms, including direct aggression, self-destructiveness, withdrawal, passive aggression, and victimization. Direct aggression occurs when we use our anger to attack the person who seemed to hurt or threaten us. Sometimes we are so wounded and angry, we lash out at everyone around us, whether they have hurt us or not. Self-destructiveness is an act to hurt or harm ourselves in some way in order to express our anger at another and ourselves. We become suicidal, insane, depressed, ill, careless, reckless, or fantasize dire things happening to us, because "then they'd be sorry!" We set up a form of self-attack as emotional blackmail to let them know how badly they hurt us or how they didn't take care of us.

I once counselled an athletic young man in his first relationship. He felt shattered when he found out his girlfriend was sleeping with someone else. When he confronted her, he reported that he barely restrained himself from picking up a very sharp knife to slice it across his chest to scar himself for life, while crying out, "This is nowhere near as bad as the pain I feel inside." He also told me how he had been driving his car fast and recklessly. He was even fantasizing about driving into a telephone pole, sometimes walking away from the accident, sometimes not, just to make her sorry. It took him a while to get over this dramatic but extremely painful stance. He was able to do so only after cleaning up some of his childhood heartbreaks, and learning that how he'd been acting and thinking was self-defeating if he wanted success in relationships.

Other forms of anger are withdrawal, depression, and even insanity. We are so angry, heartbroken, and disappointed that we withdraw from and quit life and sanity, and we may even choose death. I once knew a woman married to a psychiatrist. Every time she got really angry with him she went crazy. It was quite embarrassing for him in front of his colleagues. He'd fight back by having her carried off and committed each time, sometimes leaving her in the asylum just a little bit longer than necessary to try and teach her a lesson.

Anger also shows itself as independence, self-withdrawal, and controlling behavior. Our anger causes us to demand life on our own terms, because of our past heartbreaks and sacrifice. As independent people we rarely venture to give ourselves, which causes our partner to become dependent. As a result of our dissociation and lack of sensitivity or commitment, they end up experiencing the same heartbreaks that led us to be independent in the first place.

Passive aggression is a form of anger where under the pretence of being nice we are actually attacking. We appear acquiescent, yet the tone, energy, and sometimes the body language can be quite aggressive. The passive aggressor is typically blind to their own aggression, and acts like an innocent victim when someone finally unloads on them. I saw some dramatic examples of this when I worked as a psychologist doing drug rehabilitation for the U.S. Navy. A sailor could do something as simple as walk down the hall with such passive aggression that the head of each officer in every office would turn to see who was going by. All too often I would later see that sailor flunked at inspection for the most minor thing or court-martialled for being one minute late from weekend leave. He invariably asked, "Why me?"

Victimization demonstrates another form of hidden anger. In victimizing ourselves we use the aggressive energy against ourselves to become ill, to injure ourselves, or by getting someone to attack us. In this way we get revenge on them or someone else, by using our pain. I have found just as much anger in the victim as in the victimizer, only the anger is turned inward instead of outward.

The forms of anger that include independence, depression,

self-destructiveness, passive aggression, and victimization are typical for those of us who consider our anger to be bad, immature, or unenlightened. When we are judgmental or when we resist anger, they take these more surreptitious forms. Yet the anger is still locked away inside us along with the pain.

HEARTBREAK PRINCIPLE

Heartbreak comes from the anger hidden in us being the victim. It also makes for more anger, creating a vicious cycle. Anger comes as a result of heartbreak, hurt, guilt, and fear. It may take some form of attack or self-attack, both of which are self-defeating. If we deny our anger it will still affect us, but we won't have the awareness we need to heal it, or to recognize its more hidden effects.

HEALING PRINCIPLE

Recognizing, accepting, and letting go of our anger will allow us to transform its effects of attack, self-destructiveness, depression, independence, passive aggression, and victimization.

HEALING SUGGESTION

If we deny our anger, we can be blind to its effects, even while we are attacking. If we clearly see the effects of anger, we will clearly see that it's a mistake.

HEALING CHOICE

Today, I commit to seeing the effects of my anger, recognizing it as self-defeating, and changing it.

HEALING EXERCISE

Examine your heartbreaks for signs of residual anger. Whether this shows itself in attacking others or yourself, it will create self-defeating patterns. Choose and imagine as vividly as possible that all of your angry attacking selves are melting together into one. Imagine that all your self-destructive selves melt into one big destructive self. Imagine that all your depressive selves become one big depressive self. Imagine that all of your independent selves melt together and become one big independent self. Do the same with all the passive-aggressive selves and the victim personalities. They can only remain negative by being fractured from the whole. Embrace each one until it completely melts into you, returning your energy to you in a positive way.

58.

HEARTBREAK AND HATRED

It is not unusual to feel hatred at the time of heartbreak. We may feel hatred toward others or ourselves. When a need has been thwarted, when we have been badly hurt, betrayed, frustrated in a major way, or when we have suffered shattered dreams, hatred can easily set in. Gradually over time or as we forgive and move forward in our lives, the hatred melts away. Hatred is such a powerful negative emotion that it sets up a strong emotional pollution around us, even though we think we are only directing the hatred to the one by whom we feel hurt. Hatred is a major defense the ego has set up so that we do not hear calls for help. Because hatred blinds us to others and to their needs, the ego uses hatred to keep us singularly self-involved. We become blind to where and how we could help others and ourselves, because we are so caught up in feeling wounded and in our hatred. We all have major gifts that can help others and the world around us. The ego uses hatred to prevent us from finding them and fulfilling our true purpose by giving them.

This is how we know that there are still the effects of hatred left over from a certain heartbreak—if at the end of a heartbreak we lost our health, energy, youth, optimism, zest for life, poetry, art, music, sexuality, sharing, availability, generosity, love, or adventure, and we haven't got it back, we have evidence that hatred is still there. The hatred comes between ourselves and our lost gifts of love, creativity, sharing, and so on, and it prevents the emergence of new gifts. We need to recover those gifts to heal the heartbreak and clear the hatred that surrounds it.

HEARTBREAK PRINCIPLE

Hatred affects us by having us throw away a gift, such as love, compassion, and sharing, that we gave to our ex-partner. It blocks the emergence of new gifts. It also prevents us from hearing a specific way in which we can help others.

HEALING PRINCIPLE

Letting go of our hatred, forgiveness, and self-forgiveness gives us back our gifts and allows new gifts to emerge. Forgiveness and letting go are choices.

HEALING SUGGESTION

Since hatred is an emotion that is strong enough to keep us fractured, in conflict, and cut off from ourselves and our gifts, it is advantageous to let this hatred go.

HEALING CHOICE

I commit to finding and cleaning up my hatred with all its effects in my life.

HEALING EXERCISE

Examine your heartbreaks for lost gifts. Imagine, if you will, the hated person or persons standing before you. Imagine yourself opening your heart and mind, and giving them the gift that would transform and heal their behavior. See and feel yourself undertaking this heart-to-heart with them. Then imagine yourself embracing the gifts that you threw away, one by one, until you have brought them all back. Now, imagine that a new gift is unfolding from inside you. Sit quietly for a few minutes to see if there is a call for you to help in a certain way.

59.

HEARTBREAK AND SEX

It has been said that the longest twelve inches in the world is from our head to our heart. I would amend that to say the longest eighteen inches in the world is the distance between our heart and our sex.

All too often our heartbreaks involve sex. Jealousy, anger, possessiveness, unworthiness, independence, dependence, and sacrifice can all have their effect on our relationships, and on our sex life. The effect of heartbreak on sex can be devastating. We can have our dreams of sex and true love shattered. We may have made an idol of sex, and when it comes crashing down, we can effectively move away from sex or throw it away. By not resolving the issue and by covering over the pain, the idol is left in place—but our dreams are shattered. We can completely cut the connection between our heart and our genitals and withdraw from life, which affects our health, relationships, and careers. When disconnected from our heart, sex either cuts out or becomes promiscuous. We must let go and put into perspective what sex means in our lives.

We live in an age where sex is out of balance. We either exaggerate it into pornography or diminish and control it, leaving it ineffective as a vehicle of communication, transformation, and healing. All too often sex is used as part of a power struggle. We use it to control others or ourselves. To misuse such a powerful tool in this way always backfires.

People can spend decades after their first heartbreak trying to recover the gift of their sexuality. All too often sex has lost its power, because we don't want to be responsible for anything that is so powerful—something that can hurt us that much. Many times, the loss of sexuality occurs after a series of heartbreaking incidents. When we withdraw so much from our sexuality, it becomes an area of energetic, emotional, and even physical disconnection. This manifests itself as a relationship drought in our life.

Sex as a form of communication can be a bridge builder, a means to convey love, fun, and sharing. It can be tender, sweet, passionate, or inspiring. It can be used manipulatively to get what we want or as a weapon to defeat others or ourselves. We can withdraw from sex, which leaves us dead, listless, enervated, frigid, or impotent. Sex can add a great deal of life and spice to a relationship, or it can be one of the first lines of communication that is cut—an unused bridge considered too perilous or frightening. The bottom line is that we can choose and have chosen what sex will mean to us. And today there is almost no one who doesn't need some form of sexual healing. Sex can be a place of winning and losing, power struggle, abuse, and role playing—such as "sacrificer," or "playboy." It can be a place of guilt and shame, taking and emptiness. It can be unrequited, frustrating, disappointing, or lost in fantasy. It can be a place of control or a place of trying to prove value, worth, and specialness. We can use the body to attract and trap others as a means to try to reinforce some concept about ourselves. These dynamics can make sex a recipe for disaster, rather than a means of loving, healing, and joining. When sex becomes linked with or a source of fear, or another venue at which we expect to have our needs met, its purpose and its healing power are destroyed.

HEARTBREAK PRINCIPLE

When our heart is broken, so is the connection between our heart and our sexuality. What is illusionary in sex can turn to pain, and the true meaning and function of sex in a relationship can be lost.

HEALING PRINCIPLE

When sex is a place of giving, loving, and sharing, or used as a means of joining, it can bring healing and joy.

HEALING SUGGESTION

Assess the quality of sex in your relationship. What does it mean to you? How do you use sex? Do you use it to give or to take, to get or to love? How much have you withdrawn from sex since your childhood, adolescent, young adult, or adult life? Do you tend to exaggerate or diminish sex? If you are more prudish or prurient, this can be a sign that sexuality is unbalanced within you.

HEALING CHOICE

I commit to healing my sexual issues so that it becomes a gift in my life and my relationship.

HEALING EXERCISE

Ask yourself how much, on the scale of 1 to 100, you have withdrawn from sex. Begin with your childhood. Review significant incidents throughout your life where you may have withdrawn through guilt, shame, or pain. If this is not what you want, make another choice. Ask Heaven or your higher mind for help in healing these incidents and bringing them to understanding. Recover what was lost for your love, your health, and your general life energy.

60.

HEARTBREAK, ROLES, AND DEFENSES

When we have a situation from the past that is unfinished and full of pain, we attempt to compensate for it by playing a role. A role is based on a grievance, and it is a defense to handle the old pain, feelings of failure and guilt. Unfortunately, it doesn't work. It keeps us from receiving, and acts in such a way that will eventually bring the pain up to the surface again. A role is neither authentic nor alive. We can spend years not receiving, because it is a sacrifice, a compensation, and not true giving.

The three basic roles that we use to defend against the old pain are: dependence—leaning on the other because we don't value ourselves enough, while trying to get them to meet our needs; independence—pretending we don't have needs, which leads us to project our neediness onto others while surreptitiously taking; and sacrifice—where we try to become indispensable to our partner or others. This leads to deadness and turns our partner into someone who is continually needy. All of these attempts to play it safe will eventually lead to deadness, pain, or heartbreak. Our roles put us either above or below our partner because of our fear of intimacy. While it is much more frightening to be equal to our partner, it is the only way to bring about intimacy and partnership. Even though we fear that equality would make us feel more vulnerable, it brings about more openness, joining, confidence, excitement, intimacy, and love in our relationships.

HEARTBREAK PRINCIPLE

The three major roles of dependence, independence, and sacrifice, which are used to cover old pain, are dysfunctional because they prevent us from receiving. They lead to burn-out, and they bring about the eventual return of all the buried pain.

HEALING PRINCIPLE

Realizing that any role eventually brings about pain or deadness can motivate us to deal with the pain hidden under our roles, and instead to act by authentic and sincere choice. This brings life, availability, and the ability to receive.

HEALING SUGGESTION

Set the goal of equality and intimacy with your partner. Realize that you have the power to balance the relationship if you are willing to heal your fear of equality and intimacy.

HEALING CHOICE

I choose to be equal to my partner. I choose to let go of all roles that I sought to protect myself, which only made the problem worse.

HEALING EXERCISE

Imagine that you are using the Sword of Truth to cut through every role that you and your partner take on. Now use the Sword of Truth to cut through any pain underneath so that you can join your partner as an equal.

61.

THE TWO MAJOR CAUSES OF CHILDHOOD HEARTBREAKS

Over the years as I explored heartbreak patterns and their root in our childhoods, two major dynamics kept coming to light time and time again. The first dynamic was that of independence. After a childhood heartbreak, we had less reason to listen, acknowledge, or recognize our parents as the authority in our life. If independence is the key factor in childhood heartbreak, we usually have an independent conspiracy. A conspiracy is a trap that is set so well it seems we cannot get out of it because each heartbreak reinforces the pattern. The more heartbroken we were, the more we were forced to "raise" ourselves, because our parents had done it wrong. We think that independence will give us freedom or autonomy.

This pattern sets up a dynamic in our first relationships where we either act independent, thereby making our partners dependent, and us less satisfied, or we go into our first relationships naïvely, seeing our first partners as the answer to all that was missing in our childhood. Here, finally, is someone who will love us, save us, and be the very center of our lives. We are now the dependent partner and ripe for heartbreak. The independent conspiracy is a fracture that goes to the very depth of our mind. It is a pattern that goes all the way to our relationship with God where we are acting like a prodigal child. This authority conflict is a root dynamic in all problems.

The second major aspect of childhood heartbreak is the Oedipus complex. This is one of the strongest conspiracies dreamed up by the ego to trap us. The Oedipus complex has its roots in separation and lost bonding. It sets up feelings of scarcity, when we believe there is never enough of something, such as love or understanding—or anything we value—and competition for our opposite-sex parent. This pattern is passed down from generation to generation. What our parents did not resolve with their parents is carried over to us, and then on to our children.

One of the surprises I found as a therapist was that most childhood heartbreak was a defense against the Oedipus complex. In other words, the childhood heartbreak was actually a way of hiding or denying a deeper, more tortured and troublesome pattern. The Oedipus complex is an ego trap of guilt. It has to do with attraction and competition for the parent of the opposite sex. The Oedipus complex sets up guilt, competition, loss, withdrawal, fear of winning, guilt over winning, triangle relationships, heartbreak, power struggle, no relationships, dead relationships, fusion, separation, dilemmas, and loss of sexuality. For the most part, it is a completely subconscious aspect, and there is a great deal of denial surrounding it.

While sexual feelings are natural for us in regard to anyone surrounding us, we are affected by societal taboos against sex or sexual attraction to anyone in our family. Because of this we suppress and bury our feelings, repress or forget any situations or feelings in this regard. When a family is bonded, the natural attraction of sex is put in its proper place and balanced by the love that is present. Love allows sexual feelings and attraction to be innocent, natural, and subsumed in the love itself.

At the root of the Oedipal conflict there are the dynamics of competition and fusion, the over-closeness with another that come from separation and lost bonding. Competition, which is based on fear and feelings, is actually a form of delay. We seek to win over someone in the misguided belief that this is the way forward. We confuse winning with success, and set up comparison and win–lose dynamics, which is a sure-fire way of experiencing pain. Fusion is an over-closeness that blurs our boundaries, and keeps us in sacrifice. Re-establishing bonding in present or past relationships is a healing antidote to the hidden Oedipus conspiracy. Bonding is the natural balance and equal connectedness of all family members or partners. It encourages the centeredness of each individual and the family itself, so there is a grace and graciousness in all family interactions. Cooperation, partnership, and fun are natural characteristics of bonding. Lack of bonding is typically passed from generation to generation, along with the symptoms of independence and the Oedipus complex. Any generation can improve bonding or fall deeper into the trap of competition, power struggle, heartbreak, fear, fusion, or the deadness that lack of bonding brings about.

HEARTBREAK PRINCIPLE

The heartbreak pattern typically begins as a result of the desire for independence, which we thought would give us freedom to rule ourselves, or as a result of the Oedipus complex, a conspiracy against love, success, and our purpose.

HEALING PRINCIPLE

As we become aware of our independent and Oedipal conspiracies and how they have failed to protect us or make us happy, we reach the beginning of a new, more successful path.

HEALING SUGGESTION

Begin to examine your life for evidence of heartbreaks that may have provided you with the excuse for independence. Is there an aspect of the Oedipal fear of commitment, success, intimacy, and purpose?

HEALING CHOICE

I choose to become aware of the independent and Oedipal conspiracies in my life, and how they have held me back. I choose to heal them, so I might learn of my greatness, my purpose, and my power.

HEALING EXERCISE

Choose seven of your major heartbreaks and decide whether the main conspiracy was independence, Oedipal, or both.

Major heartbreak   Major dynamic

1. _____   _____
2. _____   _____
3. _____   _____
4. _____   _____
5. _____   _____
6. _____   _____
7. _____   _____

62.

HEARTBREAK AND THE OEDIPUS COMPLEX

While in graduate school, I studied the Oedipus complex but I didn't really believe it. I thought that it was just another theory that didn't have much to do with life. After ten years as a therapist working a great deal with the subconscious mind, I began to see what a genius Freud was. After fifteen years as a therapist, I committed to discover the ways beyond such a destructive trap. I learned that this complex was a conspiracy: a trap of the ego set up so well that it looked as if we would never get out of it. I found that it went along with fusion—a confusion of identity boundaries—and independence, which is a reaction against the sacrifice that comes from fusion.

Fusion is an over-closeness, even a super-closeness, that mimics bonding. It is a result of the family conspiracy in which we left the center within us and our balance in an attempt to save our parents from pain or problems. As we left our center—our place of grace and inspiration—we went into levels of guilt, feelings of failure, areas of fusion, and over-identification with one or both parents. If we were too burned out in the fusion (counterfeit bonding), or felt too guilty about being closer to one of our parents, especially the parent of the opposite sex, we set up some form of heartbreak or loss, to hide the evidence.

The Oedipal conspiracy is a subconscious trap set up as a conspiracy by the ego to prevent change and to block our purpose. A conspiracy is a trap set up so well by the ego that it is often never discovered. The Oedipus conspiracy is symptomized by no relationships, dead relationships, triangle relationships, or power struggles. It is generated by fusion and competition stemming from lack of bonding. Competition is based on a belief in scarcity, tied in with our ego that states we have to have more of something than anyone else has, even if it's the worst thing. Fusion is a lack of boundaries stemming from guilt, and its symptoms are sacrifice and unworthiness. It creates an inability to say no, and doesn't know true individuality. It is counterfeit joining and love.

Here is an example of how it works. Girls who felt closer to their father than even their own mother did, may have set up a heartbreak with their fathers to ensure that they couldn't be blamed for stealing him from their mother. Oedipal guilt has been passed down through the generations. The Oedipal guilt that began with our parents, around their relationships with their parents, caused a distance between our parents. As a result, it seems we could easily put ourselves in the vacuum with the parent of the opposite sex. Since the Oedipus pattern dictates we can't have the love of both parents equally, that we can't have it all, we believe we might as well get what we can and competition begins. Yet sometimes the guilt is so strong that we don't even bother to try.

When an Oedipus pattern is extremely strong, it can show up as divorce, affairs, loss of one parent early on, sexual abuse, and incest. It begins with our parents and can also be continued with our brothers and sisters. There can be either enormous competition or a refusal to compete within the family. This sets up a pattern of the Oedipal winner and Oedipal loser. The first typically succeeds in life but not all the way, or they succeed and can't feel or enjoy it, as it would be tantamount to stealing the parent of the opposite sex. The Oedipal loser, on the other hand, is afraid to win because it is tantamount to stealing the parent of the opposite sex, while killing the parent of the same sex.

The Oedipus complex hides both aggression and sexuality, because of our guilt about them. In this way, it effectively keeps us from healing them. We can only move forward, bond with our parents and families, if we recognize the roots of our complex and release the feelings of guilt that surround them. We can then share our gifts and receive gifts and love in return to reach a state of wholeheartedness and peace.

HEARTBREAK PRINCIPLE

While hidden, the Oedipus conspiracy can wreak havoc in our relationships.

‖ HEAL YOUR HEARTBREAK ‖

HEALING PRINCIPLE

Awareness of any conspiracy is the beginning of dispelling its power over us. New choices are the beginning of moving beyond its effects.

HEALING SUGGESTION

Examine your childhood story and pattern to see how much the Oedipal conspiracy dictated it. The Oedipus conspiracy is typically healed layer by layer until we finally reach our center of peace.

HEALING CHOICE

I choose to be aware of this Oedipal conspiracy and heal it easily layer by layer as it comes up in my life and relationships.

HEALING EXERCISE

Examine your last major heartbreak and one of your major childhood heartbreaks to see if the symptoms of Oedipus were present. If you enjoy this exercise, examine some of the other heartbreaks and major upsets in this light.

Last major heartbreak	Major childhood heartbreaks	Symptoms of Oedipus conspiracy (check if these were present)
_____	_____	Triangle relationships
_____	_____	Dead relationships
_____	_____	No relationship
_____	_____	Power struggle
_____	_____	Fear of intimacy
_____	_____	Lack of sex due to fear, guilt, or deadness
_____	_____	Betrayal

_____	_____	Dilemma, such as choosing one person over another or inability to choose
_____	_____	Imbalance of work and relationships
_____	_____	Lack of success at work
_____	_____	Competition for the partner
_____	_____	Competition with partner
_____	_____	Separation
_____	_____	Denial
_____	_____	Not having equal love of mother and father
_____	_____	Separation, divorce, death, or loss
_____	_____	Sexual guilt
_____	_____	Repressive atmosphere regarding sex
_____	_____	Competition of parents
_____	_____	Competition with siblings (if you were the winner you may be denying you were competing)

If you are a man, imagine yourself giving your mother back to your father at your birth. Do it again as a child, at puberty, and then as a young adult.

If you are a woman, imagine yourself giving your father back to your mother at your birth. Do it again as a child, at puberty, and then as a young adult.

Ask your higher mind to bring you back to your center and to bring your family back to its center so that balance and harmony can be restored. Using the light within you at your spiritual core, connect with the lights within the whole family so that bonding is restored.

63.

A RELATIONSHIP MODEL OF REALITY

If we understand how relationships work, we can transform the problems that arise. The "Relationship Model of Reality" provides a breakdown of how relationships and reality interface. We can, therefore, use it as a basis for making changes.

Everyday Life

Relationships (Interpersonal)

Relationship to Ourselves (Intrapsychic)

Relationship to God (Spiritual)

The first layer of this model is "everyday life." At this level, heartbreaks are caused by perceived wrongdoings—in fact, anything that relates to life on a day-to-day basis, including accidents, successes, money problems, and the normal ups and downs.

But everything on the everyday level occurs because of what is going on at the "interpersonal" level. Relationships generate our successes or failures, our prosperity or victimization—everything—on the everyday level. At the interpersonal level, we are conscious of some of what is going on, and the rest is kept below our level of awareness; heartbreaks can be the result of:

- power struggles
- win–lose attitudes
- manipulation to get needs met
- others not living by our scripts
- jealousy
- old pain
- breaking out of deadness
- projection
- subconscious communication
- giving to get
- the surfacing of old pain
- personality beliefs and self-concepts
- the desire to persist in victim and revenge patterns
- hidden agendas
- the desire for independence
- avoiding our purpose
- hiding and punishing ourselves for our guilt, especially for feeling that we failed to save our families as we grew up

In many cases we are unaware of these reasons, which lay behind our heartbreak.

The dynamics of our relationships (the interpersonal level) determines the quality of our everyday life. This concept became clear to me twenty-five years ago when I studied the subconscious mind. I could see that the pain of relationships, both childhood and adult, whether conscious or hidden, affected our lives in crucial ways. This level of relationships is the realm where communication, forgiveness, trust, letting go, true giving, receiving, acceptance, innocence, responsibility, accountability, joining, choice, and commitment take place, and they are all very important for success and happiness in our lives. Everything holding us back in life could be cleared through our forgiveness at this level. Everything stopping us on the everyday life level can be transformed by healing our relationships on the interpersonal level.

The interpersonal level deals with what is between ourselves and others. It is a "transference" stage, in that what we have taken from past significant relationships is disguised in people and issues in the present. Anything of importance now is actually a past pattern of unfinished business transferred to present circumstances. Identifying and becoming aware of these issues helps us to heal them.

Taking it a step further, everything that goes on in our relationships is a result of what is going on in our relationship to ourselves. What is happening at an interpersonal level is a reflection of our "intrapsychic" level. Those around us act out our relationship to ourselves—we act in exact correlation to the selves or personalities within us. Everyone is a reflection of part of our mind. No one is doing to us what we are not doing to ourselves, and no one is doing to us what we are not also doing to others.

We can heal problems at the everyday life level by healing our relationships (the interpersonal level) through joining and forgiveness. We can heal the intrapsychic level by finding the parts of our mind that people around us act out and then changing them by integrating them. Changes at the intrapsychic level affect the interpersonal level (our relationships) which in turn affects the everyday life level. We need to heal the personalities within ourselves and become aware of how what is happening with outside people and relationships is in fact a mirror of our subconscious. The world reflects our mind, so we can change our minds to help the world. Our healing changes our perception, and thus the world is changed. It is our responsibility to do so, and we have the power.

At an interpersonal (relationships) level, we become upset when someone doesn't live by our scripts, but at the intrapsychic level, we learn that people reflect our mind and, therefore, *are* actually following our scripts. No one is doing to us what we are not already doing to ourselves because, at this level, what people do reflects parts of our minds. These parts of our minds have a strategy or purpose to complete. Each different self or personality within is doing exactly what it thinks is necessary to help us—acting for what it thinks it or we need.

At the intrapsychic level, everything outside us is a mirror for our own mind. If we find and heal the conflict within, the conflict outside us disappears. It is here, at this level of healing, where we find the parts of our mind with different, or mistaken, strategies, and make new choices. Once we have pulled up what we have hidden from ourselves we can integrate the parts of our minds that have been fractured. Integration is a core healing principle that joins together fractured or suppressed parts of our minds into one whole entity. Integration joins the energy in a positive direction, and whatever was negative now becomes a type of "vaccination" against further negativity of this kind.

Besides being a reflection of our relationship to ourselves, our relationships to others are also a reflection of our relationship to God. By changing and healing our relationship to God, we can also change our relationship to ourselves and others.

I have found that people who have problems or conflicts with others have those same problems with God. The qualities that the problem, situation, or the person with whom we are in conflict seems to have are the same qualities that we have attributed to God. People are usually surprised when this is pointed out to them, but they can readily see and acknowledge it. Then, of course, it becomes clear that it is not God who has negative qualities or is doing these negative things, but, instead, it is we who are projecting these things onto God. As we improve our relationships to God, or our spiritual side, we improve our relationships with everyone.

Take, for example, the case of a client who came in to my office very angry with one of his co-workers. As we worked, it was easy for him to see that he had transferred feelings from his childhood relationship with his brother to his co-worker and, as we continued, he could soon see he had the same feelings against God. He was surprised to find that he was so angry with God, but he could readily see that each of the things he had named against his co-worker and his brother were feelings that he had against God. It took only a moment for him to realize that God was not doing these things, he was. It was then easy for him to forgive God, as well as himself, his brother, and his co-worker.

HEARTBREAK PRINCIPLE

Not only do heartbreaks come from relationships, but every problem comes from relationships.

HEALING PRINCIPLE

All problems can be solved by healing our relationships with ourselves, others, and God.

HEALING SUGGESTION

Acknowledging the primacy of relationships gives you the power, the ability, and the responsibility not only to help yourself, but also everyone around you. Your own healing—and helping others in their healing—is what brings you happiness.

HEALING CHOICE

I commit to heal and forgive all of my relationships, and recognize that they are how I feel about myself and about God.

HEALING EXERCISE

Choose a person who really bothers you. You know who it is! Then, recognize which person from the past you have transferred onto this present person. Now, explore which qualities of both people are yours. Do you act them out, or do you compensate for them? When you have done this, examine how this relates to how you feel about God.

Problem & present person	Transference (past person)	Self	God

Now, forgive yourself, the present person, the past person, and God.

64.

HEARTBREAK AND FAMILY ROLES

There are five major family roles that can affect us from birth until death: the Hero, the Martyr, and the Scapegoat—which are based on guilt—and the Charmer and the Lost Child—which are based on feelings of inadequacy. Usually all of these roles begin from heartbreak, or a series of heartbreaks.

The Hero, because of heartbreak and the resulting blame and guilt, attempts at all times to do his or her very best in the hope of helping the family. Heroes may be the most popular, academic, intelligent, athletic, artistic, or musical which is all an attempt to make their family proud, and to "save" it by being successful. Unfortunately it is ineffective. Heroes are playing a role which is, as we know, compensation. It covers the guilt of *not* being able to save the family.

The Martyr is the one who sacrifices anything to the family in an attempt to save others or to make things better. If this doesn't work, Martyrs may go to greater extremes to try to distract the family from its problems or sacrifice even greater things to help. I have seen sexual abuse and incest issues tied to this role. I have also seen cases where Martyrs sacrifice themselves through accidents, illness, or death. The one thing more important to a child than their sexual integrity, their health, or even their life is their family and its well-being.

The Scapegoat plays the role of the "black sheep" in the family. Scapegoats are the ones who are always getting in trouble. They attempt to absorb all the "badness" of the family, and to act it out in the hope of relieving some of the burden, or at least distracting them from their problems by getting into trouble. Everyone in the family is usually angry with this person. They tend to look down on the Scapegoat or talk about him behind his back. But the Scapegoat, though typically unaware of it, is just as dedicated to helping and saving the family. As a last-ditch resort, he may get into serious trouble outside the family, in a subconscious attempt to bring in the authorities to help.

The Charmer, also known as the "mascot" or "clown," seeks to keep the family together by their charm, wit, cuteness, sweetness, entertainment, humor, and fun. Many times, the Charmer doesn't feel loved except for his entertainment value, because this role is based on feelings of inadequacy. If a Charmer does not feel that he is successful enough in helping the family, he may take on the self-destructive aspects of the Martyrs.

The Lost Child, also known as the "invisible child" or "the orphan," takes on the role of disappearing, being invisible, or being left or abandoned by the family in an attempt to help. "Lost" children have the ability to disappear in large groups. I have seen this occur most dramatically in large Taiwanese families where there wasn't enough food for everyone. The Lost Child became ghostlike, eating little and, therefore, taking up even less space. Lost children keep their heads down to avoid being the cause of any family problems. They often feel that they are unworthy of a place within a busy family and feel that by "disappearing," they are easing the family burden. One classic example of the Lost Child is when a child is sent to boarding school. Time after time when working with adult clients in UK workshops, I have heard heart-rending stories of children going to boarding school and its effect on their confidence and sense of lovableness.

Some of our greatest childhood heartbreaks can come about from these five family roles. Yet the family roles had already come about from earlier heartbreaks, and the primordial guilt of not having been able to save the family and its members from their pain or problems. These family roles can permeate our whole lives. Although we may think we have played only a few of the family roles growing up, we have actually played them all. We will go through our life healing them until we find evidence of and clear the most hidden ones.

Family roles carried into our adult relationships can lead to heartbreak. Under each of the roles there are buried feelings of guilt and inadequacy that are tied to the pain of the heartbreaks they caused for us as children, which hid the even deeper heart breaks that generated them. Like any defense that eventually brings about what it was designed to defend against, the more a family moves into exaggerated roles, the more dysfunctional it becomes.

While the Hero and Charmer roles may be most attractive initially, they still limit intimacy and equality in our relationships. People playing roles give but can't receive, because roles are compensation—they keep us busy making up for and hiding bad feeling. Compensating and never receiving can lead to dissatisfaction and the inability to feel. The sacrificer attempts to ward off rejection by providing support to others, but before very long this leads to feelings of deadness. Without the intimacy and equality that comes from living honestly without roles, there is no attractiveness and excitement. Roles keep relationships static and unmoving, which means that they become stagnant and die.

The Scapegoat also feels undeserving of love. While they act in independent or heartbreaking ways, they can still be shattered when they leave someone they really love, or are left by them. The Lost Child role believes that no one really sees who they are, cares about how they feel, or really loves them, which can bring heartbreaks to their adult relationships.

HEARTBREAK PRINCIPLE

Family roles, which are based on heartbreak, guilt, and inadequacy, can start a nasty pattern of heartbreaks in childhood that carry into our adult relationships.

HEALING PRINCIPLE

Understanding the importance of family roles in our heartbreaks is the first step in making new choices and healing the old family patterns still affecting us.

HEALING SUGGESTION

Since family roles are a key element in heartbreak patterns, it is important that you understand them. Instead of acting from recipes and rules for living, which bring about the feelings of deadness and burn-out that roles foster, it is important for you to be yourself, to give by choice, and to have courage to be intimate.

HEALING CHOICE

I commit to understanding and healing my family roles.

HEALING EXERCISE

Examine your childhood for the roles that you and everyone else in your family were playing. These can change over time, so remember to explore all possibilities.

Roles for myself (at what ages): _____

Role my family members played:

    Father _____

    Mother _____

    Siblings _____

In your adult relationships and family, if you have one, what roles were or are you playing?

    My roles _____

    My partner's roles _____

    My children's roles _____

_____

_____

What family roles are you and your work colleagues playing? These are a continuation of your family roles.

    My roles _____

    My co-workers' roles _____

_____

_____

_____

What roles did you play at different times in your life? _____

_____

Examine the significance of your family roles in childhood or adult heartbreaks. Now, make new choices. Choice can lead to acting sincerely and to the ability to take as well as give. Now, as a result of your understanding of the roles that you and others played to save the family or your relationships, forgive yourself and these people.

65.

HEARTBREAK AND FAMILY PATTERNS

All heartbreak comes from the past. Victim patterns come from negative relationship patterns, which in turn come from family patterns. Family patterns come from soul patterns and ancestral patterns or, in other words, what learning challenge our souls set up for us for this lifetime.

Ostensibly, our heartbreaks began in our families. They began, at one level, because our parents did not respond to our needs—they didn't live by the script we assigned them to make us feel totally special. At some root level, all of our issues come back to family dynamics. Typically, it is these hidden or not-so-hidden conflicts within the family that lead to outside heartbreaks. For example, when the needs of the family are not being met, or conflicts within the family are not being resolved, it could easily lead to such incidents as sexual abuse, accidents, or failure.

Of course, all parents *do* want to meet the needs of their children. The places where they are consistently unable to give to their children are their own personal blind spots or broken places within them that were caused by their own old heartbreaks. When we suffer from wounds as a child, it is because everyone in that situation (our parents) is feeling the same thing inside them (heartbreaks) carried over from their childhood.

If we return to the root where our heartbreak began, and end the separation through love, bonding, willingness, giving, understanding, acceptance, forgiveness, or bridging, we can then heal this particular heartbreak pattern for ourselves and for our parents. We came to save our parents from their wounds, and we ended up catching their heartbreaks through our misunderstanding. Yet, all along we were the one who had the gift within us to change the situation. We can re-establish the bonding lost in the past, because we have carried that part of the past with us in our minds. The pattern of past heartbreak is so strong that it can completely cover the present, so we are actually living in the past—seeing and reacting to the past while trying to navigate the present. If we are not happy or feeling love, we are not even living in the present, but actually dealing with some past pattern.

HEARTBREAK PRINCIPLE

Negative relationship patterns stem from our family patterns.

HEALING PRINCIPLE

Healing the root pattern in our family will transform our negative relationship patterns.

HEALING SUGGESTION

The root of present pain will be found in the family. For instance, any core problem with a girlfriend or wife will also exist in your relationship with your mother. When a man heals the issue with his mother, his relationships will leap forward. When a woman heals an issue with her mother she heals her issue with her self and her self-confidence. Underneath your pain, grievance, and guilt you still have the healing gift that would release your parents from their heartbreak pattern and save you from repeating it further.

HEALING CHOICE

I commit to finding and healing the root patterns of my childhood.

HEALING EXERCISE

Choose three present problems. Explore each in terms of how it is related to a childhood pattern in your family where you judged and have held a grievance against one or both of your parents. What gift is the grievance hiding?

Present problem	Childhood pattern	Grievance with parent	Gift
1. _____	_____	_____	_____
2. _____	_____	_____	_____
3. _____	_____	_____	_____

Now, take five minutes and imagine yourself connecting heart-to-heart with your parents. Give the gifts that only you can give to free them. Once you give them this gift, it will become theirs and a part of you. There is now no one to whom you will not be able to give this gift. Healing this childhood pattern gives you some of the gifts necessary for your own life's purpose. Don't underestimate your own power to change situations, even those in the past. The power of the mind and the power of perception are profound and you will find that gifts given now can change whole patterns that have cast a shadow on your life, the lives of your parents, and other members of your family.

Once you have given these gifts to your parents, they will own them and be able to share them with you and with others. Perhaps your parents need the gift of love or forgiveness or acceptance. If you are not sure what gift you have, simply decide what you think your parents need. This will be the gift within you that has been buried under the pain and grievances. When you are able to give these gifts, they can experience their healing power and they will have gifts for you—the gifts you have not been able to receive from them because of the pain or sacrifice. They will be freed and so will you. By healing these childhood patterns, you will receive some of the gifts that you need to move forward in life.

66.

THE MIRROR PRINCIPLE

In the chapters, "Heartbreaks—the Script Taken" (no.53) and "A Relationship Model of Reality" (no.63), we related how everything that happens to us mirrors our mind, or comes from our hidden scripts. Our childhood experiences demonstrate this as well. All the aspects that others act out around us reflect the play of hidden personalities within us. Our family members act out the major fractures of our soul that we can now heal and integrate. Our parents, siblings, spouse, and children represent key parts of our mind that we can win back by releasing the pain and sharing the gifts we all have to offer, which are hidden behind the problems. As we integrate these parts of our mind at the intrapsychic level, or forgive these people at the interpersonal level (see "A Relationship Model of Reality" p. 252), negativity falls away, and the positive is enhanced for everyone involved.

As we become adults, we build our egos to gain a sense of ourselves and how to deal with the world. Our ego can become hardened and stuck when we suffer heartbreak. Having created strong egos, we now need to heal and integrate the fractures of our minds. Through this we will become more open and flexible, and we will loosen our egos' hold on us. Our egos are built up through separation, defense, fear, guilt, and competition. To have successful relationships we must melt away these defenses through forgiveness and joining. This heals the fractures within us, which makes us more whole, loving, and successful. As we evolve, our egos lose their power to control us, and we experience more love and wholeness. This type of healing restores our lost bonding and helps us to become closer to our families, others with whom we are in a relationship, and even those at work. It provides more success for all of us as partners, individuals, or as members of a team. As the family patterns are changed, the very nature of our minds is changed. As our relationships change, the fabric of our lives is transformed. When someone in our family or relationships seem to be really stuck, they reflect aspects of us which may be hidden, and which are still stuck in pain, fear, and guilt. As we change, transform, and give our gifts, our families heal so we no longer have to carry them on our backs or run away from them through independence. No matter how far we run, we carry our patterns with us, and they are waiting to be set up again in new relationships. We carry the patterns into our own adult families, and in spite of our compensations there is nothing we can do unless we heal.

Imagine that the whole world is a mirror reflecting what is within us. What we do in the world, we do for ourselves. What we heal within ourselves has an effect on the world.

"As within so without" is a principle that can empower us to change the world. This means we make changes within us and it has an effect on our lives and on the world around us. When we make changes to our own lives, we become more aware and we feel more accountable. The knowledge that we can make broadscale changes allows us to go on to share our gift with others.

Our relationships mirror our mind. We can try to change

the mirror, but if we want real change we will have to change the person in the mirror. We can never really change others, but as we change and heal ourselves, others *will* change, even if it is in our perception of them. Consider Mark Twain's comment: "When I was sixteen I thought my father a fool, at twenty-one I was surprised how much he'd learned in five years."

Our family reflects not only our potential and purpose, but also the pattern we have come to unravel to become ourselves and live our purpose. However much we heal and realize this potential will be the extent to which we are living our purpose, and our family will be correspondingly loving and successful. When we become adults, we bring unfinished business in our family pattern into our relationships with our partner. We also continue our parents' relationships with our children.

Remember that we project the things for which we have judged ourselves and hidden within us. Sometimes, when we are dealing with another's negative behavior as a projection, we might realize that we also do that behavior. If we have a compensation to hide it, we might feel like we'd rather die than act in that way.

When our partners in relationships are our opposites, they represent a core part of our mind that fractured in a major heartbreak in childhood. We effectively rejected that part of ourselves. We thought that if we acted in the way they are acting now, we wouldn't survive, so we broke this part off and repressed it. As adults we go looking for our missing part, find someone who is acting it out, and feel greatly attracted to them. We feel as though they will complete us. Of course, they are simultaneously, but conversely, finding their missing piece in us. After the honeymoon stage these differences can lead to major problems because, after all, we vowed never to go near this part of ourselves again. When we do, we re-experience all the reasons why we had to bury this part in the first place.

In a relationship, we struggle to change our partners so that they do things "our" way. We feel threatened by their differences, which recall, usually subconsciously, painful fractures of the past. Our partners, in turn, feel the same way, leading to conflict, withdrawal, or even deadness. When our needs and our partner's needs are not met, it leads to fights, withdrawal, or deadness.

I recently ran into a classic case of this concept in a workshop where a young woman who was an artist and an adventurer was complaining about her live-in engineer boyfriend who slept all the time. Once she recognized that he represented the safe, engineer part of her that was lost in a childhood heartbreak, and integrated this part so that she no longer judged him or herself, she fell back in love with her boyfriend. Having seen this happen hundreds of times, I knew that when she went home with that look of love blazing in her eyes, she would have found him significantly changed.

HEARTBREAK PRINCIPLE

Our family and the most significant people in our lives represent key parts of our own minds. Our problems or heartbreaks with them represent problems and fractures in our own minds.

HEALING PRINCIPLE

The significant people around us represent key parts of our minds that we have come to heal. As we succeed, confidence, love, and fulfillment increase in our lives. As we heal either inside or outside it has a corresponding effect on those around us. We see them differently, and we behave differently toward them. They respond to our new awareness. They have changed in kind.

HEALING SUGGESTION

Today and for the rest of your life begin to explore this mirror principle. It will help you forgive, and empower you to change seemingly impossible situations, by finding the corresponding piece of your mind and healing it.

HEALING CHOICE

I commit to recognizing that everyone around me is a reflection of myself. I choose to use this for my healing and growth.

HEALING EXERCISE

This is the simplest and most basic exercise to heal projection (when we paint a part of ourselves that we have judged and rejected onto someone else). Choose someone around you, and choose a negative quality that you have projected onto them and wish to heal. Now, begin to examine that behavior, or quality, as your own belief, albeit a hidden one, about yourself. Try on this characteristic for size. Determine if it is how you behave, or decide whether you act in the opposite way in compensation. You may say: (A) "Yes, I am this way too" or (B) "Yes, I used to be that way, but I buried it" or (C) "I must have this self-concept very strongly, and have defended it as if I'd rather die than act it out." Remember the most negative figures around us can reflect our core negative self-concepts. Experience this negative behavior and the feeling that goes with it. Own this feeling. Burn it emotionally until it's gone. Forgive yourself for being this way. You will know when you have completed this, because you will feel at home with the characteristic. Now, instead of it being in the foreground of your mind with pain and judgment, it will be integrated as part of the background. You will feel at peace with it.

67.

FEAR AND INDEPENDENCE

Old heartbreaks that remain unresolved can cause distance between us and our partners. They can result in a fear of intimacy and while this fear belongs to both of us, it may be acted out by just one of us. This is a fear of love which has become "normal behavior" in the modern world. Believing that we would lose something in love is what causes us to act like the original "desperado."

Some of us are afraid that we will lose ourselves or our freedom and spirit of adventure if we have partners. We feel that we will be trapped with one person when there is so much to do and explore with so many others. This is actually our fear parading as independence. Even in my most independent days, I recognized that my independence was a rather thin veneer over my fear. This independent behavior—basically an exploration of possibilities—is stage specific. The more heartbreaks we have had, or the less we've healed, the more we are stuck in the independent stage. We fear that coming back to love would mean returning to the same heartbreaks, jealousy, and sacrifice that we experienced before.

Fearful of losing our sense of adventure, freedom, choices, relationship buffet, purpose, or ourselves, we act so independently that we inadvertently cause heartbreak in current relationships. This heartbreak is almost exactly the same as that which led us to become independent in the first place. We actively resist being possessed by someone who is acting possessive or needy, as we used to be. Our dependent self has been rejected, and we compensate by becoming independent. The extent to which we are independent relates to the level of heartbreak, dependency, sacrifice, and burn-out that we carry inside us. It can be recognized as dissociation, control, fear, and even running away. We cannot forgive our dependent self because it caused so much pain. By being blind to the pain and needs of this self, we become insensitive to those around us. This concept also explains parents' insensitivity to their children's wants and needs. In covering over our own needs and heartbreaks, we become insensitive to our children in a similar fashion.

HEARTBREAK PRINCIPLE

We are afraid of love, intimacy, and partnership because we mistakenly fear we would lose something. The extent of our independence is the extent of our hidden fear, dependency, and heartbreak.

HEALING PRINCIPLE

Our commitment, paradoxically, gives us the freedom and success we thought would come through independence.

HEALING SUGGESTION

As you realize that every forward step you have taken in partnerships and relationships has truly made your life better, you will be motivated to take the next steps.

HEALING CHOICE

I commit to healing my fear, dependency, and heartbreak so that I can move through my independence and step into partnership.

HEALING EXERCISE

Examine how independent you are (according to how unsuccessful you have been in committing to an intimate relationship). Recognize that independence is a compensation for neediness, heartbreak, burn-out, and fear. Complete the following statements:

If I were to guess how many independent personalities I have, it's probably

_____

If I were to guess how many of these compensating independent personalities are covering other painful personalities it's probably...

fear personalities, it's probably _____

needy personalities, it's probably_____

victim personalities, it's probably_____

jealous personalities, it's probably _____

heartbreak personalities, it's probably _____

sacrifice personalities, it's probably _____

burn-out personalities, it's probably_____

Now, melt the fear personalities and their compensating independent personalities together into one. Then, melt the needy personalities and their compensating independent personalities together into one. Continue this process with the five remaining personalities and their compensating independent personalities. When you have finished doing this, integrate each of the seven combined personalities back into you, thereby healing the conflicts, bringing you a greater ability to receive, and feeling more whole as you take a giant step toward partnership. Visualizing the melting or combining of various personalities saves us time because instead of tackling each personality one by one, we can deal with the overall pattern.

68.
HEARTBREAK AND INTROJECTION

Introjection is an ego defense that we use to try to save our families. Like all defenses it does not work. Introjection is our attempt to help those we love by taking their pain into us. We attempt to swallow the heartbreak, guilt, or even death temptation to help our parents or others whom we love. For instance, if we see our mother experiencing a heartbreak with her in-laws, we try to swallow as much of it as possible. Depending upon our level of psychic ability, we can swallow differing amounts of pain. The most psychically gifted of us have the potential to swallow dangerous even life-threatening amounts of pain.

One way to know if we have been introjecting in our relationships is to examine whether we have typical scenarios operating in our life. If we are with a friend who is really down, and after ten minutes they are feeling much better, while we are suddenly feeling down, it is most likely that we have been introjecting. Whenever we feel exhausted or even ill after being in the company of someone who has inexplicably made a sudden recovery from pain or illness, chances are we have absorbed it into ourselves. That's introjection.

In a workshop, I once worked with a woman who was skilled at swallowing other people's pain. She had befriended a struggling artist, and was swallowing his pain so much that she ended up having fainting spells. It would usually take her months to dispel the pain, but she had noticed that in the last several months it had been disappearing more quickly. We discovered that her own son had been swallowing *her* pain. He had started having epileptic seizures about six months earlier, at about the same time that the effects of her introjection began to lessen. When I asked her how much emotional pain she had in her from growing up with her family, her ex-husband, and her artist friend, she intuitively replied, "Tons!" Her intuitive response to my question about how much her son had swallowed was, "Even more." The awareness of her son's pain and predicament finally motivated her enough to give up the misguided form of helping. She let go of all the accumulated emotional pain that she had, and then she gave up the swallowing mechanism itself. Her son's epilepsy soon disappeared without a trace.

I discovered the introjection mechanism in operation about twelve years ago, when I was working with some clients who had recurrent feelings of heartbreak and guilt. They had worked with fine therapists and had let go of heartbreak only to have the feelings return in a week or two. Even the most gifted and dedicated therapists become frustrated if they do not realize that introjection is operating in their client. Because the pain is not really the client's, after it is emptied, it simply balloons back in a short time. Once the introjection is discovered, it is easy to clear it by simply letting go of both the pain and the swallowing mechanism. One of the oldest forms of healing is taking on another's pain and healing it for them, but as you can imagine, there is a high mortality rate for such healers. One of my teachers, who was gifted in the healing and psychic arts, told me that healers of this type usually did not last more than five years before succumbing to some mortal illness.

Introjection seems to begin with those who have some basic healing or psychic ability. As a child they may have witnessed a family heartbreak or crisis. In the face of such pain, they tried to play "God" and the swallowing began.

A successful man who was working through the "dead zone" (see page 42) area of his relationship with his wife, discovered that he was an introjector. He described the incident where he first began to do this. At four years old he had walked into his parents' bedroom, even though the door was shut. When he opened the door, he found his mother, who was a doctor, staring at a pair of surgical scissors and looking at her wrist. In an instant he realized what his mother was contemplating, and he reached out and grabbed her death temptation and swallowed it. He was able to swallow the problem so completely that his mother never had such a strong temptation again. Although his mother scolded him for coming into her bedroom when the door was closed, he knew that this was not really what was going on. In an attempt to save his mother he had not only introjected, receiving her pain and death wish, but he had also gone into sacrifice to a point where he was caught in fusion which only mimics bonding.

As a result of this experience, he was now closer to his mother than he was to his wife, which was what was causing the deadness in his marriage. He was able to heal the dead parts of his mind, and to give up the pain he still had within him. He gave up the swallowing mechanism by symbolically handing the responsibility back to God. He then went back to his center, where he re-established the bonding with his mother, and he was able to give her a gift of love and forgiveness to free her of her problem. Needless to say, his relationship with his wife took a huge jump forward as a result of healing the introjection.

HEARTBREAK PRINCIPLE

If we introject someone else's pain, or heartbreak, we can never fully heal it until the mechanism itself is healed.

HEALING PRINCIPLE

It is important to let go of the swallowed pain and the swallowing mechanism, and to put this gift in God's hands so that we won't use it to abuse ourselves.

HEALING SUGGESTION

Examine your life for introjection. It could have a major effect on your life by keeping you locked into pain or heartbreak.

HEALING CHOICE

I commit to letting go of all pain that I have swallowed and to putting the introjection mechanism back in God's hands.

HEALING EXERCISE

If you recognize that you are a "swallower," complete the following statements:

If I were to know how much pain I swallowed...

from my mother, it was _____

from my father, it was _____

from my siblings, it was _____

from friends, it was _____

from my lovers, it was _____

from my spouse, it was _____

from my children, it was _____

from anyone else, it was _____

Take all of this emotional garbage and the introjection mechanism, and put it in God's hands to let it go. Now, ask yourself if any parts of you died, or went into a coma, with your heartbreak incidents. Intuitively find the areas of your body that you put these selves in, and go to them and blow the sacred breath of life back into them. Love them until they grow up to your present age, and melt back into you.

69.

HEARTBREAK, INDULGENCE, AND AFFAIRS

We cannot have a heartbreak unless we have been indulging ourselves—we have made our needs more important than our love. Our indulgence is a strategy that we use to be happy, but it actually leads us to heartbreak. We have made our indulgence more important than our partners, especially where we tried to make our partner responsible for our happiness on earth, and to take care of our needs. Even though our partners may be perceived as "the bad guy" through affairs, alcoholism, abuse, or leaving us, for example, the responsibility for the heartbreak is, in fact, our own. We are usually able to hide our lack of integrity because our partner's lack of integrity is so blatant.

When I was a marriage counselor in California, I regularly saw a couple in which the man had a drug problem. They recognized that they would make much better progress if they healed together. As a couple they worked hard and, as their relationship got stronger, his desire for drugs abated. This continued until one weekend when she was on a business trip, and he had a cocaine binge. As we worked on the problem, we discovered that while she was away she had been flirting. While she never carried it further than that, she realized that she had not acted with integrity either. Both had equal levels of lack of integrity, though he was ostensibly "the bad guy."

More than twenty years ago I realized that the best policy to adopt when working with couples or individuals who are in a relationship is a "No fault, no blame" policy.

Not only does our indulgence lead to heartbreak, but we use our heartbreaks as an excuse for indulgence. In many cases I see partners having affairs, which breaks the heart of the other partner. The "victimized" partner uses this to go and have an affair of their own. Later, they secretly admit to me that they had been wanting to have an affair all along, but hadn't until they discovered that their partner was having one. This gave them permission to indulge themselves. Another common example is using a partner's affair as an excuse for a break-up or divorce, so they are able to live an independent lifestyle.

When some people acknowledge their indulgence and lack of accountability, the ego attempts to exchange responsibility for guilt. The ego uses guilt to allow us to do two things—to stop exploring our own mind, and to encourage us to continue doing what we have been doing all along. Guilt gives us the excuse to avoid change, just as long as we continue to beat ourselves up for what we are doing. In other words, as long as we feel guilty, we are absolved of responsibility for our actions. This keeps us stuck and fragmented. Because guilt is the negative emotion, it keeps the positive compensating self from integrating with the negative self underneath the role. It allows us to pretend that we are really the "good" one.

HEARTBREAK PRINCIPLE

Heartbreaks come from power struggles which are actually the result of fighting for our own indulgences and needs.

HEALING PRINCIPLE

When we realize that our indulgences do not make us happy, and that they keep us in a vicious cycle of indulgence and sacrifice coupled with a negative self-image, we are motivated to choose the peace and love that would really make us happy.

HEALING SUGGESTION

The extent to which you indulge yourself is the extent to which you will sacrifice yourself and feel "bad" to make up for it. These feelings lock you into the cycle. By realizing that what you get in indulgence does not make you happy, you may want to make another choice. Examine how the indulgence level of your life, the sacrifice level, and the core negative self-concepts are all tied together. Is this indulgence a strategy that really makes you happy?

HEALING CHOICE

I commit to what really makes me happy. I let go of my strategy of indulgence, and ask to be shown what really makes me happy.

═══════════════════════

HEALING EXERCISE

Examine your heartbreaks for indulgence and lack of integrity. Let this motivate you to forgive those involved, including yourself, so that everyone is free.

═══════════════════════

70.
GIVING UP SACRIFICE THE HARD WAY

Heartbreaks can occur as an excuse to give up a certain sacrifice situation that we are in. We have come to the end of our rope, so we create some kind of heartbreak to get us out of the sacrifice situation. We felt we needed some outside permission—a heartbreak bad enough to finally justify running away from the situation.

I have seen many examples of heartbreak stemming from a partner's affair, which finally allowed the other partner to leave or to get a divorce. The affair was "the straw that broke the camel's back," allowing them to go into their independent stage. They needed a heartbreak to give them the assertiveness that they lacked to stand up for themselves or to leave. One man explained that he had been married for twenty-seven years, and had fought with his wife for the last ten of those years. He felt very abused by her, but didn't want a divorce, even though she had threatened it a thousand times. Finally, in one of her attacks, she said, "You don't have the balls to get a divorce." That afternoon he called his lawyer and began divorce proceedings. She had provided him with the excuse he needed to act.

In 1976, I was one of the facilitators on a retreat for military service members and their families, and I developed a strong rapport with one of the sailors. Through music and sharing, he got in touch with his heartbreak and the rage that he had toward his mother. His father had been killed, and his mother became wild and crazy in her grief. At one point, when his brother was five and he was seven, the sailor's mother had "flipped out" and chased them around the house with a kitchen knife. She caught his brother and cut off his penis. Seeing this, he ran away from home and got help. After the pain of the heartbreak, a layer of guilt began to surface. He felt guilty that he hadn't been able to help his brother, even though he could not have done anything to stop his mother. As he explored this incident, he realized that he had wanted to run away from home all along, but he felt he couldn't do it until his mother went too far. This dreadful incident was the thing that finally allowed him to run for help. This awareness was the beginning of forgiving himself and his mother.

When the dynamic of giving up sacrifice the hard way is understood, it allows us to give up part of our victim experience around the heartbreaks, and to win back our power. When we can forgive ourselves for using others for this painful strategy of giving up sacrifice the hard way, and forgive the others involved, we win back a tremendous amount of confidence, which allows us to move more into partnership.

HEARTBREAK PRINCIPLE

We sometimes use heartbreaks to justify giving up sacrifice. Our heartbreak is a strategy that allows us to give up our sacrifice, albeit the hard way.

HEALING PRINCIPLE

Acknowledging how we were able to give up sacrifice allows us to more easily forgive ourselves and the other person for doing it the hard way.

HEALING SUGGESTION

Examine the situations where you have been in sacrifice in your life, and look at how you got yourself out of them. Did you use heartbreaks to do this?

HEALING CHOICE

I commit to giving up sacrifice the easy way.

HEALING EXERCISE

Choose five heartbreaks you have used to give up sacrifice the hard way. Respond to the next three headings for each heartbreak to discover your hidden choices for this mistaken strategy.

Heartbreaks	Sacrifice I got out of	What the heartbreak allowed me to do	What I didn't have to do as a result of the heartbreak
1.			
2			
3.			
4.			
5.			

Now, with your new understanding, forgive yourself and the other person involved for your mistaken strategy, so you can free yourself of the past pain and the pattern of giving up sacrifice the hard way.

71.

HEARTBREAK AND EXPECTATION

Expectation and heartbreak go hand in hand. Expectations are demands that come from our needs. Expectations will create problems sooner or later—because when our partners bow to them and give in to our needs, we will remain dissatisfied and our partners will become more unattractive because they are acting from pressure rather than choice. If our partners do not meet our needs, we will be frustrated, disappointed, or even heartbroken. Expectations put demands and stress on others, and no matter how well people attempt to satisfy us, it is never enough. The extent to which we feel stressed by others' demands is the extent to which we put those same demands on ourselves. It is also the extent to which we put those demands on others. Expectations are compensations against our needs, fears, and losses. They are pictures about how others and life should be to make up for what was and what is missing in our lives. Unfortunately, the more we expect, the less we are able to receive and to be satisfied. This causes increasingly more stress, because we push ourselves and others to live up to our expectations in an attempt to fulfill what was missing.

Even with the best partner in the world, expectations limit our ability to enjoy them. If they meet our expectation, we will expect more in the attempt to get our needs met. No matter how good they are, and how much they fit our picture of how they should be, we will not be fully satisfied, so we keep changing our picture, thinking that maybe a new picture would finally satisfy us. The more we demand from our partner, the less we can receive from them, and the more they will resist us, which leads to power struggle. Even if they felt like giving to us, the constant demands eventually steal the enthusiasm and willingness from people around us, because they feel they have no choice. We always expect from others what we are not giving. What we need to do is to let go of our expectations and give what we are demanding to our partners. In doing so, we invite our partners to do the same in return, rather than demanding that they do so.

My friend and mentor, Sam Hazo, wrote in his poem "The First and Only Sailing": "Expect nothing and anything seems like everything. Expect everything, and anything seems like nothing...."

Demanding in any form is a fast formula for heartbreak. Our expectations are based on what we perceive to be lacking in our lives. We believe that we can only be happy when our expectations are met. But even if they are met, somehow we will not be happy, so we go on and make a new set of dreams or expectations. It goes on and on. When we have a great deal of expectations, we are usually so dissociated that our relationships feel like a desert. Expectations are effectively fantasies. A fantasy puts us in our head, and cuts us off from our heart and the ability to really join with another. A person like this can have no partners, many partners at the same time, or many partners one after another, because they just can't be satisfied.

When we have high expectations we push ourselves and those around us, causing present and future trouble for ourselves and our relationships. Expectations lead to perfectionism, where we feel inadequate because we never have and never will get it perfect. Neither will our partners. If we let go of our expectations, setting realistic and achievable goals instead, our lives will be easier, and those around us will feel happier and more successful. Perfectionism means that nothing is ever good enough because, at the heart of it, we feel that we are not good enough.

HEARTBREAK PRINCIPLE

An expectation is a demand based on need that can never let you succeed, receive, or be satisfied. In a relationship, an expectation leads to stress and resistance.

HEALING PRINCIPLE

If we are willing to let go of expectations or give what we have been expecting, we will move forward and receive.

HEALING SUGGESTION

Look for expectations in your life at points where others resist you. Examine your attitude and your language for words like "should," "have to," "got to," "need to," "ought to," and "must," as they reflect expectations. Instead use words like "want to," or "choose to," which takes the pressure off of you and those around you. With an expectation, nothing is ever good enough. Your partner will be discouraged if they feel they can never succeed with you.

HEALING CHOICE

I commit to letting go and making choices and commitments in my life, rather than pushing myself. I commit to inviting and enlisting my partner, rather than expecting from them.

HEALING EXERCISE

Make a list of what you feel you have to do. Let go of the attachments about them, the pressure and the picture or fantasy of how they should be. Now choose what you want. Make a list of the expectations that led to heartbreak. Then list the expectations you still have (in other words, what my partner has to do to remain my partner). Let go of these expectations and choose what you want, so you can let go of the stress and resistance. Paradoxically, this will allow you to succeed and receive more, and your partner will feel happier and more successful with you.

72.

HEARTBREAK AND DEPRESSION

Depression often sets in after we have suffered a heartbreak. Depression is a psychological tantrum where we refuse to let go of the past. It is a mixture of many feelings bound together, and characterized by lost trust and an inability to put faith in the future. We are still holding on to someone or something lost through heartbreak. We have not yet chosen to accept, let go, and move forward in our life. We feel as though we have been knocked out of the game of life—and it can be a time of intense suffering, little energy, and meaninglessness. Unless we let go of the heartbreak and the attachments, or we heal them in some way, it seems inevitable that depression will set in. In many cases, we may not even realize that we were depressed until we have begun climbing out of it. A heartbreak has not been fully transcended until all traces of the old heartbreak are gone, and we are able to move to a whole new level of life and relationships. This means clearing depression.

HEARTBREAK PRINCIPLE

The extent to which we do not let go after heartbreak is the extent to which we fall into depression.

HEALING PRINCIPLE

Our decision to let go and move on will move us forward from loss to a new birth.

HEALING SUGGESTION

Examine your life for losses from which you have not recovered. For each loss you suffered ask yourself how much of your energy is still not recovered. To reclaim that lost energy, forgive and let go.

HEALING CHOICE

I commit to letting go of all of my losses, so my life can begin.

HEALING EXERCISE

If you have experienced loss, imagine yourself back at the time, just before the loss occurred. Now, from the light within you, connect to the light within the other person, situation, or thing. Then put this person, situation, or thing in Heaven's hands, and ask for the grace to begin anew.

73.
HEARTBREAK AND SELF-DESTRUCTION

Heartbreak combined with vengeance and the feeling of being unwanted leads to self-destruction. Self-destruction is a form of throwing ourselves away, while hoping both to exact some revenge on our partners *and* to get them back. All too many people, especially young men, have reported getting drunk or driving recklessly after a heartbreak, while thinking to themselves, "If I'm hurt and killed, then they'll be sorry...then they'll miss me." Self-destruction states, "If they won't love me the way I need to be loved, then it is not worth living."

I have worked with many people who had accidents after a break-up. On one level they were trying to get their ex-partners back, and on another level, they were throwing themselves away. I have worked with women who had cancerous or pre-cancerous conditions, and part of the dynamic that emerged was an attempt to hold on to, or to bring back lost loves. Once these dynamics were brought to her conscious attention, she was able to let go of the attachments. The physical healing was swift or immediate, as a result of healing the heartbreak. About twenty years ago I heard a talk by Dr. Carl Simington, a foremost cancer specialist, who was speaking on research into cancer and relationships. It was discovered that in many, many cases of cancer there had been a trauma with a significant person six to eighteen months before the onset of the cancer. The self-destructive pattern that occurs in adulthood is often one that we have carried since childhood. When the root of this self-destruction is cleared, a new level of success, self-worth, and confidence begins in our relationship.

HEARTBREAK PRINCIPLE

Many times after heartbreak, we throw ourselves away because we feel that we weren't loved or valued enough. Our death or something equally dramatic seems to us, in our heartbroken state, a fitting punishment for the perpetrator.

HEALING PRINCIPLE

Returning to the root of the self-destruction patterns is an effective way to change them. Usually, this level of self-destruction speaks of high levels of past heartbreak; the heartbreak in the present that led to self-destruction is part of the pattern.

HEALING SUGGESTION

Take a look at your life, especially over the last two years, in regard to illness, injuries, and self-destructive energy or patterns. Who were you punishing by throwing yourself away? How strong is the sense of self-destruction in your life? Make new choices.

HEALING CHOICE

I commit to clearing all of the self-destructive patterns in my life.

HEALING EXERCISE

Complete the following statements to get to the root of your self-destructive patterns:

If I were to know where the self-destruction began in me, it was probably at the age of _____

If I were to know who was involved, it was probably _____
_____

If I were to know what occurred to cause this to begin for me, it was probably
_____

If I were to know what I decided about myself, it was _____
_____

If I were to know what I decided about life, it was _____
_____

If I were to know what I decided about relationships, it was _____
_____

If I were to know what I decided that I would have to do from then on, it was
_____

If I were to know if I made any other negative decisions that may be affecting me now, they are _____

For any decisions you do not like, make a new choice for yourself. The question about what you would "have to do" was a trick question. It showed an expectation you made as a result of the event. Any answer would be a trap, because it comes from a "have to" rather than a "choose to" scenario. Now, choose what you want. In the original incident, ask your higher mind that everyone be returned to their center. Bond with them, light to light, spirit to spirit. When you are all connected with rays of light, help each person out of their heartbreak and self-destructiveness. In the painful situation, the negative feeling that you came away with was exactly the pain that they had within them. Now, imagine that you have a healing gift, and that its beautiful color is moving back through both sides of your family line to heal. It also moves forward into your life to help those around you.

74.

LOSS OF CENTER AND SELF-DESTRUCTION

Years ago while I was studying guilt, I found that a layer exists beneath the guilt that comes from our actions or inaction. This guilt is associated with core family dynamics deep within our minds, and is the place where family pain and family patterns are passed on. It is here that we leave our centers, and fuse in sacrifice to the family member in trouble. The more we leave our centers and fuse, the more we go into illusion and sacrifice; we feel like a failure. The more this occurs, the more valueless we feel, and the more self-destructive we become. Through our fusion and misunderstanding we take on the pain of a family member, which means that we end up with the same problems that we could have healed. Sometimes the fusion or pain is so great that we finally burn out and become independent. This sets up layers of independence and grievance over the heartbreak, covering the guilt and our ability to heal ourselves and others.

Our centers are a place of innocence, grace, and true value. At our centers we live in the present, connected with life and others, and we are able to receive in an almost childlike way. We feel at peace and we are able to recognize and follow our own spiritual guides. Our centers accomplish by the grace of being, rather than through the compensation of doing. We leave our centers through misunderstanding or misperceptions, in order to try to help those around us. The more we leave them, the more unsuccessful we become. My studies indicate that if we moved off our center by up to 29 percent, illusion and mistaken responses occurred in our lives. Shifts from 30 to 79 percent mean going into higher and higher levels of sacrifice. When we are 80 to 99 percent off our centers, there are levels of self-destruction. At 100 percent we experience the death of a self or selves within our minds. I also found that we are often born "off our centers," which sets up self-destructive patterns that carry on through our lives. As my trainer and engineer friend Jeff Allen says, "To change the course of a stream, put a pebble near its source, rather than a boulder downstream." So, going to the root of the self-destructive pattern and returning to our centers has the greatest healing effect. The valuelessness we feel from losing our centers can turn into death temptation. To avoid feeling this, we hide it by doing, being busy, and other forms of compensation.

When a person has lost his or her center, I have them ask their higher mind to carry them back to their center, along with the others in the situation. Some had to be carried back to successively deeper centers to find a sense of peace. It was from this center that they were peaceful enough to recognize the gifts that they have for others. These gifts, paradoxically enough, are often the very things that they felt they needed and had been trying to get from others around them. They were seeking the same things in their present relationships, but the satisfaction of their needs remained elusive. As we find the gifts in ourselves and give them, first to our families and later to our partners, our old wounds and needs disappear in satisfaction and success.

HEARTBREAK PRINCIPLE

Our deepest heartbreak and guilt patterns come from losing our centers in an attempt to help our parents and family. Once we leave our centers, we enter into sacrifice, and we take on the very wounds we are trying to help them with.

HEALING PRINCIPLE

When we are returned to our centers by our higher mind, and our family is also returned to their centers, we lose the self-destructive patterns, and the on-going pain and compensations. We are returned to grace, peace, effectiveness and to a state of being rather than doing. In this place we are effective, rather than self-sacrificing and self-destructive.

HEALING SUGGESTION

To remove your heartbreak, guilt, and self-destructive patterns, you must return to your center. The sacrifice that comes from leaving your center is ineffective and self-destructive. The ego attempts to replace the bonding that is lost when you leave your center with fusion—a muddying of your boundaries with others. Fusion is counterfeit bonding, which increases your sense of failure and guilt, and creates an "over-close" or smothering relationship. It is important that you heal these primordial patterns to get rid of heartbreak, deadness, and valuelessness.

HEALING CHOICE

I commit to returning to my center with grace and ease.

HEALING EXERCISE

Choose a current problem. Ask your higher mind to return you to your center, and everyone else in the situation to their centers. Visualize this happening, in whatever way you see it. Repeat this at deeper centers, if necessary, until you feel at peace. Now, ask your higher mind to bring you back to the root where this problem began, and when you are there, ask that everyone in that situation be returned to their centers. When you have reached that place of peace, imagine yourself going through that center within you. It is a gateway. Typically, you will find a place of beauty or light. Bring the people from both the current problem and root problem situations to this place, so they, too can be filled with beauty and grace. Finally, return everyone to the original situation, and see how everything works out. This helps them by allowing you to see them differently. As the old way of helping them or sacrificing changes, so they change in their response to you and to others.

75.
ABORTIONS, STILLBIRTHS, AND MISCARRIAGES

I have worked with many hundreds of people who have gone through an abortion or the painful loss of a stillbirth or miscarriage. All of these cases had one thing in common: a self had died for all of them as a child. In other words, something was so spectacularly painful for them as children that the self in charge was overwhelmed and killed. The mind is so prolific that as soon as one self dies, another self comes to take its place. When this happens, however, we find ourselves further away from our centers. It is as if we started off in one bowling alley marked "Success in Life" and now, through loss of selves, we are in alley number 6 trying to get a strike in alley number 1.

I have found that at the time it happened, some men and women were very nonchalant about having an abortion. Later, raging guilt would spring up for what they had done. I have seen this guilt cause the break-up of relationships and families, and have people withdraw in deadness, closing off life, because that is all they felt they deserved. Similarly, I have seen stillbirths emotionally tear up a family, or lay a pall of guilt and depression over a family for years. I have seen couples have successive miscarriages because they felt guilty about an earlier abortion.

Abortions, stillbirths, and miscarriages are often an attempt by the mind to clear feelings of guilt and fractures. It often seems that we set out—subconsciously or consciously—to create a heartbreak that will bring the pain and guilt to the surface to heal it. Of course, the ego will attempt to use the new problem, the next eruption of pain, as a good opportunity to increase guilt and self-destructiveness.

Unfortunately, most people who have abortions, stillbirths, or miscarriages don't get in touch with the lost or dead child within them; they just feel bad, sometimes terribly guilty, sad, and tragic. If they heal the dead self within and regain their innocence from childhood, it is natural to let go and forgive themselves now.

In almost every case, either in my office or in a workshop, remarkable things occurred in healing these situations. We would feel an energy shift. Many times the soul of the aborted, miscarried, or stillborn baby would become present so that my client could palpably feel their presence. My clients went on to see the "lesson" they were being taught, and to experience an amazing healing energy, so there was always a dramatic understanding and sense of relief. They would be able to release the self-destructiveness and guilt, and move on with their life in a new and healthier way.

HEARTBREAK PRINCIPLE

Miscarriages, abortions, and stillbirths are our souls' attempts to heal the dead selves and self-destructiveness within. They are also an attempt by the ego to increase guilt and self-destruction.

HEALING PRINCIPLE

When some strong pain, guilt, or self-destruction arises, it is always an opportunity to heal both our past and our present.

HEALING SUGGESTION

Examine your feeling about abortions, stillbirths, and miscarriages, if you've had one. Or examine judgments you may have held about people who have experienced one. Judgments hide guilt and block grace. Use this opportunity to heal yourself and to find if there are any selves that have died within you. The family dynamics where this would occur is affecting you now as a destructive pattern.

HEALING CHOICE

I commit to healing any family patterns or lost selves, so that I can free myself, and bring about my total innocence.

HEALING EXERCISE

If there are any experiences of abortions, stillbirths, or miscarriages in your life, complete the following statements:

If I were to know how this event is still holding me back, it's by _____

_____

If I were to know how many incidents in childhood needed to be cleared to resolve this painful pattern, it would be _____

_____

If I were to know where the first one began, it was at the age of _____

_____

If I were to know who was involved, it was probably _____

_____

If I were to know what it was that occurred, it was probably _____

_____

If I were to know what I decided...

about myself, it was_____

about life, it was _____

about relationships, it was _____

If I were to know what I decided I would have to do, it was _____

_____

The nature of an expectation, or "have to do," that the above question contains, makes any decision a false one. Sometimes, you have done what you decided you had to do, and sometimes you did not do it because of the feeling that you "had to." Or, sometimes, you did it half the time and refused to do it the other half. Whatever your choice, your expectation was trapping you. Let it go and choose what you want. Make new choices about what you want for the other decisions that you made. Your decisions become your beliefs, and your beliefs determine your perception. In this original event, ask that your higher mind return you and everyone to their centers until you all achieve a state of peace. Visualize this process for everyone involved. Feel the light within you connecting to the light within everyone else. Now go to those places inside where selves might have died, and blow the sacred breath of life into them to restore them. Love them until they grow up to your present age and melt into you. Now ask yourself what gift you have to heal the people in the situation—there may be more than one. Pass the gift to the people in the painful scene, and fill them with it. Now, see it passing up to your and their ancestors, healing the whole family tree. You can repeat these questions if there was a significant event like this that affected your family while you were growing up.

76.

PLAYBOYS AND PROMISCUOUS WOMEN

I came of age during the sexual revolution and besides being a late bloomer (I didn't leave the seminary until I was almost twenty-one years old), I had shyness to get over. After a few heartbreaks and a move to California to begin my doctoral studies, I began to make up for lost time. I certainly enjoyed the seventies as much as anyone could after a few heartbreaks. While I had all the independence I wanted, I also had an equal amount of dissociation.

I had enthusiastically gone through each relationship until I got to the place where I felt there was a terminal problem with the relationship. Then I would give up, and move on. Not being able to figure out how to heal the deadness in a relationship, I gave up on having just one relationship at a time. Although from time to time afterwards, I would find myself in just one relationship, I was usually dating two or more women at any given time. Finally, at the end of all this, I realized that I was not heading in the right direction, and began to look for alternatives. I made a principle for myself: "Don't go to bed with someone unless you believe there's a possibility for marriage." I began to see that the only hope for my long-term happiness was a committed relationship. I moved more and more in this direction, healing childhood and adult heartbreaks alike to regain my trust, not just in women, but also in myself.

Research has shown that girls whose fathers did not pay attention to them are sexualized early. It has become a cliché that a woman trying to get her father's love through other men becomes promiscuous. It is certainly a key factor in nympho-mania. I once had a client who had slept with every professor she had at college, except for the one who referred her to me. She successfully completed her therapy when we healed some core misunderstandings and heartbreaks she'd had as a child, and when she could feel my love without having to go to bed with me. Within the year I received an invitation to her wedding.

Playboys, Peter Pans, and other such clichéd roles are played by men who are desperately trying to be loved, but don't really believe that it can happen. They are filled with heartbreaks that are covered over by compensation. They have a good life, although they just cannot feel it, and it is almost impossible for them to say the word *commitment*, much less *marriage*.

The heartbreaks that were passed from fathers to daughters were then passed onto sons. The heartbreaks that mothers passed onto their sons made some pretty nasty "heartbreaking machines" out there. And these men eventually passed it on to their daughters, if they got that far. This is a heartbreak pattern where heartbreaks proliferate until someone has the courage to heal it. Without healing our hearts, cynicism springs up to blight relationships and even the ability for them to occur at all. Cynicism is a result of the burn-out that comes from defending independence, which also covers heartbreak. Cynicism is a defense built on fear, and when we are lost in cynicism, we are a "walking wasteland."

HEARTBREAK PRINCIPLE

Sexual promiscuity is the result of heartbreak and a lack of bonding that discon-
nects our heart and our sexuality.

‖ Heal Your Heartbreak ‖

HEALING PRINCIPLE

We must have the courage to see what is necessary, in order to live our lives and to fill our relationships with love, commitment, and success. This will ensure that we have fulfillment in our lives, rather than having lives built upon our egos.

HEALING SUGGESTION

Assess your life and relationship in light of the following questions. How happy are you? How happy are you in your relationship? How committed are you? No matter how well you are doing, you could be doing better, because life and relationships are a continuum. In the same way, if your life and relationships are a disappointment, you can make them better if you have the courage or the willingness to be willing, which allows your higher mind to help.

HEALING CHOICE

I commit to heal all of my broken bonding between my heart and sexuality, myself and others, and me and myself, so that I may live a life of happiness, and pass on a legacy of love to my children.

HEALING EXERCISE

This exercise will help you to heal experiences in your life where the connection between your heart and sexuality was broken.

If I were to guess who was involved when I broke the connection between my heart and sexuality, it was probably with _____ and _____ and _____

If I were to know what probably happened to cause me to break the connection between my heart and sexuality, it was _____ _____

What did this broken connection now allow me to do? _____ _____

What did I avoid doing or facing as a result of this broken connection? _____

_____

What fear did I try to protect myself from? _____

_____

What excuse did it give me? _____

Why was I trying to control myself? _____

Who else was I trying to control? _____

If I were to know, what was I trying to control in others? _____

_____

If I were to know, what gift was I frightened of giving? _____

_____

If I were to know, what guilt was I trying to pay off? _____

_____

If your strategy did not make you happy, make another choice. Now, go back to the heartbreak, and ask your higher mind to center you. Bond with the other people in the situation by connecting your light with their light, from your spirit to their spirit. When this is complete, give them the gift that you have for them in this situation.

To heal the broken bonding between yourself and others, use the person with whom you have your biggest lost bonding in the following exercise:

If I were to know, this person is probably _____

_____

What probably happened to cause me to break this connection?

_____

If I were to know, what did it allow me to do? _____

_____

If I were to know, what did I avoid doing or facing as a result of this?

_____

If I were to know, what fear did I try to protect myself from? _____

_____

If I were to know, what excuse did it give me?

_____

If I were to know, what was I trying to control about myself?

_____

Who else was I trying to control by having this happen? _____

_____

What was I trying to control in others? _____

_____

If I were to know, what gift was I frightened of giving? _____

If I were to know, what guilt was I trying to pay off? _____

_____

If your strategy did not make you happy, make another choice. Now, go back to the heartbreak and ask your higher mind to center you. Bond with this person by connecting your light with their light, from your spirit to their spirit.

To heal the separation with yourself:

If I were to know, when was the time I most separated from myself?

_____

It was probably with _____ and _____

and _____

If I were to know, what happened to make me want to break this connection?

_____

If I were to know, what did it allow me to do? _____

_____

If I were to know, what didn't I have to do? _____

_____

If I were to know, what fear did I try to protect myself from? _____

_____

If I were to know, what excuse did it give me? _____

_____

If I were to know, what was I trying to control about myself? _____

_____

If I were to know, who else was I trying to control by having this happen?

_____

If I were to know, what was I trying to control in others? _____

_____

If I were to know, what gift was I frightened of giving? _____

_____

If I were to know, what guilt was I trying to pay off? _____

_____

If your strategy didn't make you happy, make another choice. Now, go back to the heartbreak, and ask your higher mind to center you. Bond with yourself by having lines of light reconnect you and yourself, your mind and heart.

HEALING CHRONIC HEARTBREAK
–Healing The Unconscious Patterns

77.
HEARTBREAKS AND MASTER EGO PROGRAMS

Master Ego Programs are the core issues of the mind that determine the pattern of our life. These patterns come from the deepest, most hidden areas of our minds, although it is only their ability to hide themselves that makes them seem unchangeable. Sometimes these programs are set up so well that they seem foolproof, but although they may seem foolproof, they are not grace-proof. I have found that any problem, given time, dedication, know-how, willingness, and grace, can be opened for healing.

The Master Ego Programs include "Dark Stories," "Personal Myths and Shadow Stories," "Core Negative Self-concepts," "Conspiracies," "Ancestral Patterns," "Past Lives," "Shamanic Tests," and "Idols." These are the deepest and nastiest traps that the ego uses to keep itself in charge. The only thing that all of the programs have in common is that they each have a strategy. Our strategies are the core "accountability" questions that help us to understand the underlying dynamics of any situation or program.

Dark Stories are the negative and painful stories that provide the main scripts for our lives. Personal Myths and Shadow Stories are also key scripts built along archetypal lines. They are compensations for pain, failure, and guilt and, at a deeper level, they cover our true goodness. The Core Negative Self-concepts are key areas of self-attack and self-hatred. Conspiracies are traps that seem inescapable. Ancestral Patterns are the problems that have been passed down to us through the generations. Past Lives are metaphors and stories from the deepest levels of our minds. Shamanic Tests are tests set up by our souls in an attempt to leap to a new level of consciousness. Idols are the false gods that we worship, such as drugs, money, lust, power, romance, suffering, illness, and crucifixion. We believe they will make us happy or fulfill us.

Each of these programs has a purpose that they are trying to accomplish. Sometimes, they accomplish what they attempt, but mostly they don't. They always fail to bring us happiness, which is the ultimate measure of success. After we discover our mistaken strategies, we can make a new choice.

All of our Master Ego Programs, at some level, are attempts to avoid our purpose, and to protect ourselves from the primordial fears of death, love, losing ourselves, having it all, and God. We all set out to love and to be loved, but the traps set by our egos prevent us from attaining this because of our fears. In other words, our egos hold us back from giving situations because we think there may be danger on the path ahead. By tricking us into believing that happiness can be found in other ways and by other means, our egos convince us that loving and joining are not worth the effort, and that they will lead to heart-break. Of course, heartbreak occurs when we cannot love or give wholeheartedly. It is our willingness to recognize these patterns and how they are serving us that allows us to move through them to heal them. In so doing, we evolve. This ongoing evolution is our expression of love.

HEARTBREAK PRINCIPLE

Our Master Ego Programs, the deepest patterns of our minds, contain strategies that try to protect us, have us get what we want, and make us happy. They become traps that lead to heartbreak.

HEALING PRINCIPLE

Becoming aware of the Master Ego Programs and how they serve us is the first step toward making another choice, because they will always spectacularly fail to make us happy.

HEALING SUGGESTION

Become aware of your Master Ego Programs and the effects that they have had on your life. The ego hates awareness, and some of these programs will collapse as soon as you become aware of them. All of the programs are choices that halt the flow of grace. They are places where you would rather follow your own bright ideas, than be inspired or guided.

HEALING CHOICE

I commit to become aware of and to heal my Master Ego Programs so that I can evolve and express my love.

HEALING EXERCISE

To free yourself from any traumatic event in your life, or any Master Ego Programs, examine your strategies closely. To unveil your strategy, complete the following statements using your intuition:

If I were to know what I was trying to get from this program, it's probably

_____

If I were to know how I thought this would make me happy, it's probably

_____

If I were to know who I was trying to defeat, it's probably

_____

If I were to know what I was trying to prove, it's probably

_____

If I were to know what fear I was trying to protect myself from, it's probably

_____

If I were to know what excuse this gave me, it's probably

_____

If I were to know what I was trying to control in myself, it's probably

_____

If I were to know what I was trying to be right about, it's probably

_____

If I were to know who I was trying to control and about what, it's probably

_____

If I were to know what guilt I was trying to pay off, it's probably

_____

If I were to know who I was getting revenge on, it's probably

_____

If I were to know what it ultimately allowed me to do, it's probably

_____

If I were to know what it was that I ultimately didn't have to do, it's probably

_____

If you do not like the results, make a new choice to let go of your program and its strategy to keep you from your fear; to keep you in control. Then spend a few moments in silence to see and feel what is given to you in its place. If you have realized that this event, or program, was a mistake and that it did not bring you happiness, then it is time to let it go and receive the real answer to your situation. You can change this core issue so that you move toward wholeheartedness.

78.

HEARTBREAK AS A STORY

We are storytelling creatures, mythmakers, and legend-spinners, and our lives are our greatest stories. We write the stories of our lives. We are the stars; we direct the action and we are the producers. We are ultimately responsible for our lives as we have made them. There are two general categories that encompass all of our stories: the Healing Story, where the purpose is to use everything for joy and transformation, and the Death Story, where we turn away from life. Some of the other main stories that come up time and again are the Hero Story, the Success Story, the Victim Story, the Revenge Story, the Redemption Story, or the Awakening Story—which is enlightenment, the waking up from our story.

Stories come from the deepest parts of our minds and, for the most part, we are unaware of them. This does not mean that they affect us any less. Stories are one of the key unconscious patterns that direct our lives. Ultimately, we can choose the stories we play out, rather than simply following the script we assign to ourselves.

We also have the power to change the script as the story is running. Think of your unfolding story as a film: if you wanted to change the film you were watching on screen in a cinema, you would not go up to the screen and try to change the images. You would go to the projection room. But changing the film would change only the images on the screen, not the film itself. It would be much more effective to go to where the film was made—Hollywood, for example. Go no further! Our minds are both the projection room and Hollywood in one.

The first step toward clearing any of the core traps is awareness. If we realize how a story serves us, we can change it. The final step is to let go of a negative story and choose the type of story that we want our lives to be. We all tell positive and negative stories at the same time. If we are unaware that we are telling a negative story, we might heal parts of ourselves only to have the next chapter in our negative story come back to haunt us at a later time.

I once worked with a Japanese workshop participant, who realized that she was telling a "Heartbreak Story." I asked her how bad it was and she said, "It's not that bad. It's *good*. It's a four-handkerchief story." When I asked her what purpose she had in telling that story, she replied, "It makes me feel alive, otherwise my life would be boring." For her to let this story go, I had to show her that excitement and adventure could also come from a "Healing Story" or a "Love Story." She didn't need heartbreak to keep her going. In fact, as soon as she started learning about herself and began to heal, she found few things as exciting as seeing the new story unfold.

HEARTBREAK PRINCIPLE

A Heartbreak Story can go on chapter after chapter, for year after year in our lives because we don't realize that our lives are the sum total of our stories. We need to understand that we are storytellers and that we have a purpose in telling these stories.

HEALING PRINCIPLE

It is important to become aware of the stories that we are telling and to change the ones that don't serve us. If we are happy with some stories and they lead us toward wholeheartedness, then they are healing stories.

HEALING SUGGESTION

What is the film of your life like? Is it a comedy or a tragedy? Is your life a love story, a fear story, or a heartbreak story? Is it a spiritual odyssey or a soap opera? Is it a mystery or a horror story? Do you like the story of your life? Does it make a good film? Is it an adventure or is it so boring that you would fall asleep in the middle of the performance or spend most of your time at the concession stand? Is your film so bad that you would leave halfway through it? What kind of film is the film of your life? What would its title be? What elements are in the film? Is it an exciting film to you and to others? What would you change about it? Examine your life to determine what negative stories have been affecting you and let go of the ones you don't like.

HEALING CHOICE

I commit to finding and letting go of all of my "death stories" which turn me away from life, and I commit to writing my life as a masterpiece.

HEALING EXERCISE

This exercise is best done together with a friend or, if that is not convenient, you can use a tape recorder. At the end you will have a record to listen to. It works best with a friend, and you can take turns telling your stories to one another over the phone. Try to tell one or a number of stories a day. To get the full benefit, complete the exercise. The quicker you get through the darker stories, the better you will feel. It is important to become aware of whatever story you have been telling, and to know that your stories are one of the deepest ways you program your life. Our stories represent our perception of our lives—the way we see them. If we look at them differently and we perceive them differently they are, effectively, rewritten.

Tell your story dramatically. Take twenty minutes for each life story as you tell it. If you have taped your story, listen to it later. Take time to reflect on how this program is affecting your life. Begin the first twenty minutes by telling your life as a victim story. If you are working with a friend, have them tell their life as a victim story, and keep alternating back and forth. Then take twenty minutes to tell your life as a heartbreak story. Then choose five from this list and continue with twenty minutes each for the stories:

- horror story
- drama or soap opera
- revenge story
- martyr or sacrifice story
- fear story
- war story
- scarcity story
- tragic story
- tantrum story
- death story
- a story where you planned everything that happened to you in your life
- healing story

Choose five from this list and take ten to fifteen minutes to tell each one:

- comedy story
- hero story
- adventure story
- success story
- spiritual journey story
- redemption story (where you are saving others, rather than judging them, and they are saving you)
- happy story
- abundance story
- a series of awakening stories
- masterpiece

- beautiful life story
- love story

You will definitely be tired of your stories by the end of their telling, but you will also be aware of them, and you will probably have the power to have your story be any way you want it to be. If you are really committed to your healing, go back and complete the exercise for every category. Notice which story you knew by heart because you've been telling it so frequently to those around you. It is time to make new choices about the stories you want to tell. Find out what your strategy is for telling a certain story by completing the following statements:

Did it work?   Did it make me happy?

If I were to know what I am trying to gain by my story, it is probably _____
_____

If I were to know what fear I am trying to protect, it is probably _____
_____

If I were to know what guilt I am trying to pay off, it is probably _____
_____

If I were to know what I was trying to be right about, it was probably_____
_____

If I were to know who I was trying to defeat, it was probably_____
_____

If I were to know what this gave me an excuse for, it was probably _____
_____

If I were to know what I was proving by telling this story, it was probably _____
_____

Why? _____

(If you are proving anything you don't fully believe, or why try to prove it?)

If I were to know who I am getting revenge on, it is probably _____

_____

If I were to know how this helped me avoid my purpose, it was probably _____

_____

Once you realize that this story did not give you what you really wanted, because it didn't make you happy, you can choose to let it go. All of our stories are of our own making and we can choose to change our past stories by altering our perception of them or the way we tell and see them. We can change our present and future stories by directing them and telling them in a way that makes them positive and purposeful. If we discover and delete our negative stories and make new choices for healing stories, we move toward wholeheartedness.

79.

HEARTBREAK AS A PERSONAL MYTH
OR SHADOW STORY

Key patterns operating in our unconscious minds are our personal myths and shadow stories. We experience personal myths when we live our life scripts as a myth, a legend, or a fairy tale. The script can be a powerful directive in our lives, but it is also compensation—in other words, it is an attempt to make up for what we consider to be bad or unacceptable about ourselves. No matter how hard we try to do things right, and no matter how good we might appear to be, we will get no real rewards for it. A personal myth is usually hidden, so the crucial element is to become aware of it and then to make new choices to heal the heartbreak that it comes from and causes. Our personal myths will have begun at the time of a trauma. It was a time so painful, so full of failure, that we thought we could not handle it, but a character or hero in our personal myth *could*. We started living the script of this character to cover the trauma, as a kind of compensation.

For example, you may have suffered a serious heartbreak and found yourself left with a broken marriage and two children. You believed that the old "you" couldn't handle that situation, so Superwoman emerged from the ashes. Superwoman can cope with anything and, on the surface, appears to. But this role prevents you from receiving.

We have all built barriers around ourselves and the positive elements that we have created to fulfill our roles. Underneath we believe that we are failures. We believe that we are unworthy of receiving because we are living a lie—playing a role that hides a weak or bad character.

Similarly, a shadow story is typically well hidden and possibly even more destructive. These stories are some of the fundamental negative self-concepts that direct our major life stories and set our whole life patterns. We talked about shadow figures on page 38, and the same concept holds true here. Shadow stories contain some forms of self-punishment, such as heartbreak, failure, ill-health, or defeat. In a shadow story we fracture off the "bad" shadow self and blame it for the situation rather than blaming ourselves. Shadow stories are controlling, although we are not usually conscious of them, and they prevent us from experiencing life and love to their fullest. It is a script that is usually mythical, coming from legends, fairy tales, or historical characters, and it follows the patterns or metaphors of that script in a strict fashion. Shadow stories are effectively stories that we believe about ourselves. We might have read a fairy tale as a child and secretly identified with the nasty or evil character. We pocket that story away, experiencing guilt or fear about such feelings, but that story remains within us and it becomes a metaphor for our lives. We follow *that* script because we subconsciously believe that it pertains to us and to our lives.

At its deepest level, a shadow story also hides our true goodness, power, mastery, and our identity as someone worthy of all the love there is. The ego uses these shadow stories to keep us stuck and to punish ourselves. By becoming aware of these stories that are hidden in our minds, we can make another choice.

HEARTBREAK PRINCIPLE

We have personal myths and shadow stories that provide the scripts by which we live. They can be heartbreaking or tragic. We do not understand why certain events keep happening to us, but the scripts of our myths and stories can dictate these events. We cast ourselves as a certain type of character and get stuck in this role. As great as some of our roles might be, we reap no reward, other than a momentary pleasure, for even the positive myths.

HEALING PRINCIPLE

Awareness of our personal myths, shadow stories, and unconscious scripts gives us the power to choose the truth.

HEALING SUGGESTION

Discover your personal myth by asking yourself, "If I were a legendary, fairy tale, or historical character, who would I be?" To find your shadow figure, ask yourself, "If I were to know the character I would most hate to be in all the legends, fairy tales or history, who would it be?" Write down your responses in the exact order that they come to you. Sometimes you will get two or three responses for each question. People who are super-positive sometimes deny and hide the answers that come to them. If you do this it prevents you from changing the patterns holding you back. Your inability to face things is yet another example of your effort to look good—even if it is only to yourself. You may do this so automatically that you don't even notice yourself censoring and editing everything to fit your self-image.

HEALING CHOICE

I commit to discovering my personal myths so that I can heal the original heart-break that I thought I could not cope with myself and reap the rewards for my positive actions. I commit to discovering my shadow stories and integrating the shadow self so that I can live my true goodness, power, and mastery.

HEALING EXERCISE

This exercise is also best done with a friend or a tape recorder. Tell the story of the character who is your personal myth. If you don't know the exact story of this particular character (say Joan of Arc or Robin Hood), fill in the details intuitively. Explore how your personal myth has been a key script in your life. Examine how and where you acted like your mythical figure. Did you encourage your family or the people around you to act out different characters in your myth? Recognize that you are all the characters in your personal myth. Tell your life story from the standpoint of each character including the shadow characters (such as the French monarchy or the Sheriff of Nottingham), if you have one in your personal myth. The shadow will be typically the most hidden, but also the most powerful. This idea may seem strange, but I have found that unearthing our personal myths—the "goodies" as well as the "baddies"—allows us to step out of our deepest traps easily and gracefully. Now, complete the following statements:

If I were to know how old I was when my personal myth began, it was probably at the age of _____

If I were to know who was around when it happened, it was probably

_____

If I were to know what was happening that I decided I couldn't be me, but had to be the character in my personal myth, it was _____

_____

Now use the strategy method to find motivation to have this happen by completing the following statements:

Did it work?   Did it make me happy?

If I were to know what I am trying to gain by my personal myth, it is probably

_____

If I were to know what fear I am trying to protect, it is probably   _____

_____

If I were to know what guilt I am trying to pay off, it is probably   _____

_____

If I were to know what I was trying to be right about, it was probably   _____

_____

If I were to know who I was trying to defeat, it was probably   _____

_____

If I were to know what this gave me an excuse for, it was probably   _____

_____

If I were to know what I was proving by telling this story, it was probably   _____

_____

Why? _____

Remember: whatever it is that you are trying to prove, you don't really believe it. Why else would you try to prove it?

If I were to know who I am getting revenge on, it is probably   _____

_____

If I were to know how this helped me avoid my purpose, it was probably   _____

_____

Once you realize that this myth did not give you what you really wanted, because it didn't make you happy, you can choose to let it go. Make a choice for truth and see what would happen if you let go of the Personal Myth and its strategy. What do you choose now about yourself? In the situation where the myth began, ask that your higher mind carry everyone in this myth back to their center. Have the light inside you join with their light. Give them the gift that you intuitively know will heal this situation. Is it love? Forgiveness? Understanding? Imagine yourself taking all the characters in your Personal Myth and melting them into you.

By accepting them all as part of you and your story, any hold they have on you dissolves. You are free to reclaim the part of your heart that was broken when you created the personal myth.

Now, tell the story of your shadow figure. Explore how this shadow story has been a key script in your life, and examine how and where you acted like your shadow "mythical" figure. Tell your life story as this shadow figure, but notice how you probably played all the different characters in your shadow story. Now, complete the following statements about your shadow story:

If I were to know how old I was when the shadow story began, it was probably at the age of _____

If I were to know who was around when it happened, it was probably

_____

If I were to know what was happening that I decided it wasn't really me doing this, it was my shadow, it was probably _____

_____

To find your mistaken motivation for having this happen, complete the following statements:

If I were to know what I am trying to gain by my shadow story, it is probably

_____

If I were to know what fear I am trying to protect, it is probably _____

_____

If I were to know what guilt I am trying to pay off, it is probably _____

_____

If I were to know what I was trying to be right about, it was probably _____

_____

If I were to know who I was trying to defeat, it was probably _____

_____

If I were to know what this gave me an excuse for, it was probably _____

_____

If I were to know what I was proving by telling this story, it was probably _____

_____

Why? _____

Remember, what you are proving, you don't really believe, or you would not need to prove it.

If I were to know who I was getting revenge on, it was probably _____

_____

If I were to know how this helped me avoid my purpose, it was probably _____

_____

Once you realize that this story did not give you what you really wanted, because it didn't make you happy, you can choose to let it go. Make another choice for a positive story or ask for spiritual guidance to get you through the letting go process in order to reap the rewards. What do you choose now about yourself? Ask that your higher mind carry everyone back to their center in the incident where the shadow story began. Have the light inside you join with their light. Now, give them the gift that can heal this situation. Again, ask your higher mind to help, and imagine taking all the characters in your shadow story, and melting them into you.

80.

HEARTBREAK AND CORE NEGATIVE SELF-CONCEPTS

Our core negative self-concepts include areas of self-hatred and they represent every deleterious belief we have about ourselves. We use these core negative self-concepts to attack ourselves and to hold ourselves back. We even hide behind them. We use these painful self-concepts as an excuse to avoid responding to calls for help, because we are too busy and involved in beating ourselves up, and we use them as excuses to avoid going forward in life and relationships. They do, however, provide us with a certain amount of control, which we use to protect our fear so that we do not have to risk intimacy or living our purpose.

When we have these negative self-concepts, we usually compensate for them to avoid consciously suffering them. Typically, we compensate for them by acting in the opposite way—maybe by being good, working hard, or being a perfectionist. We play roles in an effort to cover over these dark personalities. The negative self-concepts seem to disappear under these roles which are really forms of sacrifice. We sacrifice our true selves and our true feelings. We can discover where these negative self-concepts are hidden if we look at the areas in our lives where we give, but don't allow ourselves to receive. Our roles are a form of compensation that hide our negative beliefs about ourselves, and our negative self-concepts are a form of compensation that hide our true goodness, innocence, and identity as someone who deserves every good thing.

Good, Nice, Sweet Role—
Deadness—Can't Receive

This hides _____

Bad, Evil, Nasty Personalities—
Self-Attack—Receives Punishment

This hides _____

True Goodness, Peace—
Spiritual Love—Receives Grace

We hide our evil or dark personalities from the light so that we can do things our ego's way and hide from spiritual light and peace—our true state of being.

These negative selves are beliefs that lead to feelings of unworthiness. They block love and success, and eventually lead to heartbreak. Our heartbreaks are fractures that give us even more negative beliefs about ourselves, which gives us a sense of control. As a result of these areas of self-attack, we do not have to share ourselves and we get to do what we want, just as long as we feel guilty enough and continue to punish ourselves. Core negative self-concepts are one of the Master Ego Programs that are the chief generators of heartbreak, and heartbreak is one of the chief generators of negative self-concepts, so this leaves us caught in a vicious cycle of pain and self-attack.

HEARTBREAK PRINCIPLE

Our core negative self-concepts stop love and abundance, and generate heart-break to give us control, negative attention, and further negative self-concepts, which creates a vicious cycle.

HEALING PRINCIPLE

Once we realize the purpose of these negative self-concepts, we can see that they will never fulfill us. They are indulgences for which we have paid a deadly price. We can choose to have love and the success, which would make us truly happy.

HEALING SUGGESTION

Much of our hard work and over-exertion, which we undertake as part of the general sacrifice of roles, covers our core negative self-concepts and wears us out. It is a sure sign that we would rather search endlessly for happiness than have true love in relationships, or spiritual peace and love in ourselves. We can choose to give up the vicious cycle that prevents peace and holds back love and spiritual oneness.

HEALING CHOICE

I commit to give up the hoax of my negative self-concepts, which is what I use for indulgence, self-attack, and forgetting my true identity as a "child of God."

―――――――――――――

HEALING EXERCISE

Explore the vicious cycle of indulgence, self-attack, sacrifice, and heartbreak that attempts constantly to recycle itself in your life. Begin with the compensations of your sacrifice—the hard work and overscheduled hours that do not seem to pay off. Or, explore the cycle by looking at your methods of self-attack and the negative beliefs you hold about yourself. Or, explore the vicious cycle by examining your indulgences—the "toys" that you think will make you happy. Once you realize how each of these areas reinforce each other and fail to satisfy you, you can make another choice.

When you find one aspect of this vicious cycle in your life, the others will be present. Their roots are tied together. You may recognize evidence of your indulgence, your poor self-image, or self-attack, or you may notice how hard you work, how good you are and how little you get in return. Typically, one side of you is more prominent and you hide the others. Some examples are:

Recognition:	Negative ▶ leads to ▶	Indulgence ▶ leads to ▶	Roles ▶ leads to ▶	Heartbreak
	self-concept			
	I'm evil	Control, laziness,	Exhausting job,	Heartbreak
		food and drink	no balance	

Recognition:	Roles and ▶ leads to ▶	Indulgence ▶ leads to ▶	Negative ▶ leads to ▶	Heartbreak
	Compensation		self-concept	
	Helper	Super busy	,Failure,	Heartbreak
		trying to swallow others'	it's all my fault	
		pain, food, drink, work		

Start in any area, and you will begin to find what you have hidden from yourself. If you have a partner, you will typically be acting out one side while they act out the other side. For example, you may tend toward the "sacrifice" side while they are in the negative self-image side. Both of you feel guilty and then hide your indulgent sides more. The vicious cycle will continue until you realize the high price you are paying for something that is not making you happy. You can make another choice.

81.
CONSPIRACIES

Conspiracies are the traps that the ego set up for us. They are so convincing that it seems like we will never get out of them. They are an attempt to hide our purpose in life, out of fear that we are not "big" enough to carry out these deepest promises. They also hide our fear of our own gifts, which hold so much potential for ourselves and others.

Our conspiracies are excuses not to be ourselves. They are ways of hiding, staying small, and running away from our potential, sometimes because we fear that we would do more harm than good if we tried to help. Yet every conspiracy is a mistake, a triumph of the ego in its effort to delay and distract. The ego exaggerates us into either self-aggrandizement or self-effacing smallness. Our conspiracies demand that we be small, and we all have supposedly good reasons for being small. We live in the age of excuses. The opposite of smallness is not the glamour of fame, but the real truth of our greatness, which is ultimately the truth of who we can be. Having worked with so many thousands of people, I know that we all have the potential for genius and greatness within us but, in our fear, we have used myriad problems, woven into conspiracies, in an attempt to hide from our purpose.

Some of the many conspiracies that surround heartbreak include the heartbreak conspiracy, the victim conspiracy, the revenge conspiracy, the jealousy conspiracy, the independent-dependent conspiracy, the sexual conspiracy, the feelingunwanted conspiracy, and the Oedipus conspiracy. Conspiracies were set up so well by the ego to prevent us from getting through them, so the primary healing element is awareness. Once we become aware that we are hiding, we can make more conscious and judicious choices. In whatever ways we try to gain something or to protect ourselves through our conspiracy, we must realize that they are mistakes that have led us into further pain and darkness.

HEARTBREAK PRINCIPLE

Our conspiracies are traps so big that we don't usually find our way out of them. They hide our purpose and our potential for giving gifts and lead to heartbreak.

HEALING PRINCIPLE

Any conspiracy can be healed when we recognize it and our purpose for having it. Once we realize that it is a mistake, we can let it go and make a new choice.

HEALING SUGGESTION

Examine your life for problems that are so big they look insurmountable. Commit to healing them, and ask that it be done easily and gracefully.

HEALING CHOICE

I commit to finding and healing every conspiracy I have. I ask for a miracle in this regard.

HEALING EXERCISE

Meditate on your purpose and consider how great it must be that your ego set up such a great defense to hide it. Make the choice for your purpose, letting go of any conspiracies of which you are aware. Examine each conspiracy. What is the major gift or potential that it hides? For example, if you are caught in a revenge conspiracy, in an episode such as fighting a long court battle for justice, your major gift may be forgiveness. If your conspiracy is jealousy, the major gift may be giving or love instead of possessiveness. When you find what it is (look for hints throughout your day), embrace it. Commit to your gift, and put the conspiracy in the hands of the gods. Choose your destiny!

82.

THE HEARTBREAK CONSPIRACY

A heartbreak conspiracy is a heartbreak—or a pattern of heartbreaks—that is intended to last a lifetime. It is one of the ego's strategies designed to delay and distract us. It is our ego's attempt to keep us from further pain, but it rarely works, and it never makes us happy. The heartbreak conspiracy is a destructive ego defense that removes us from life, from contact with others, and from the connection of love. Without this joining, the illusion of separation is strengthened, as is the ego itself. With bonding, separation melts away, reducing the ego's impact, which brings more love and success. Ease and effectiveness characterize inspiration, truth and grace, which are the opposite of the ego. Any difficult area of our lives signifies a place where our egos are working hard to keep themselves entrenched.

The difficulty we have accomplishing or completing anything when we are pulled back from life can be explained by the following analogy. When we are asked to pick up a heavy load, we are instructed to keep our backs straight and to lift with our thighs so that we do not strain our backs. If that heavy load, instead of being right in front of us, was two feet away, imagine how much strain there would be on our backs as we lean forward to lift it. If that burden was four feet away, we would be on our knees trying to lift it, and we'd feel even more strain. At six feet away, we would be stretched out full length, and at ten feet it would be impossible to lift the load. The same concept applies to the heartbreak conspiracy. We become so removed from life that the task of learning about love and relationships seems beyond us. Emotionally, even the brightest and healthiest of us have backed off from life, because of our personal history of heartbreaks and those we have inherited. As a result, we live dissociated lives—out of touch, independent, objectifying, cold, and disconnected. Unless there is healing, the fracture from one generation is passed on immediately to the next generation at the behavioral, emotional, and self-concept levels. You can see this in action when emotional traumas become illnesses, and the symptoms of, or predilection for, certain illnesses are passed on.

The heartbreak conspiracy may repeat itself over and over again like a heartbreak story. The difference is that the heartbreak conspiracy will typically occur just as we are about to take a significant step forward. It becomes our excuse not to change. The heartbreak conspiracy subverts the surge of vibrant, eager energy that is present as we fall in love, while the heartbreak story comes up as a chapter from time to time because it is a way of life.

HEARTBREAK PRINCIPLE

A heartbreak conspiracy is a heartbreak so big or complicated that it seems impossible to escape from it.

HEALING PRINCIPLE

Finding and healing a heartbreak conspiracy can be relatively easy if we have the courage for love and intimacy, and if we use our own potential for grace.

HEALING SUGGESTION

Ask for Heaven's help to heal yourself and to regain your heart. Ask for a miracle to heal your heartbreak conspiracy. A miracle is an act of love and faith that looks upon the problem as an illusion.

HEALING CHOICE

I commit to healing my heartbreak conspiracies, winning my heart back, and fulfilling my purpose in life and relationships.

HEALING EXERCISE

Use the same strategy method as in previous exercises of this section to find your motive for having the heartbreak conspiracy by completing the following statements:

Did it work?   Did it make me happy?

If I were to know what I am trying to gain by my story, it is probably _____
_____

If I were to know what fear I am trying to protect, it is probably _____
_____

If I were to know what guilt I am trying to pay off, it is probably_____
_____

If I were to know what I was trying to be right about, it was probably_____
_____

If I were to know who I was trying to defeat, it was probably_____
_____

If I were to know what this gave me an excuse for, it was probably _____
_____

If I were to know what I was proving by telling this story, it was probably _____
_____

Why? _____
If I were to know who I was getting revenge on, it was probably _____
_____

If I were to know how this stopped me from my purpose, it was probably _____
_____

If I were to know how this stopped me in relationships, it was probably _____
_____

If I were to know what major gift it hides, it is probably _____
_____

When you discover the motives behind your strategy, you will recognize how it trapped you in heartbreak. You can make another choice now and open the door to your heart and to true love.

======

83.
THE FEELING UNWANTED CONSPIRACY

Feeling unwanted is a type of heartbreak that frequently turns into an "unwanted conspiracy." It starts at the beginning of our lives and is the forerunner of many destructive patterns in relationships. I have worked with people who—through hypnosis or by using their "intuition"—described traumas that occurred in the womb or at the moment of conception. When traumas begin in the womb, there is always a level of self-destructiveness that accompanies them.

I was working with John, a sailor at the rehabilitation center, who had a nasty heartbreak-rejection pattern. Through regression and healing we traced the heartbreaks of this pattern to his conception. At that time, his father was feeling rejected and, as a result, was acting in an aggressive, forceful manner. His mother in turn began to feel rejected and, as a result of this, John began to feel unwanted. He also interpreted his father's behavior as rejection, the same misunderstanding his mother had. John carried these feelings as he grew in the womb, and they were compounded at birth by the painful force used to bring him into the world. His feelings were reinforced throughout his childhood by a number of major misunderstandings causing heartbreak. These heartbreaks led him to the drug rehabilitation center. When we healed the original rejection at conception, John was able to see that his father had felt rejected, and he could understand why his father had acted the way he did, because John had this same fear of rejection. He was able to see now that *he* had rejected his father rather than the other way around. John was able to let go of this whole misunderstanding and, for the first time, feel that he was loved and wanted by his parents. This was the key to his rehabilitation.

Like any negative emotion, feeling unwanted is always destructive. Feeling unwanted as a child leads to adult heartbreaks. It is a mistaken belief that almost always leads to conspiracy.

This has shown up quite dramatically in women who feel unwanted because of their gender. I've treated many hundreds of women who felt unwanted or undervalued because they were women. This is a particular trait of the Chinese culture, where women were once considered less valuable than men. It is no wonder that these remarkable Chinese women have become so practical, entrepreneurial, and driven to success in order to prove that they are useful. In family roles some of these women commonly chose to be the hero—succeeding for everyone—or the invisible child, who seemed almost to disappear in order to take up less space. Others chose to be sacrificers in the family, always taking care of others because they felt guilty for being alive or for receiving anything at all. Many times, feeling unwanted made them extremely competitive, especially with their brothers.

Unhealthy competition always suggests broken bonding and the need to do something to prove we are desirable. Many times, I have seen competitive women become highly successful chief executive officers, but their love lives never seemed to work out, because their men seemed to fail them. Their sense of competition led them to believe they were better than the men, and underneath the competition was a broken heart caused by feeling unwanted.

When I worked with women who had expressed this dynamic, we were able to trace back to the point at which the unwanted feelings began. It usually occurred at birth or soon after, or sometimes in the womb. The whole cycle began with the feeling of being unwanted by their mothers, fathers, or both. If the feelings of rejection stemmed from the mother, it was normally because the mother needed to prove her own worth by having a son to gain her husband's or family's approval. When the feelings stemmed from the father, he often needed to prove his strength or worth by having a son to make up for his own feelings of rejection or unworthiness. Frequently, I would ask my client to conduct an experiment by imaginatively supplying the needs of the family such as food, money, self-worth, confidence, and resourcefulness. I would ask my client how her mother or father felt about her now that their family's needs were handled. In every instance, they felt happily welcomed into the family.

I found that as babies we often took our parents' feelings of fear or worry as rejection against ourselves. When our parents suffer from the same feelings of rejection this experience is increased. Once the misunderstanding was cleared up, it became obvious that the gift these career women had brought to the family was exactly what the entire family had believed a boy would provide—in other words value, abundance, or success. As these women felt the misunderstanding and heartbreak clear up, they began sharing the gifts they had brought for their families. A new level of confidence, self-worth, irresistibility, success, and abundance would emerge. When these early incidents were healed, the women often continued to act in the same successful way, but now they were able to receive, enjoy, celebrate, and feel lovable, wanted, and successful, because it was not just a compensation to prove their worth. They can feel the rewards and celebrate them. The key is feeling better—then we know it is the truth. Compensation, as we have seen, has a habit of being uncovered at some later stage—it is doing the right thing for the wrong reasons.

If we feel that our parents did not want us, we will typically feel that no one will want us, and in this way the unwanted pattern becomes the "unwanted conspiracy." This can cause heartbreak after heartbreak throughout our lives. Whenever I ask in a workshop how many people felt unwanted by their parents, about one-third of the people typically raise their hands. The unwanted conspiracy is compounded by the independence conspiracy, but once it is examined and healed, the gifts are spectacular. These gifts usually include the gifts of irresistibility, irrepressibility, and true love.

HEARTBREAK PRINCIPLE

Feeling unwanted begins as a mistaken assumption and ends as a conspiracy sabotaging our relationships.

HEALING PRINCIPLE

There is no truth to our belief that we were unwanted. It is a result of our misunderstanding of our parents' behavior—how they acted because of their own pain and lack of bonding, which triggered it in us. When we imaginatively supply the needs that were causing our parents' pain, their behavior becomes welcoming.

HEALING SUGGESTION

Give what is needed without expectation and you cannot feel rejected. If you reject someone because they acted negatively, you will also feel rejected.

HEALING CHOICE

I commit to healing the feeling of rejection and bringing out my gifts of irresistibility, irrepressibility, and true love.

HEALING EXERCISE

In any situation where someone has acted less than hospitably, ask yourself what pain they are feeling or what needs they want to have met. Imagine supplying those needs with the energy of your gifts pouring into them. Notice how the behavior changes when the pain is gone and the needs are supplied. In any situation where you feel fear, notice that all those around you are feeling the same fear. In any situation where you feel unwanted, notice that others are also feeling rejected. What is the gift that they would need to heal these painful feelings? Imagine yourself giving that gift.

84.

I RUINED THEIR LIFE CONSPIRACY

This conspiracy typically appears in tandem with a few other conspiracies. It can include patterns or conspiracies of failure, sacrifice, and valuelessness. I once worked with a young man who had the "I ruined their life conspiracy" along with a heartbreak conspiracy and an unwanted conspiracy. As a boy, he had heard his parents fighting over him, and they went on to discuss divorce. The fight was about his mother wanting to go back to work. She worked as a professional and valued her life outside the family. She felt like she had lost her freedom when she had become a mother. The young man had grown up believing that he was a burden to his mother; he believed that he owed women, that he had to sacrifice his life, that he didn't deserve a happy relationship since he had wrecked his family, and that no woman really loved, wanted, or valued him.

When this young man realized that his mother had felt valueless and unlovable—exactly what he was feeling now—and that she was using work to counteract these feelings, he could forgive her. He imagined his mother feeling lovable, valuable, and free and was, for the first time since he was a child, sure she had really wanted and loved him. He recognized that his mother's words of rejection were the result of her pain, feelings of valuelessness, and needs, and not about him. He could see that part of his purpose was to save his mother from this very trap and to help her feel free and loved. He imagined himself giving her these gifts heart-to-heart, and at the same time could feel his mother giving him her love. Instead of feeling like he'd ruined his mother's life and destroyed his family, he began to act and feel irresistible.

HEARTBREAK PRINCIPLE

The "I ruined their life conspiracy" sets up a pattern of feeling that we do not deserve abundance, success, or happiness in relationships, and that we have to give up our life in sacrifice and repayment.

HEALING PRINCIPLE

Understanding is a key to releasing the heartbreaks and their conspiracy. The conspiracy was nothing more than a strategy to avoid facing fears, or an expression of guilt about avoiding their life purpose.

HEALING SUGGESTION

In any painful situation, to understand why someone is acting the way they are, ask yourself what you or anyone would have to be feeling to act a certain way. If you have ever felt those same feelings, you know how crippling they are. Would you still hold it against this person, or would you have compassion for them, reach out to them, and forgive them?

HEALING CHOICE

I commit to living my life and embracing my destiny. I commit to clearing up any misunderstanding by realizing that I am 100 percent responsible for what happened in the past, but I am also 100 percent innocent.

HEALING EXERCISE

Recognize that the "I ruined their life conspiracy" is compensating for a major gift. What is your gift? Can you think why you would need such a big conspiracy to hold it back? Now, imagine that the compensation you have used to hide the conspiracy is melting into the gift, so the gift becomes bigger and more attractive. We can give gifts by seeing ourselves giving them—as we think, healing is accomplished energetically.

Just as we can tell when people dislike us or are suspicious of us, we can also tell when people appreciate us. When we feel wanted and appreciated, we behave differently. So if we appreciate others, their behavior becomes less defensive and fearful. Others change as we perceive them differently.

85.
THE JEALOUSY CONSPIRACY

Jealousy is an emotion that is based on the insecurity that comes from lost bonding, old heartbreaks, and dependency. Jealousy is made up of feelings of loss, fear, anger, abandonment, hurt, rejection, vengeance, unworthiness, possessiveness, guilt, and competition. It is made up of so many painful feelings that it can easily tear us up inside and lead to heartbreak. If we let it affect our behavior, we can bully or badger our partners to such an extent that they want to leave us. Jealousy can start a vicious cycle of destructive and self-destructive feelings. It very easily becomes a conspiracy because of its consuming nature.

Many times, we dissociate ourselves from our jealousy and become independent, because jealousy is such an extreme and painful feeling. It may have begun as jealousy for a sibling, or a trauma such as losing a parent, and being jealous of others who have two parents. To protect ourselves, we lower the importance of partners, relationships, love, and sex so that we do not, or cannot be, hurt as much. We become isolated or dissociated, which can make us so independent that we make our partner dependent and jealous. For obvious reasons this does not create a happy relationship. The only effective way to heal jealousy is to begin a path of healing the old wounds that led us to such heartbreak. Jealousy makes us want to control our partners to make them safe. If we succeed, they become safe and boring but, more often than not, our control leads to fights and power struggles, which only causes more hurt.

The jealousy conspiracy is one of the most common causes of heartbreak. In the worst cases, the pain can be so strong that it is difficult not only to act maturely but also sanely. Unless our partners are highly mature and answer our sometimes desperate calls for help, our attractiveness is greatly lowered and we drive them out the door. If our partners are very independent, it becomes frightening to them, because it is this very neediness, dependency, and jealousy within them that drove them to be independent in the first place. Too often, we choose independence to compensate for jealousy, which only delays the healing.

Healing the jealousy is the only thing that will truly work, otherwise our partners will just act out our hidden jealousy.

HEARTBREAK PRINCIPLE

Jealousy is a painful and volatile emotion that easily becomes a conspiracy, which almost always leads to heartbreak.

HEALING PRINCIPLE

Only through forgiveness, letting go, acceptance, understanding, joining, and healing old fractures can we act confidently and effectively.

HEALING SUGGESTION

When you recognize jealousy in yourself, commit to healing the root of it, or it will return again and again. If your partner is jealous, recognize that it mirrors your own buried fractures and dissociated jealousy. If you respond as a good partner, you will act with compassion, give love and support, raise your partner up, and continuously reassure them. They may act like they are not listening to your reassurance, but they are listening to every single word you say. As they are lifted out of their jealousy, you are both moved forward, and your hidden jealousy is healed. The one thing worse than having a jealous partner is for you to be jealous. If you help them through their pain by reaching out and joining them, you can save a lot of pain for both of you.

HEALING CHOICE

I commit to heal my jealousy, whether it shows up in my partner or me.

HEALING EXERCISE

Forgive yourself and your partner. Let go of your needs, and join your partner again and again. See and feel yourself connecting with him or her heart-to-heart, mind-to-mind, light-to-light. Now, complete the following statements to heal the root of your jealousy:

If I were to know where the pain of my jealousy began, it was probably when I was
   at the age of _____

If I were to know who was involved, it was probably_____

_____

If I were to know what it was that occurred, it was probably something like_____

_____

In this situation ask your higher mind to carry everyone back to their center, the
place of peace, lovableness, and grace. If, for some reason, you do not feel peace,
then ask to be carried back to a deeper center. Do this until everyone in the scene
is centered and at peace. Now, from the light or spirit within you, connect with lines
of light to join everyone present in the situation. Now imagine what need they
would have to be feeling to be acting in that way. Typically, the pain that you picked
up is the same pain that they were feeling, which caused them to act this way. What
is the gift that would heal the pain? Give them that gift heart-to-heart, so you will
both be free from this pain. Assess how you feel after the experience. You may feel
completely, somewhat, or only a little better, depending on how many incidents
there are yet to heal within. Repeat this exercise as necessary. Now ask yourself the
following intuitive question: "If I were to know, how many jealous shadow figures do
I have inside?" Melt all those figures into one big jealous shadow figure and ask
your higher mind to heal and transform this figure. Now let it melt back into you.

86.

HEARTBREAK AND THE ANCESTRAL PATTERN

Many of our heartbreak patterns were passed down from generation to generation. Sometimes, these painful patterns can
have the same or different outward symptoms in each generation, or sometimes the symptoms are experienced internally
and manifested as lack of confidence or a high level of self-

attack. I have seen the patterns of children who were born to parents out of wedlock pass on from generation to generation. I have seen rape occur in generation after generation because the feelings and painful patterns were passed down through the generations. I have seen the predilection for a certain disease, such as cancer, pass down intergenerationally, and I have seen heartbreak patterns continue on generation after generation.

Twenty years ago, I worked with an eighty-year-old woman who came to see me at my office as a birthday present from her son. She wanted to work on her allergies, because she was allergic to almost everything. As we began working, we found that part of the problem stemmed from a summer romance heartbreak that she had suffered at twenty years old and still carried within her. We traced the next part of the problem back to an ancestor during the time of the civil war, where the problem that occurred and affected each succeeding generation had also been heartbreak. His heartbreak had ultimately led to his death on the battlefield. His death and the resulting heartbreak for the family was passed down intergenerationally, mostly as loss and heartbreak, but shifting to physical symptoms with this woman's mother. We went back to the original ancestor and energetically healed the traumatic heartbreak, which transformed the story into him having a long and happy life, thereby passing down the positive, healing effect to each generation. When this ancestral pattern was changed within and the healing energy reached her, she could feel a palpable difference. I later heard from her son that all but one of her allergies had cleared up, leaving only her allergy to cats.

It says in the Bible that the sins of the fathers will be visited down to the third and fourth generation. This is a metaphor that means problems will be passed on intergenerationally. If the pain can be passed down, the healing also can be passed back, or so I have found. Therefore, it also means that we can energetically *heal* the misunderstanding of previous generations.

It may sound like an odd concept, but it is absolutely possible to heal patterns back across our family lines. Consider, for a moment, a spiritual healer. He or she uses the power of spirit or the mind to effect healing in individuals. There is a profound spiritual energy that is our life force. Some people call it our soul, others call it our spirit. What we do know is that it can be used to heal.

All of us have the ability to heal when we learn how to use it, and by getting in touch with our spiritual centers—the core of our being, or our spirit—we can harness that healing love and energy and spread it. This is very much the same idea as giving "gifts." We all have within us a power to change ourselves and the world around us. Looked at slightly differently, it is clear that our minds are powerful instruments. Our perception of our lives is what makes them what they are to us, and we can choose to perceive them any way we want. By changing our perception, we can change other people's perceptions because our minds are connected and we share truth so as we feel differently, we act differently, we experience differently, and we have effectively rewritten the script so that the scripts or "realities" of others are rewritten too. When we give the gifts of love or forgiveness, for example, we release a burden in someone else that might have been the root of a painful pattern. They in turn are able to give gifts back along their family lines and to perceive things in a very different way. This healing pattern can go back up the family lines to heal and to encourage the kind of forgiveness and understanding that makes love and healing possible.

For example, when we understand what a parent felt, and why they behaved the way they did, we are able to forgive them and to feel their love. When we get rid of a mistaken belief, our whole perception of the event and our lives changes. Our relationships change, and anyone involved in our lives feels the benefit of that change. This perception is, in fact, rewriting history, and as we change the script back along family lines, everyone is freed from the negative patterns that have caused the heartbreak and pain. Again, this may sound fantastic, but that is only because it is. I have seen it happen hundreds of times with grandparents, parents, children, and grandchildren, who were changed as the story through the generations was changed.

Some of the biggest breakthroughs I have seen came through healing an ancestral pattern. Many of our childhood heartbreaks were hand-me-downs from our parents' relationships with their parents, which were hand-me-downs from their parents, and so on. I have seen ancestral patterns get better with each generation through healing and forgiveness, and I have seen ancestral problems get worse, even compound, with each generation when there is no understanding. With healing, there is the chance to free ourselves and our ancestors. We are the culmination of our families' love and wisdom and also their painful, unlearned lessons. As we heal and free ourselves, we not only heal and free our children, but we also heal and free our ancestors from their ancient karma. It is a two-way process.

HEARTBREAK PRINCIPLE

Heartbreaks and other problems leading to heartbreak can be passed down from generation to generation.

HEALING PRINCIPLE

Ancestral patterns are no more difficult to heal than any other pattern. We can free ourselves and our ancestors by healing these patterns.

HEALING SUGGESTION

Examine what has been passed down to you from your mother's and father's sides of the family. Enjoy the gifts and commit to healing the rest.

HEALING CHOICE

I commit to healing all the negative effects passed down through my family, thereby freeing me and my ancestors.

HEALING EXERCISE

Once you have identified a problem that you want to heal, especially heartbreak, respond intuitively to complete the following statements:

If I were to know...

which side of the family it was passed down through, it was probably _____

_____

how many generations back it began, it was probably _____

_____

if it began with a man, a woman, or both, it was probably _____

_____

what it was that occurred that set up this problem, it was probably _____

_____

what effect this had on their life, it was _____

_____

what got passed on to their children and how it turned out in their life, it was probably _____

_____

what got passed on to their children and how that turned out, it was probably

_____

(Continue this line of questions down through your grandparents, parents, yourself, and your children, if you have any.)

Now, imagine yourself as the point at which all of your family's gifts culminates. Feel your gratitude to them. Ask yourself, "If I were to know, what gift did I bring into this life to free them from this problem?" Open up this gift inside you. Imagine that it has a color. What color is it? Now see and feel this gift and color filling you, and being passed down to your children and grandchildren. Then see the gift and color being passed up into your parents, then grandparents, and all the way up until it goes back to the original ancestor with the original problem, healing and filling everyone with color and love.

87.

HEARTBREAK AND PAST LIVES

Many people have spontaneous recall of past or simultaneous lifetimes, whether or not they believe in past lives. These stories can come up vividly in dreams, sometimes as a certain knowing, or more vividly in flashbacks. I know that the mind can fabricate these stories, just like it does in dreams, as a metaphor of our soul's journey through time. In a session, I will use whatever model works best for my client. With a fundamentalist I'll pray and it will work. With a believer in past lives, I'll use a past-life model. Both have served their purpose. I know that the metaphors or belief systems by which a person lives will be the way they experience the world. What is more important than beliefs is a strong healing bond between us and a willingness to change, so that what is painful can fall away. This helps my clients to move forward, to learn and to grow in a healing session.

I was quite unprepared for my first experience of the phenomena of past lives. I was finishing up the last of my classes at the United States International University in San Diego before beginning work on my dissertation. I certainly had heard of past lives—after all I lived in California—but I had not realized that they could show up in a therapy session. It left my professional view of the world shattered but, since then, I have had so many thousands of professional experiences involving past lives that I am certain of their authenticity as a personal experience that affects their world. Whether we use other lifetimes as a powerful metaphor or as the way things are, I know that it has a major healing effect on core patterns.

If we believe in other lifetimes, then we also believe in karma, which are patterns that are passed down by our souls, lifetime after lifetime, until they are healed. Karma is the belief that we are all at the mercy of a kind of retributive justice. Our present lives are determined by past deeds in previous lives or incarnations.

If we do not believe in other lifetimes, then we might believe that the challenges we face in this lifetime are set up by our souls so that we learn our lessons and train ourselves in our life's mission. We might then view the phenomena of past lives as parts of our unconscious coming to the surface. Just like dreams are produced, the unconscious produces stories or metaphors to describe the soul's mythic journey. No matter what we believe, the past-life pattern will show up in our family, relationships, or victim patterns.

In early 1975, I took a hypnosis class as part of my doctoral program. I loved the insights I received from working with this model of the mind but, being basically a lazy guy, I did not want to go through the ritual of hypnosis constantly, especially when not everyone was amenable to it. Soon, I had developed what I call my "intuitive method," which is accessible and agreeable to everyone, since we use our intuition all day long. Many questions begin with "If you were to know…" because this opens up our intuition. When we use our intuition we bypass our "surface" minds, which are heavily defended by our egos. This allows us to go straight to the issue while we are fully conscious. There have been only two people over all the years with whom this method did not work, but that was mainly because they really didn't want it to work.

I began using the intuitive method to take people back to traumas where they made certain decisions about themselves and their lives, and about relationships, men, women, success, sex, and money. I helped people to understand the power of their decisions and how they set up both beliefs and negative patterns in our minds. When people make new choices or change the image in their mind they are able to heal the trauma. I had been using intuitive regression to heal traumas for many, many years, taking people as far back as the womb to heal nasty mistaken patterns. When a person reaches the root trauma and heals it, the whole pattern dissolves. Using this technique I soon found myself taking someone back to a root trauma that existed beyond the womb.

Over the last twenty-five years, thousands of these past lives or stories have come up, and I have discovered that these are just some of the patterns that can lead to the most dramatic breakthroughs when they are healed. Past lives are a common root characteristic of heartbreak and, even more sinisterly, one of the core elements in the dynamic of serious illness. Healing back along the lines to our past lives or the stories we hold about them, can make profound changes that affect our health, happiness, and ability to love and accept love in the present.

HEARTBREAK PRINCIPLE

In heartbreaks, other lifetime stories can sometimes figure predominantly as a main issue.

HEALING PRINCIPLE

Other lifetime metaphors can be cleared as easily as any other issue.

HEALING SUGGESTION

Be curious about this metaphor. It describes one of the deep patterns of the mind that sets up other patterns. It is an ego pattern. Even if you don't believe in "other lifetimes," you will nonetheless be fascinated by the stories that come up, whether you consider them to be dreams, something out of the unconscious, or real descriptions of other lifetimes. These ego patterns, or whatever you would like to call them, set up some of the primary patterns of your life.

HEALING CHOICE

I commit to healing all the patterns of other lifetime metaphors.

HEALING EXERCISE

This is one healing method used in the other lifetime model. Whether or not you consider this is a metaphor, I invite you to explore this area. Choose a symptom in your lifetime that you would like to work with, such as heartbreak, health, money, success, or whatever springs to mind. Use your intuition to complete the following statements:

If I were to know how many core lifetimes I would have to clear to resolve this
    problem about_____ it would probably be
    _____ (If you think that there is more
    than one lifetime, just repeat the exercise with each core lifetime.)
If I were to know in which country I was living in this core lifetime, it's the country
    that's now called_____
If I were to know if I was a man or a woman, I was probably a _____
    _____

If I were to know how long ago it was, it was probably _____

_____

If I were to know what occurred in that life that's affecting me now, it's probably

_____

If I were to know the lesson I had come to learn in that lifetime, it was probably

_____

(If the answer to this question about your lesson seems to be a dark lesson, it means that it's what you learned, not what you came to learn. Ask the question again if this has occurred.)

If I were to know what percentage of that lesson I learned, it was probably _____

_____

If I were to know what gift I had come to give, it was probably _____

_____

Now that you have the story and can see the pattern, imagine yourself going back to when you were a very little child in that life. Ask your higher mind to take you back to your center, that place of peace and grace. In major traumas, you may need to ask your higher mind to carry you back to even deeper centers to achieve peace. Once you are peaceful and returned to a place before the conflict, open your heart and mind, and give the gift that you were destined to give. What gift could define your purpose for living that life? If you are not sure what the gift might have been, consider what spiritual gift you could have given in that lifetime that would have changed its course. Give the gift to yourself and to everyone and everything around you. How does that life turn out now? If it's not completely better, there is probably another gift you were also meant or destined to give. Repeat this part of the exercise until there is a strong positive feeling. Bring the healed energy back into your life, filling you up in the present.

88.

HEARTBREAK AND THE SHAMANIC TEST

Long ago, Shamans would give their apprentices tests and, if they passed, they would be initiated into a higher level of consciousness. Shamans were people who had mastered the powers of the mind. In some cultures they are also known as medicine men or witch doctors.

A Shamanic test is the root of heartbreak for some people, but it is very difficult to pinpoint, and may seem obscure to some readers. If this section resonates with you, it is possible that it may apply to your particular situation.

The Shamanic test is a gamble in which we have set a test for ourselves in order to win back a part of our minds that has been lost. For most of us, when this occurs, this test is undertaken without conscious awareness, and we attempt to win back this part in order to move forward to a whole new level of consciousness and power. In a Shamanic test we lay everything on the line in order to succeed, and this attempt is entirely governed by our desire to leap to a new level of awareness and power.

We subconsciously believe that if we pass this test we will reach higher states of consciousness. We gain new levels of confidence and even powerful new abilities by succeeding, but when we fail we feel as though our heart has been ripped out or our world has collapsed upon us.

As children we may have set up these tests for ourselves and failed. We then covered over our failure and emotionally limped or crawled away from the scene. But it doesn't end there. We compensate in order to make up for our great feelings of failure and pain. But within us the test continues until we succeed. In actual fact, we relive the test over and over again in our lives in a painful cycle of failure and lost hope. This process is so painful that we set some type of defense over it, to avoid being conscious of such pain. This creates deadness and sterility in this area of our lives. Yet, we carry on trying to pass the test in order to heal ourselves through that process.

To give an example of a Shamanic test, consider the case of a small boy who is witnessing his parents violently arguing. While this scene is common in many households at some time, the difference is that this particular child has set a test for himself. Against all odds, he is "testing" himself in order to heal the breach with his parents. If he succeeds in bridging the gap, his level of confidence, wisdom, intelligence, awareness, courage, communication skills, healing, and capacity to love grow. There are even psychic or artistic gifts that can develop as a result. If he fails he can carry this experience as a major heartbreak or crushing experience within himself for the remainder of his life, until they can be healed. He will subconsciously try to pass the same test throughout his life, setting up similar situations in which to do so. The success of a Shamanic test leads to our greatness and a leap to a visionary stage of evolution which we are all seeking.

I have worked with many thousands of heartbreaks and I find the dynamic of a Shamanic test cropping up from time to time—usually with people who have a strong sense of mission in their lives. In many cases, when many layers of heartbreak and fractures have been healed, and there is no obvious cause for the continuing pain or inability to move forward, I find a Shamanic test at the root. I realized that if we can understand that this experience was a test that we set *ourselves*, we can then go back and pass it by looking at it differently or by bringing in grace.

At the unconscious level, everything becomes metaphoric. Metaphors then become the best vehicle we have to work on our heartbreaks. Appreciating the power of metaphoric exercises saves us months or even years of conventional therapy and moves us forward in our healing—sometimes in huge jumps. This is ground-breaking work and those of us brave enough to tackle unfamiliar concepts will benefit ourselves and those around us, as I have experienced countless times over the years.

HEARTBREAK PRINCIPLE

Some of our worst heartbreaks may have been Shamanic tests that we set up for ourselves to jump to a new level of power and confidence.

HEALING PRINCIPLE

We can go back now, complete, and finally pass the Shamanic test. The heartbreak is the test still going on within us until we pass it.

HEALING SUGGESTION

Examine your life for tragic heartbreaks and resolve to succeed now in the test with your healing.

HEALING CHOICE

I commit to successfully completing any Shamanic test I set up for myself.

HEALING EXERCISE

Ask your higher mind to be with you and go back to the time of the heartbreak. Ask for Heaven's help so that this test might be passed easily and with grace. As you return to the test with the help of this love and grace, how does the test turn out now? How are they directing its completion? What gift do you succeed in winning? How do you feel with the added part of your mind and heart that you recovered? Feel this renewed energy and gift moving through your life from the start of your Shamanic test to now. The Shamanic test can be a life or death experience, so it is always a good idea to call in your friends in high places, so it can be accomplished easily and lightly.

89.
HEARTBREAK AND IDOLS

We cannot be heartbroken unless we are looking for happiness outside ourselves. The purpose of every relationship is love, healing, and happiness, but when we begin to think of a relationship as the *source* of our happiness, we believe that we will be *given* something, rather than *giving* something ourselves. Giving manifests itself as joy, while expecting to receive sets the stage for pain. Buddha stated that only happiness that came from within could be sustained; the rest is ephemeral.

When we look for happiness in a person, situation, or thing, instead of in spiritual peace, we create an idol. Idols are the things outside us that we think will bring us happiness. Idols begin with needs that become indulgence and turn into an addiction that eventually becomes an idol. They can seem positive, in the form of relationships, sex, money, or power, or they can be negative idols, such as sickness, suffering, and death. Idols contain a tempting dark glamour. They may glitter but they are not gold.

When we focus on things outside ourselves as a source of happiness, we experience disappointment and frustration. For many of us relationships have become idols. They then become the greatest source of our disappointment, and they give us an excuse to quit both relationships and living wholeheartedly. Having been disappointed by one idol, we will seek another; we seek idol after idol, and incur disappointment after disappointment, until we finally give up and want to die. It is here that the ego has won and we have lost love. The ego, which fights for us to remain separate from each other, has won against love, which invites us to join each other. The ego is intent on keeping us from the experience of joining with others so that it can survive as an individual entity and govern us. There is a crucial change that occurs in our life when we seek to give, rather than get; to understand, rather than be understood; and to recognize, rather than be recognized. When we reach out to others in need rather than finding ways to get our own needs met.

All too often our youth, beauty, sexuality, creativity, and passion for life do not survive the disappointments that occur when we make idols of relationships and sex. Idols lead to shattered dreams which are the hardest aspects of heartbreak to let go of, leaving us helplessly dependent, hopelessly independent, or indentured in sacrifice.

An idol is seeking God in some form. This is the place where we are seeking the satisfaction and happiness that only God can give. We know that there is something missing in our daily lives, and we search for it in all the wrong places. Unless we let go of our disappointments, the future becomes as dismal as the past. The process of giving and receiving helps us to let go of idols and illusions that stand between ourselves and receiving all that we want. True peace and happiness can only exist within us, within our own giving and receiving in a relationship, or within a spiritual relationship with our God. We will never find them in the false idols we create for ourselves.

Every time we let go, we take the source of our happiness back within ourselves. This returns us to a place of giving and receiving, rather than a place where we just attempt to get. We move one step closer to our God and to spiritual peace. Letting go of heartbreaks means letting go of our lost dreams and idols. Heartbreak is a place of illusion where we mistakenly act in a way that does not respond to the truth of the situation. We respond to things as we want them to be, not as they are. If we do not fully let go of the pain, we still have our idols. Holding on to the pain is just a way of holding on to an idol. We may defend ourselves from future pain by being independent, which is another indication that we haven't let go of our idols or their incumbent pain.

The dissociation that makes us independent also keeps us from recognizing our idols. We think that our plans for happiness or our plans for preventing hurt will work. Sometimes they may appear to succeed in keeping us from hurt, because we are dissociated enough that we don't notice we are actually locked into and compensating for old pain. Defenses may or may not be successful in keeping us from the pain, but they are always successful in keeping us from love. Unless we heal these idols and let them go, we think the darkness of the past will continue to darken our future. As we heal and let go of the past, this darkness transforms into understanding, wisdom, worthiness, confidence, humor, openness, and taking ourselves lightly. These are the qualities that characterize true happiness and spiritual peace.

HEARTBREAK PRINCIPLE

Our heartbreak pain shows us the presence of an idol. An idol is something outside us that we use in order to try to get something, such as happiness.

HEALING PRINCIPLE

Our love and happiness comes from the love and happiness we give. Giving love and happiness allows us to feel love and happiness, and opens the door to receiving.

HEALING SUGGESTION

Every situation can be healed and made successful by giving. Every situation where you are trying to take, or get, begs for rejection and disappointment. Look at the situation for what you can give. Ask for the guidance and grace to give what is necessary to change the situation.

HEALING CHOICE

I choose to use every heartbreak situation as a means of letting go of idols, and moving forward toward my God and spiritual peace.

HEALING EXERCISE

Examine two heartbreaks in your childhood, your youth, and in adulthood. What idols did you have?

Childhood heartbreaks　　　　　**Idols**

1. _____　　_____

　　　　　　　　　　　　　　　　_____

　　　　　　　　　　　　　　　　_____

2. _____　　_____

　　　　　　　　　　　　　　　　_____

　　　　　　　　　　　　　　　　_____

Youth heartbreaks　　　　　　　**Idols**

1. _____　　_____

　　　　　　　　　　　　　　　　_____

　　　　　　　　　　　　　　　　_____

2. _____   _____
                            _____
                            _____

Adult heartbreaks   Idols

1. _____   _____
                            _____
                            _____

2. _____   _____
                            _____
                            _____

Remember, idols may be body fitness, money, or fashion, or they may be idols of fear, power, or heartbreak. They always represent an attempt to find a source of happiness outside ourselves. For instance, the idol of suffering could be used because we want people to feel sorry for us and pay attention to us, to get revenge, to try and control or defeat someone, including ourselves, because we think this will keep us safe and make us happy.

90.
THE HEARTBREAK IDOL

Heartbreaks typically stem from a relationship idol, where we worship relationships in an attempt to find happiness or to feel valued. But a heartbreak idol is something more. In this situation we worship pain, and the fine line between pleasure and pain has dissolved. It might occur because we are trying to pay off guilt with pain, or we may have made a heartbreak into a "peak" experience. We remember peak experiences as moments when we came alive; the vividness of our pain made life into poetry. We may love the thrill of riding the wave of relationship until it crashes us on to the beach—and the relationship and heartbreak with old "what's-his-name" becomes just the background for this exalted agony or dramatic loss. But the glamour of this scenario also finally pales, and we go off again seeking the perfect relationship for our next climactic shattering. Whatever our reason for seeking thrill and vivid feeling, it ultimately fails because, in between the pain, we become increasingly fragmented and dead.

Sometimes we set up a heartbreak idol to punish ourselves for a relationship that we lost long ago, and to which we have now built a shrine. Of course, we fail to see that we would never have chosen this loss if the relationship had been able to meet all of our needs. It is important to examine our strategies to find what is *really* behind our heartbreak idol and how it serves us. All idols are supported by unconscious pockets of agony from the worst times in our lives, or they are carried into this life by ancestral patterns. We might have one idol holding up another, such as the heartbreak idol holding up an independent idol, but if we were to unveil any idol we have, we would find the face of death. Any idol takes us in a death direction, away from an expanded, truthful existence.

HEARTBREAK PRINCIPLE

The heartbreak idol is a celebration of disappointment and self-destruction. It is a false god we worship, thinking that it will somehow make us happy.

HEALING PRINCIPLE

As we become aware of all the attempted secondary gains and hidden agendas surrounding our heartbreak idol, we realize that they never worked. This is the beginning of choosing what would really make us happy.

HEALING SUGGESTION

Examine your life for where you have made something into an idol because you thought it would bring you happiness. Be willing to let it go and to allow into your life what would bring true happiness.

HEALING CHOICE

I commit to finding and letting go of any heartbreak idol I have.

―――――――――――――――――――――――

HEALING EXERCISE

Use the strategy method to find your mistaken motivation for having this happen, by completing the following statements:

Did it work?   Did it make me happy?

If I were to know what I am trying to gain by my heartbreak idol, (which means I have a recurring heartbreak story) it's probably _____

_____

If I were to know what fear I am trying to protect, it's probably _____

_____

If I were to know what guilt I am trying to pay off, it's probably _____

_____

If I were to know what I was trying to be right about, it was probably_____

_____

If I were to know who I was trying to defeat, it was probably_____

_____

If I were to know what this gave me an excuse for, it was probably   _____

_____

If I were to know what I was proving by telling this story, it was probably_____

_____

Why?   _____

If I were to know who I was getting revenge on, it was probably _____

_____

If I were to know how this stops me from my purpose, it's probably _____

_____

If I were to know what excuse this idol gave me, it was probably _____

_____

If I were to know what or who I was trying to hold on to by having this idol, it was

probably _____

If I were to know what this heartbreak idol allowed me to do, it was probably

_____

If I were to know what this heartbreak idol allowed me to avoid doing, it was

probably _____

If I were to know if this heartbreak idol supports any other idols, they are probably

_____

Imagine yourself entering the temple of your heart. Look on the altar. How many heartbreak idols and others supported by them are there? If you are willing, take the idols off your altar, and get rid of them. Put the lilies of forgiveness on your altar for everyone involved in the hells that you have used to keep the idols going. As you do this, embrace all the selves that are now free from your hells. Then, see a light shining from above on to your altar. The gifts that the idols hid are now there. Embrace your gifts and use them for your own and others' joy.

THE TOOLS FOR HEALING HEARTBREAK

91.
COMMUNICATION

Communication is one of the greatest joys of a relationship. It is also a fundamental characteristic of any successful relationship. Communication builds the bridges that turn differences into the basis of understanding, forgiveness, and joining. It adds spice and interest to our relationships, which enhances their life and length. Clarification can clear about eighty-five percent of all our problems; the remaining fifteen percent are chronic or past issues that have been transferred on to the present situation, and call for deeper transformational communication.

I once knew a couple in which the wife was beginning to stray. She began to flirt with other men, and then her husband caught her seriously kissing one of his closest friends. The husband realized that his marriage was slipping. They were just about to move and had planned to take a week to drive across the country. Ten minutes into their journey, the husband opened up communication with his wife about what had been going on for both of them. He said that they talked nonstop across the country, and when they got to the East Coast, they were both recommitted.

There are certain successful principles of communication that will help us to avoid the biggest mistakes that we can make in our relationships. These mistakes usually center on making the other person responsible for what we are feeling, blaming them for our emotions, and trying to force them to meet our needs. These painful emotions were usually brought into the relationship as baggage and date back to before we met our partner. They are often transference or replays from our childhood. When they occur, we blame, transfer, and project our "baggage" onto our partner in an attempt to heal our old pain. Even if they succumb to our demands, the relationship can only become dull, and it will not resolve our old pain.

But there are ways to communicate that will resolve our problems in the present *and* heal the old pain, and it is important for us to learn these ways. Communication builds a bridge to others. Unfinished communication, because of a grievance, or a "thank you" not shared, is like a loose end that needs to be tied up or capped. It will continue to drain energy until we do so.

HEARTBREAK PRINCIPLE

Any heartbreak situation is preceded by a breakdown or lack of communication.

HEALING PRINCIPLE

Communication builds bridges to our partners. It clarifies the situation and it is the beginning of forgiveness.

HEALING SUGGESTION

Be willing to learn all you can about communication and how it builds a bridge to your partner.

HEALING CHOICE

I commit to becoming an expert in truly communicating with others.

HEALING EXERCISE

Choose three heartbreak situations in your life. Now, imagine that you are an expert on communication. With each situation, reflect on what you would have done differently. How would you have shared? What would you have said? You will know when you have succeeded, because you both see and feel everyone in the situation is happy with the results.

92.

MEN AND COMMUNICATION

When I started to write this chapter, I realized it could be very short given the subject. In my experience, men are not very good at communicating about relationships, because relationships involve feelings not just the passing along of information. For the most part, men are not very good at sharing their feelings, or dealing with their sensitivity. They'll fight off space invaders single-handedly, but they will quake at the thought of having to deal with and share their own feelings. This is largely due to the fact that boys are brought up to be "brave" and to keep a stiff upper lip. Emotional outbursts have been frowned upon, and many boys grow up never knowing how to verbalize their emotions. Men also expect communication to be rational. It is a male trait to address a problem as something that needs to be "solved," rather than as a vehicle for communication, expressing, and joining. Practical solutions and game plans simply don't address the fundamental basis of relationships—feelings. Women want communication to be heartfelt and full of feelings and as a result they are more aware of their feelings and more forthright in their communication. Nothing can drive a woman ballistic faster than rational communication.

Women are naturally better communicators and don't usually need to hide their feelings under humor—with bluffing or talking about the big game, the last game, any game at all! Women can naturally direct and educate men in the area of relationships, communications, and feelings. Women also need to educate men in sex, in spite of the fact that every man believes he's God's gift to women. Frankly, we men need to believe that!

Men just need to be motivated to learn about relationships, communication, and feelings, and we don't need to be rocket scientists to figure out how to motivate a man.

Most men hate hearing the words, "We need to talk," and most men usually cringe at the idea of communication, because they know that somehow they are going to end up being the bad guy. This is very bad news for the male psyche— we've all been trained to believe we are heroes. If this self-image is tarnished, it can break a man's spirit. If he continually finds that he's the bad guy, he'll look elsewhere for a place where he can be the hero—maybe at work, maybe in someone else's arms. If women are willing to educate their men and to let them know when they've done it right, offering the appropriate rewards along the way, they'll have willing and eager learners on their hands and the communication gates will fly open.

Women often become the leaders when it comes to communication. When a woman communicates with integrity, she will create a rapport that is vital to a successful relationship. It will be one of the tools that each partner will learn as they unfold together. However, if women use communication as a form of indulgence to get their needs met, to make their partners wrong or responsible for their feelings, then there is not much hope for a successful relationship. Men will become willing learners in communicating, if they are not constantly made out to be the bad guy. If communication is always about how men did wrong or weren't good enough, they will naturally become shy, reticent, disassociated, workaholic, independent, and, finally, uncaring. When women are willing to teach and lead the way, the relationship will progress. When a man is willing to be "educated," the relationship will progress. Of course, every relationship may be different, but this is the general trend.

Men are willing to learn to communicate if they are appreciated and motivated through sex because that's how most men experience love, just as most women experience it through romance. Men need to know that they have an equal place in the relationship, or they begin to believe that they are just there to be used for the emotional needs of their partners or as an emotional punching bag. If men try to share their deepest feelings and they are attacked for it, their partners will have lost a major chance to make things better. It might be because she's just not listening, or maybe she doesn't believe he'd ever share an important feeling, or it might be that, as with so many times, the urge to fight is just too great. If in response to what a man is sharing, the woman says, "You think that's bad, what I'm feeling is…" it will be strike one as the tone of the communication changes abruptly to indulgence, and the man's eyes go from poignancy to glaze in moments. A great opportunity has just been lost. Communication is about respectful sharing, and it forms the basis of every happy relationship.

HEARTBREAK PRINCIPLE

If a woman is more indulgent, angry, or withdrawn in a relationship than she is loving, she loses her opportunity to lead, direct, and educate for her own benefit—and that of her partner and the relationship. If a man is more interested in affairs or fantasy, and in defending and protecting himself, he loses the opportunity to move his relationship forward.

HEALING PRINCIPLE

When women value themselves and their men, they will give up attack, indulgence, and sacrifice for communication. When men value the feminine and learn from their partners more than they try to protect themselves, they will be open to communication and to moving the relationship forward.

HEALING SUGGESTION

As a man, you are called to value the feminine and to protect, heal, and save it. As you learn, reach out to, and receive guidance from your partner, rather than hiding your fears and protecting yourself, you bring about happy and healed relationships. As a woman, you are called to give up indulgence in order to lead, guide, heal, nurture, and motivate the man about the power and value of relationships, communication, the feminine, and mutual sexuality. The extent to which the masculine is dissociated, is the extent to which the feminine will be indulgent. You are totally responsible and you can bring your relationship back to balance.

HEALING CHOICE

I commit to move the relationship forward by valuing and loving my partner.

HEALING EXERCISE

Assess your partner for emotional indulgence, lack of sexual integrity, dissociation, or any form of protecting their fear. This will represent a projection of your own hidden and judged side. Wherever you are on opposite sides, each of you is in a conflict within yourselves. Choose to forgive your partner for this and, therefore, yourself. Imagine that your higher mind is taking the qualities displayed by both you and your partner and melting them down to their pure energy and then joining them together. This gives each of you the joined energy to use for healing. Do this exercise about once a week to improve the progress of your relationship. The first step is most important—valuing your partner and realizing how they will always reflect your conflicted part so that you can integrate it for healing. When you value them, rather than judge or try to control and change them, you can enlist their support in making the relationship everything it can be. Integrate the side they are acting out so you can move forward with the best of both sides.

93.

THE RESPONSIBILITY OF MEN AND WOMEN

We are each totally responsible for our relationships. As women, we project our masculine sides onto our partners. As men, we project our feminine sides onto our partners. We also project anything else we have repressed within ourselves. Our partners show us how and what we are, even though we may have hidden parts of ourselves away. We each have a function to fulfill in our relationships, and it is crucial to the success of the relationship and its purpose.

For a man to listen to his partner, he must first value the feminine. As he does so, he will recognize the importance of what she is saying, and he will boost her confidence and self-esteem. By listening to her and valuing what she says, both partners move forward. Sometimes men act out the "wounded" feminine, dependent side in the relationship, and women act out the exaggerated masculine. In this case, it will be her turn to listen, to reach out, and to value the feminine in her partner.

Men who are motivated to learn and grow, and who have developed a feminine side for rapport, compassion, and communication, are highly valued as partners. Men who truly love women and value the feminine are in high demand, because it has, in the past, been a rare event to find a man who can value and communicate within a relationship. Today, feelings and healing, rather than the suppression of needs, are beginning to be acceptable and even encouraged. Feminine attributes, such as the ability to verbalize emotion and to communicate, are increasingly treasured in our masculine, independent society. This is slowly bringing about a balance between the masculine and feminine, which is necessary for partnership.

Women who are willing to take their position as the natural authority, educators, and communicators in relationships can have their heart's desire of love, romance, and beautiful relationships, if they are willing to be the sculptor of those relationships and the leader in this regard. Both men and women with awareness are needed now to help society move forward, because society is based on family, and family is based on relationships. Consequently, the healthier our relationships, the healthier our families and society will be. As men and women, we have a function that both fulfills and sets us free as individuals, in relationships, and in our families. We are all called to do our part, because if we are not part of the solution, we are part of the problem.

As women educate their partners about feelings, respect, communication, relationships, and sex, and motivate them with rewards, they'll find willing learners. As men join and value their partners, rather than protecting their feelings, they'll be good partners. Relationships are never a fifty-fifty responsibility: each one of us has a 100 percent responsibility for our relationships. Women's leadership is needed in the relationship as much as men's willingness. If a woman is too dependent or frightened, or if she doesn't value her partner, she will not take her natural leadership position, and her partner can drift out of sexual integrity. On the other hand, if a man invests his energy into his partner instead of into affairs, fantasies, or idle wishes, he builds and raises his partner out of feelings of need, pain, and valuelessness. When a man is willing to learn, he will listen to his partner in as defenseless a position as possible. He will realize that the extent to which his partner attacks is the extent to which he is defended and dissociated. He will value and integrate his partner's communication in order to see what new truth and direction will emerge.

HEARTBREAK PRINCIPLE

If we don't assume our responsibility to heal our relationships and to contribute what we have to give, there will be blaming, fighting, and heartbreak.

HEALING PRINCIPLE

By learning from, respecting, and valuing our partners and their contribution, we can contribute our function to the function of the relationship.

HEALING SUGGESTION

In a relationship everything is equal, and you will always be in balance in an opposite way—for example, independent/dependent, positive/negative, rock/swamp, dissociated/emotionally indulgent, and sexually indulgent/withdrawing. Whatever your partner plays, you act out the opposite to keep the balance. You and your partner need to split the tasks and lessons between you, which accelerates your growth and learning. There are equal levels of integrity and neurotic behavior, maturity and fear, motivation for healing and indulgence, true giving, and sacrifice! You each have equal responsibility for how things are in the relationship, and you each have an equal ability to transform and move the relationship forward. As you realize that your partner is acting out your hidden side and that it serves a certain purpose for you to have them act in such a way, you are less likely to try to change them and you will be encouraged to change yourself instead. The tasks are split up to accelerate healing, because you have chosen to be in a relationship which cannot succeed without partnership. If you do not recognize this, there will be continued judgment and power struggles, and neither you nor your relationship will move forward. When you learn that as you judge you are only pointing your finger at the mirror, you will be motivated to change and heal yourself.

HEALING CHOICE

I commit to valuing the feminine and to bringing myself and my relationship into balance, and thus to partnership. I commit to fulfilling my function either as a man or a woman to help heal my relationship.

HEALING EXERCISE

Complete the following statements to bring the masculine and feminine parts of your relationship into balance. The extent to which they are in balance is the extent to which we are successful in our relationships.

If I were to know where my masculine side was thrown out of balance, it was
probably at the age of_____

If I were to know who was involved, it was probably_____

_____

If I were to know what occurred to throw my masculine side out of balance, it was
probably _____

_____

Go back to this place. Ask your higher mind to bring everyone back to their center. Join everyone present by taking the light within you and connecting it to the light within them. What gift do you have to give to everyone present, as a male or female, to balance and heal the masculine energy?

If I were to know where my feminine side was thrown out of balance, it was at the age of _____

If I were to know who was involved, it was probably_____

_____

If I were to know what occurred that threw my feminine side out of balance, it was probably_____

_____

Go back to this place and ask your higher mind to bring everyone back to their center. Join everyone present by taking the light within you and connecting it up to the light within them. What gift do you have to give to everyone present, as a male or female, to balance and heal the feminine energy?

Now, take a moment to relax. Go deep inside to where your masculine and feminine sides are both present. Look at how you represent them. If your feminine side is diminished, or in need, let your masculine side raise it up and provide whatever is necessary. If your masculine side is over-exaggerated, too busy, stressed, or out of balance, let your feminine side return, draw it back into balance, and save it in return.

94.
TRANSFORMATIONAL COMMUNICATION

Transformational communication is communicating in order to change ourselves and, therefore, the problem at hand. This form of communicating enlists or motivates others to support us, and it will carry us and our partners into a new level of partnership. When we learn the principles behind transformational communication, we can use them to communicate more successfully in every area of our lives, because it allows us to change without putting demands on others around us—which only leads to sacrifice, resistance, or power struggles.

Transformational communication is successful when we *ask* for our partner's support, and *take* responsibility for our own feelings by recognizing that they have been carried over from the past and are now disrupting our present peace. We can acknowledge that these feelings are from the past, commit to our healing, and ask for our partner's help in changing the situation for the better, by reassuring them that they are not to blame for our upset. This also gives our partner a chance to choose to support us. Typically, our partners are willing to help us when they don't have to shoulder the blame for a situation.

To communicate transformationally we first need to communicate with ourselves, because if we deny our feelings or our experiences we will not be able to change. For some of us, sharing our emotions in a true way may be the most difficult part of this kind of communicating, but we can motivate ourselves by remembering that a successful relationship is one in which there is successful communication. There are three gigantic traps that we can fall into: we may cover up our feelings because of fear, or we may use our sharing to meet our own needs, or to punish our partners for not meeting them. It's extremely tempting for us to unload our bad feelings on to our partner, but this simply spreads the negativity rather than engendering positive feelings. After getting in touch with our own feelings we need to take responsibility for them. Our feelings are ours alone, and we have probably had them long before we even met our partners. If we bear this in mind, we can keep our communication honest and in perspective.

When we enlist our partners' help in the communication, it is much easier to accomplish our healing, and if we share our intent with them before we begin communicating, it is much easier for them to choose to support us. It is a huge step in maturity to pull back our feelings rather than laying them on our partners, even if it seems like our upset is the result of something they did. When we have the willingness and determination to succeed, we can remain honest as we talk about our emotions and the feelings that we had at the time of the upset. As we are sharing what is upsetting us, it can help if we reassure our partners that they are not to blame for our feelings. As we explore our feelings as feelings already within us, it is helpful to share every nuance of the feelings and experiences, thereby releasing all the withheld energy. When we ask ourselves when we had experienced these feelings before, we may re-experience old emotions, but that's all a healthy sign. Let out the pain and don't be afraid to communicate it. As we talk about how we felt in that situation, it helps clear the old unfinished backlog of emotion within us.

Sharing our past emotions may remind us of other, even older, deeper experiences and feelings we have had in the past. Sometimes, these experiences come up very vividly; all we need do is share them, focusing on the feeling rather than the story. If we focus mainly on the story, the feelings are lost and the breakthrough will not be as powerful. Sometimes we may experience only strong feelings, rather than remember an actual event. This, too, is normal. Simply sharing these feelings will inspire our partners to support us, instead of running away because they think they did something wrong.

If we have previously abused communication by using it to blame or control, our partners may be quite shy and afraid that we are going to attack them again, so we may need to rebuild their trust. After we have shared our feelings, we may need to support our partners through some of their own feelings. This type of honest, open communication based on an unselfish wish to move the relationship forward for both parties leads to a sense of relief and release. The problem either disappears or, with a chronic problem, a whole layer disappears. If we are able to heal a layer of chronic problem or emotion, it is strongly advised that we put aside time to share about it every week or so. This way the feelings and emotions are healed layer by layer, and it will greatly relieve the situation and keep it from building.

HEARTBREAK PRINCIPLE

If we do not take responsibility for our feelings and experiences, and are unable to communicate in an honest and healing fashion, we become a victim and a soon-to-be victimizer using complaint, withdrawal, and attack.

HEALING PRINCIPLE

As we take responsibility and share in a way that explores the root feelings and experiences that led to this situation, and avoid blaming others or the situation, we can heal the painful emotions through our sharing.

HEALING SUGGESTION

In order to be an effective communicator, it is important to be defenseless and to avoid blaming others. This allows for openness and flexibility to receive feedback, while not giving up or compromising your position. Then, as you and your partner communicate with each other, you will find shared feelings and a satisfying solution.

HEALING CHOICE

I commit to learning the principles of transformational communication so that it can be a valuable tool in my relationships.

HEALING EXERCISE

Think of something that upset you recently. Imagine for a moment that no one was to blame, in spite of how it looked. Imagine for a moment that it actually came from feelings prior to this event. Now, respond to complete the following statements:

If I were to know how old I was when this feeling began, was _____

_____

If I were to know who was with me when it began, it was _____

_____

If I were to know what was happening when it began, it was probably_____

_____

If I were to know what other experiences in my life compounded these feelings, it

was probably _____

and _____

and _____

Now, with this information, share what you have discovered with the person that you originally thought caused you pain. Speak honestly about your feelings at the time of the upset, but also tell how your explorations led you to the root of the painful emotions and other experiences that compounded the original experience. Share in such a way that you also share all of the feelings you had in those events. If for some reason you cannot share these events and feelings with the person you originally thought was the cause, share the experience with someone close to you. Notice how you feel afterwards. Ask yourself the degree to which you now feel better and the degree to which things actually are better.

95.

STEPS FOR TRANSFORMATIONAL COMMUNICATION

Most problems in a relationship are cleared if both we and our partners clarify the reasons why we behave the way we do. This clears the air and allows us to join in understanding. This goal of sharing and clearing strengthens our belief that everything can be worked out, because if we know what we are both feeling and we are willing to share, we can build our relationships. Whatever cannot be cleared by expressing feelings and the reasons for behavior is likely to be a chronic problem, which requires transformational communication. In transformational communication, we focus on principles that work rather than engaging in disagreements, fights, and even brawls that sometimes occur in relationships. The following steps will set you on the right path:

1. If you are upset, take responsibility for your feelings. These are feelings you carried into the situation or relationship. They are yours. Changing your feelings, rather than attempting to change your partner, is the most effective way to transform the situation. Choose to make the situation an opportunity to heal yourself and your partner.

2. Ask for your partner's help. Let them know that the intent of this communication is to heal yourself through sharing. Assure them that they are not the target or the "bad guy." They are likely to be willing if they know they won't be attacked for your bad feelings.

3. Ask for spiritual help and guidance. It opens you to receive grace which makes everything easy.

4. Choose the outcome you would like to have as a result of

this communication. When you set a goal, you will then see problems that might arise as small setbacks on your path, rather than evidence that you have failed. If you don't set a goal, then any conflict that occurs could be your last.

5. Share your feelings without making your partner wrong. There are no bad guys; you can both win. Blame stops communication. If you think someone else is to blame, you won't be able to change in the way that is necessary to move forward. If you don't take responsibility, your partner will be very reluctant to communicate. It is often important to reassure your partner continually that they are not to blame. Share your feelings, stating what you are upset about as clearly and openly as possible.

6. Take back your feelings, making them your responsibility. This is the most crucial step in the communication, because it brings your feelings back to where you can deal with them.

7. When you own the feeling, talk about how it has featured in your life. Sometimes stories from the past will come up. Share them, but stay as close to the feeling as possible. This keeps you moving away from or suppressing the feeling that you have finally brought up. Keep it near the surface where it can be released more easily. As you share your feelings you will notice that they change. The more you share them, the better you will feel.

8. Consider whether your behavior reminds you of someone's from the past. Share this. If you get in touch with this and share it, you release its hold on you. When you share in this fashion, it inspires your partner to support you.

9. Choose to give up any defenses that you've used to protect yourself from this feeling. Be willing to share about it. As

you do, it will change. Accept that the feeling never worked to improve your life. It was just a mistake, and as you acknowledge it as such, it will change.

10. Ask for your partner's help in this new way of being and feeling. Thank your partner for their help, and for helping to free you of the pain. Your defense or strategy didn't work, but now you can be inspired in a new way of being.

11. This alone will often clear a whole conflict or a layer of a major conflict. With this type of healing, you have built a bridge of communication to and inspired confidence in your partner. Continuing to use transformational communication to heal negative patterns or chronic problems ensures a successful relationship.

HEARTBREAK PRINCIPLE

By blaming our partners or hiding our feelings, we build up resentments that weaken our relationships.

HEALING PRINCIPLE

By practicing transformational communication, we build our relationships and heal ourselves, training ourselves in principles and skills that we can use throughout our lives.

HEALING SUGGESTION

Communication is a vital key to your evolution and your relationship. Although it might take some courage, the rewards are the renewed love and bonding that will see your relationship through any problem.

HEALING CHOICE

I commit to become an expert in transformational communication so that I can value my partner more than my pain.

HEALING EXERCISE

Today, practise transformational communication with someone close to you. To become an expert, do this at least once a week.

96.

I'M SORRY

Never having to say "I'm sorry" is an important principle because it helps us to understand the parameters of our relationships. Never having to say sorry means that we commit never to do anything that would ever hurt our partners. This sets a standard to measure everything we do, and constantly encourages us to consider whether or not what we are doing would affect our partners. It's very much an embodiment of the lesson, "treat others as you would have them treat you." Before or within any situation, consider how it would affect you if your partner was to do the same thing. Or imagine that your partner is with you at the time: if he or she would feel happy about what you are doing, okay. If not, reconsider the action.

If your partner is very possessive and jealous, you must begin a series of communications with them in order to build a bridge. It is crucial to balance truth with your partner's pain threshold. Negative behavior is a call for love and support, and if your partner receives that support, they can take the step into a new level of partnership.

Learning to say "I'm sorry" is another crucial concept within a relationship. The two most important words that a husband can learn to say are, "I'm sorry." Women usually do this readily. Time and again I have seen the magical effect of these words, when they are spoken sincerely. They are not an expression of guilt but an acceptance of personal responsibility. If we use them to express guilt, we won't always make necessary changes. Guilt is an emotional "super glue" that encourages us to continue doing what we are doing—just as long as we feel bad about it. Guilt eases the burden of negative behavior because we feel we are "paying for it" by carrying around a guilty conscience. On the other hand, responsibility reflects our ability to *respond*. When we sincerely apologize, we are responding to our partner and to how they feel. It is a broad generalization to say that men find it more difficult to apologize, but it's very often true. Women often grow up feeling unloved while men grow up having sacrificed themselves to compensate for guilt. To compensate for their guilt, men attempt to do everything perfectly, which keeps them as far from the realm of apology as possible. For many men, apologizing is tantamount to declaring guilt, and it can bring up a host of guilty feelings and feelings of failure that they may have suppressed since childhood. As a result, men can be quite blind and obtuse in situations that call for apology, as a defense against these feelings. Women are often more sensitive and more likely to get their feelings hurt. When men can learn the importance of these words, they can create a sweet and binding rapport with their partners.

But apologizing without sincerity, without truly feeling it, is an attempt to manipulate the situation. I once met a man in a workshop who said that he knew the power of these words, and he demonstrated it by apologizing to his wife as profusely as he could. It was obvious from his tone that the words held no meaning for him. He had somehow stumbled on to these magical words, seen their effect, and abused them until they were meaningless. It was obvious that he wasn't intent on change and growth, but on manipulating the situation to his own benefit.

HEARTBREAK PRINCIPLE

The refusal or inability to apologize can lead to misunderstandings and power struggles.

HEALING PRINCIPLE

The willingness to apologize sincerely when we have made mistakes or when our partners are feeling badly, establishes rapport and shows them that we are concerned about their feelings.

HEALING SUGGESTION

A sincere apology is an important bridge in a relationship. To apologize gracefully, we must be willing to eschew any form of domination, competition, and guilt and to make joining our partners and their feelings more important. An apology shows our commitment to correct mistakes.

HEALING CHOICE

I commit to apologize when I have made a mistake.

HEALING EXERCISE

Examine your life for examples of your ability to apologize. Consider how your style of apologizing may have affected your partner. For what issues or situations do you owe your partner an apology? If you believe there are none, you are either denying their existence or you are ready to ascend! Which do you think it is?

97.

BONDING AND JOINING

All present pain is from past separation that is manifesting itself in the present. What we do with the problem depends on our attitudes. When we choose healing, there will be learning, joining and evolution, but if we choose to remain unaware, there can only be more painful separations, or fractures.

At one level, separation has its roots in the inadequate bonding we experienced with our parents. But if we blame them, we live our lives as victims or sacrificers or as overly independent partners. We won't succeed in love or work as well as we could. Almost all parents do the best they can for their children, and they often do so with their own poor bonding patterns that they carried with them from their childhoods. Broken bonding goes all the way back through our family trees and is repeated over and over with each successive generation unless the pattern is broken. When we blame our parents, we will encourage the same grievances from our own children. But we *can* change how things were and how they are now. We are not the victim of our past unless we choose to be—it is how we use the past that determines how we see it, and how we envision our future.

Every situation is an opportunity for healing, giving, and growth, or it can be used for indulgence, pain, and sacrifice as part of a mistaken strategy for happiness. We can choose whether we use the past and present as an excuse or as an opportunity to move forward. Without bonding, there is no hope for true love and true success, and we can choose whether or not we will bond. Sacrifice or using others does not count as bonding, because it is counterfeit. We can end the separation right now by bonding and joining, because only love and forgiveness will make a difference.

We do not have to agree with others to bond with them. Bonding is not dependent upon being right or wrong, but it involves moving toward our partners and allowing a just and mutually satisfying solution to evolve. We must, however, avoid making sacrifices, or another agreement out of a false sense of loyalty. It won't last. True bonding is about respecting ourselves and our feelings and not settling for anything less than a *complete* joining. Only then can there be a resolution. It is crucial that we respect our feelings and listen to them, but we must not let them rule us because they are not the whole answer. Joining is the only choice and it will provide the right answer.

Joining is the means by which we can experience pure love. Because the root of every problem is separation, there is no problem that joining cannot heal. Some problems have many layers, and an unconscious fracture can have hundreds of them. Yet, every time we join, a layer falls away.

Dr. Charles Spezzano (no relation), a psychologist from Denver, Colorado, has done some crucial research and written some important papers on bonding and the importance of the bonding process immediately after birth. He stresses that the first twenty-four hours after the birth is the most crucial time for a child to bond with his or her parents. If the bonding is accomplished, research shows that the relationship between child and parent is much easier as the child grows up. Dr. Spezzano says that the first fifteen of the twenty-four hours are the most crucial for the bonding process.

My own experience also shows that those who did not bond at birth typically have some sort of difficulty bonding with their own babies. But I also found that many damaged layers could be healed by imaginatively taking people back to their birth and having them bond imaginatively with their parents. I ask people to find the light within themselves (their spiritual core or the source of their being) and to use it to imagine the light bridging to join with their parents. I then bring them back to the point of their babies' births, and have them re-bond with them in the same way. They later reported significant shifts in their feelings about themselves and their relationships with their children.

Bonding that is lost or never established sets up further loss, misunderstanding, fear, illusion, abandonment, feelings of inadequacy, neediness, and dependency throughout our lives. In many cases, people with poor bonding start on the path of love relationships much later in life, attempting first to build a foundation of bonding, readiness, and understanding. Without early bonding, it is much easier to be heartbroken. Bonding encourages understanding of ourselves and others, and we feel more valued and self-accepting. When the bonding pattern is broken, we lose key pieces of that understanding which makes our later relationships more difficult.

Healing involves bringing what was lost or never established into our present relationships. Every time we bond with someone, we enhance our ability to bond, and some of the wires that were cut in the past can now be joined. Our present love can heal our past defeats. We can achieve wholeheartedness.

HEARTBREAK PRINCIPLE

Every place of lost or unestablished bonding sets up patterns of loss and heartbreak.

HEALING PRINCIPLE

We can establish or re-establish our bonding by joining and healing the separation.

HEALING SUGGESTION

Assess the level of bonding you have. Ask yourself the following question: "If I were to know, what was my experience of my birth and my time in the womb?" How much bonding do you think you lost? Now assess the amount of separation you carry—it will be evident by the level of need, fear, heartbreak, loneliness, illness, and chronic problems you experience. Be willing to bond now.

HEALING CHOICE

I commit to healing so that I can end all the separation within and around me.

HEALING EXERCISE

Choose a present problem or situation. Ask your higher mind to carry you back to your center, and to carry everyone in the situation back to their centers. If necessary, take them to a second, deeper center. See and feel the light within you connecting to the light within everyone present. From now until the problem is resolved, do this every time you think of the person(s). Ask yourself "Who really needs my help?" Every time you think of a person in trouble, see and feel the light within you connecting to the light within them. Make a list of their problems, and at the end of every week, examine how they're doing in this particular area. If you have any gifts that you know are yours, share these gifts with them to help them heal.

98.

WELCOMING CHANGE
AND THE WILLINGNESS TO LEARN

Whenever there is a problem, life is asking us to change, and so is our soul. Each problem represents a place of conflicted energy within us, which is projected on to our outside environments. Each of these conflicted places is calling for forgiveness on the outside and integration on the inside, in order to change the situation. Whenever we have a conflict with our partners, the message being given to us is that *we*, not our partners, need to change. We might force our partner to do things our way, which would place *them* in sacrifice instead of *us*, but we would miss the opportunity to heal something within ourselves. There may be large fractures within us, but if we continue to join and to forgive our situation and those within it, we will experience rebirth.

If we refuse the lesson, it will continue to present itself until it eventually becomes a trial. We are constantly being asked to learn new ways to address our lives and, more importantly, ways in which we can heal or unlearn something. The order in which our lessons are arranged for us is pre-arranged by our higher mind or, if we refuse to change, if we insist on being right, if we play win–lose, if we manipulate or emotionally blackmail to get our needs met, the results can be tragic.

Our willingness to learn can have spectacular results, because it builds our confidence. Each time we choose to join with our partners, rather than trying to score emotionally or sexually to prove our superiority, we are rewarded with a new level of love. Our desire to learn and our willingness to change and grow will open up new areas for us.

When we are willing to change, lessons can be assimilated easily and smoothly. When we are willing to embrace our true life path, much that was hidden will be revealed to us, saving us a great deal of time and pain. Our willingness to learn and heal allows our life to become graceful and peaceful. I was once working with a client who had cancer. One day, as he was driving to my office, he felt compelled to leave the motorway, because he felt that there was some message waiting for him. He drove through a sleepy coastal town, but nothing struck him. However, just as he was re-approaching the motorway, he saw a billboard that read, "Your change is your cure." Needless to say, he was in a profound state of reflection by the time he reached my office. His renewed determination to make changes went on to change his prognosis and his life.

HEARTBREAK PRINCIPLE

Our refusal to learn and to change can lead to spectacular heartbreaks.

HEALING PRINCIPLE

Our willingness to learn and to grow brings grace and ease to our life, which is set out in a curriculum by our higher minds.

HEALING SUGGESTION

The willingness to learn keeps you young and flexible. It allows you to continue to evolve and to show ever-new sides of yourself to your partner. This encourages a refreshing sense of ease and excitement in your relationship. Any fights, deadness, or problems within your relationship reflect a place where you are frightened to change. When you commit to change and when you are excited to learn from your partner, from their experience, from life, and from your own spiritual core, you give a valuable gift both to yourself and your partner. We don't change just for the sake of change, but to become truer, happier, easier, and more abundant in everything we do.

HEALING CHOICE

I commit to learn and to change easily, fully, and gracefully.

HEALING EXERCISE

Assess your willingness to learn and to welcome change. On the scale of 100 how willing are you to learn and welcome change...

in yourself? _____

in your partner? _____

in your life? _____

in your career? _____

Take ten minutes to imagine yourself at the 100 mark in all of these relationships. What is the difference between this and how you live now? Would you be willing to make new choices in light of your new awareness?

99.

THE PURPOSE OF RELATIONSHIPS

Every relationship has a purpose, the first and most important purpose of which is for love, joy, and happiness. When we receive love, we are encouraged to become our true selves, to live our destinies to the best of our ability, and to reach Oneness. If we haven't reached this stage, then the second purpose of a relationship, which is healing, is needed to bring us back to joy. Whenever we feel less than loving or happy, it is time to employ healing, and a relationship is the perfect vehicle to do this. Our relationships also serve the purpose of helping our friends and the world around us, by inspiring others with our love. We provide a level of service to the world not only by what we give but through the inspiration that comes from the love and joining in our relationship. Every relationship also has its own unique purpose which may differ at various stages of our lives.

Our relationships provide us with a goal of enjoying each other, finding the meaning of love, and bringing ourselves, our partners, and our relationships to a state of wholeness. Relationships can be both the stairway to spiritual peace and the means by which we can create our own heaven or nirvana on earth. Every relationship has as its purpose and its promise, the ability to help the earth evolve. Every fracture we heal between each of us in our relationship helps heal a fracture and an illusion on the earth, of which there are billions left to heal.

When we realize the purpose we have in our relationships, we work together toward a goal that inspires each individual in a partnership, and conflicts along the way become mere hiccups on the path to wholeheartedness. We begin to see problems as vehicles for healing and for positive change rather than messages that our relationships are somehow wrong. Not every relationship can last forever, but when there is love and joining between partners, its ending would be in friendship, rather than heartbreak as its purpose is realized.

HEARTBREAK PRINCIPLE

Relationships that end in heartbreak have not realized their purpose.

HEALING PRINCIPLE

Our relationships" purpose provides us with direction, sustains us and presents a gift to ourselves, our partners, and the world.

HEALING SUGGESTION

You have a purpose and so does your relationship. When you are not living your purpose, your distractions, and problems will have negative, destructive tendencies, one of which is to avoid the true purpose of your life and your relationship.

HEALING CHOICE

I commit to fulfilling my life and relationship purpose.

═══════════════════════

HEALING EXERCISE

Examine every significant relationship that you have had, including those with parents, siblings, children, ex-partners, and your present partner. What was the purpose in each relationship? What joy and happiness were you meant to bring each other? What were you meant to heal together? Did you succeed? You can still succeed by forgiving everyone involved. What was the main gift or gifts that you were meant to give them? What gift or gifts were they meant to give to you? As you give your gifts, they correspondingly give you theirs. How much of that was complete? If you have not given these gifts, do so now because it will help complete your purpose for being together. You can measure your level of fulfillment with any person or period of your life by asking yourself, "How much, if I were to know, was I fulfilled in that relationship or time period of my life?" Where you are least fulfilled, give the gifts that would bring these scenes to a happy ending. You will then be able to receive the gifts they have for you.

═══════════════════════

100.
HEALING PROJECTION

This is a radical concept that has a great transformational effect. It is a principle that gives us back our responsibility for and power to change ourselves, our situations, and the world.

Everything we see and experience is projection. Our perception of the world comes from us, and the world itself is made up of the collective perception of all of us. What we project onto the people around us and our situations, forms our perception of them. It also affects the way other people perceive things. We are all entirely responsible for our own lives, and using the power of our minds to change our perceptions, and to change what we project onto others and the world, we have the ability to make changes for us and everyone else.

Through accessing the more hidden layers of our minds we can change ourselves and, literally, change the world. All we know of the world is our perception of it, so when our perception changes, so does our world.

Earlier we learned how people and the world around us mirror our minds. A projection is a part of ourselves that we have judged and then pinned onto someone or something in our world. The word "projection" comes from the Latin *projacére*, which means "to throw forth," as in a javelin. When we project, we forcefully put our own self-judgments onto those around us. For example, when we see a particular person as being nasty or unkind, we have projected our own nasty side onto them.

But we can change our perceptions through forgiveness or by pulling back the projection and forgiving ourselves. In this way we can heal this wounded part of ourselves. When we pull back the projection we are able to receive from others, and we are able to hear their calls for help. Changing our core heartbreaks, which led to the projection, has a way of changing the people and the world around us.

Projection occurs when we have separation or fractures in our minds which set up separation outside us. In a fractured state we believe that the problems are external and unrelated to our own emotional health. Healing can mend the rifts and help to raise our own self-awareness, which will prevent projection in the future. When we are self-aware, we see ourselves and our situations in others and we can rectify problems or fractures in ourselves.

Projection originally begins when we separate a certain part of us, which causes conflict within, because whatever is separated is rejected. Then we throw these rejected, fragmented selves on to the world, causing us to separate from (and therefore be in conflict with) others or a situation as we projected these parts on to them. We see others and external situations as being "bad" and ourselves as being "good." When we deny our own part in the problem, we feel superior. Superiority, however, is not a state of joining and it engenders even further separation and conflict.

All projection is based on denial. We pretend to others and ourselves that we do not have a certain quality by compensating or acting in a way that appears to make up for it. Our "hidden" side may be evident to others, or it may be buried so deeply that no one is aware of it. In this case, we can only become aware of it by assessing the strength of our compensation. We can be sure that there is compensation operating if we are working hard, being the best people we can be, and still seem to get no further in life. The invisible barrier that is holding us back is whatever part of ourselves we are hiding, and when we compensate, we prevent that hidden belief in ourselves from being discovered and healed. In real terms, we are unable to receive anything from others or the outside world because these barriers and our compensation keep us in denial and sacrifice, which prevent reward. We are effectively punishing ourselves by compensating as much as we would be if we were acting out the negative quality, because we use enormous amounts of our vital energy (or life force) in keeping it buried.

When our denial or compensation is profound, it usually helps to go back to the trauma where the fragmentation and rejection of this part of ourselves occurred, and we need to analyze where the projection began. By healing the original incident, we can heal the hidden part and release the projection.

Basically, if we see problems, they are our problems. When we change our perceptions, we effectively change the situations. In this way, we have the ability to change others by taking responsibility and changing ourselves, and this doesn't lead to the conflict of trying to change them. Finally, it gives us an opportunity to change the life in our partner, rather than changing the partner in our life!

It is extremely important to remember that projection is not just about throwing out negative qualities. We have judged and separated more than negative qualities in ourselves—we have also rejected positive qualities through fear of losing control or because we are afraid of others" envy. Sometimes, we feel so guilty, afraid, or embarrassed about the gifts we have that we even project these on to others, and "pretend" that we don't have them. Then we dislike others we believe they have something "good" that we don't have. The projection principle is the same in this instance—we have separated or rejected positive qualities in ourselves that we are now seeing in others. It is as important to get over our fears and to integrate these qualities as it is to heal our negative qualities. Joining and integrating are forms of healing.

Several years ago, I stopped in to visit my best friend. He had some very close friends whose marriage was on the rocks, and he asked if I would help them. They spent the first forty minutes of the session telling stories and complaining about each other. Since there was only twenty minutes left to save their marriage, I decided to use the projection healing technique. I asked them both to name the three things that most bothered them about their partner. Each dutifully named the three qualities that drove them to distraction. Then, I asked them to pull back their projection and own it, and to recognize that they were doing the same thing or compensating for having done so in the past. I explained to them that they were attacking themselves for having the same qualities and asked them to choose whether they were going to keep attacking themselves or support their spouse. They chose to support and, as they did, they saw a change in their partner. In twenty minutes, they were back in love with each other and planning a vacation to Hawaii. It is truly this simple, if we choose it to be.

HEARTBREAK PRINCIPLE

As a result of old heartbreaks, we project onto those around us, which leads to separation, conflict, and heartbreak.

HEALING PRINCIPLE

When we take responsibility for our perceptions and experiences, and realize how they mirror us, we can change them.

HEALING SUGGESTION

As you see the whole world as a projection of your own self-judgment and gifts that you were frightened to give, you will realize that you can change the world by forgiving others and yourself. You can own back your gifts with confidence, and you can free yourself from self-attack.

HEALING CHOICE

I commit to give up self-attack, until both myself and my world are free of pain.

HEALING EXERCISE

Choose three major heartbreaks and, with each one, use the projection healing techniques below. You can even use the heartbreak itself as a projection. All situations in the world lend themselves to this type of healing. Start with step one by choosing one person with whom you are having trouble. Complete every step. As you feel the freedom you receive from this exercise by leaving your self-attack and separation behind, and instead, supporting and embracing your friend, you then can choose anyone on whom you are projecting to feel even freer.

1. Choose the person with whom you have the biggest projection and imagine them standing across the room from you. What are you projecting on them?
2. Now pull back the projection. In other words, own the quality you don't like about them and accept it as being yours.
3. Recognize your own style—whether you do the same things they do or if you are compensating (acting in the opposite way in an extreme reaction to something within you). If you do the same thing you will see it instantly. If you are compensating, you'll feel you'd rather die than ever do that. Go back to the place where you judged this part of yourself, fragmented it, buried it, and then projected it onto others. Simply use your intuition to see what "pops" into your mind when you ask yourself "If I were to know, how old was I when I judged this quality?" Then, "If I were to know, who was with me?" Then, "If I were to know what was going on when I began to believe this about myself, it was probably..." What did you decide to do with this quality? Once you begin to recognize how you buried this quality in self-attack, it is easy for you to proceed.

    Some people have a bit of both styles—they do the same thing part of the time and deny the behavior the rest of the time by compensating or acting in an opposite way.
4. Recognize how you've been attacking yourself for this quality and creating a wall of separation around you so that others will not see this quality in you.
5. Ask yourself whether you want to keep attacking and keeping yourself separate, or if you would rather leave the self-attack behind, step out of your self-tor-

ture chamber, past the wall of separation, and go support a friend on whom you had projected and who needs your help. It's a simple choice—attack yourself or help others. This technique always works unless you are using the projection as an excuse and a conspiracy to hold yourself back.

═══════════════

101.

HEALING THE DREAM

If we understand the radical nature of the principle of projection, we begin to realize that we can change the world as if it were a story, a movie, or a dream. I have seen how powerful this can be—for the last twenty-five years I have helped people to change their dreams.

We all live in a powerful, entrancing dream. This dream is the world in which we live and it is peopled by others who reflect parts of our minds and act according to the stories we create for them. We can choose to live in a happy dream or a nightmare, but at some level, our dreams are wish-fulfillment.

The idea of our lives as dreams is not a new one. A fundamental concept in Indian philosophy is *maya*, which means "illusion." It derives from the belief that the world is an emanation of divine energy and the product of a collective perception of reality. Thinkers such as Radhakrishnan agree that the world is mysterious and derived from God and that our lives are dynamically produced by maya. Similarly, in the Old Testament, the book of Genesis states that Adam fell into a deep sleep, upon which Eve was born and the cycle of humanity began. At no stage in the Bible does it state that Adam ever woke up.

One way to examine this concept is through realizing that

the people around us are actually *us* acting out our "dream." In other words, everything on an interpersonal level comes from our own minds—it is a reflection of our relationships with ourselves. The same phenomenon occurs when we dream in our sleep. In our sleeping dreams, all of the people are symbols of fragmented aspects of ourselves. What we accuse them of, or see them doing, we are doing ourselves. All of us do this at the same time, which creates the collective drama of life. Whatever goes on in our lives is written by everyone in the situation. For this reason, any one and all of us have the ability to change it.

This concept encourages us to take responsibility for ourselves, our partners, and whatever is unfolding in our dramas. When we take responsibility, we have the power to change things. Working on our lives, our dreams, our healing, and our lessons can make profound changes in the world around us because when we change ourselves and our perception of things, we change the "dream" that is our lives and the collective dreams of everyone around us that make up our world.

It may seem farfetched to believe that we can make broad-scale changes in the world simply by altering our perceptions, but it is important to remember that our lives are just a reflection of ourselves. When we create negative dreams, they touch on the lives of everyone around us and alter everyone else's dreams. When we create positive dreams, and are able to send out lines of love and healing, we change both our perceptions of the world and those of other people.

HEARTBREAK PRINCIPLE

Not to realize that our lives are a dream and that we are the dreamers keeps us dreaming, and, at times, dreaming nightmares and heartbreaks. This diminishes our power to change and have exactly what we consciously want.

HEALING PRINCIPLE

The willingness to change and forgive ourselves and to forgive others allows the world to transform and the collective dream to become a happy one.

HEALING SUGGESTION

Reflect on your life. What kind of dream has it been? How has it served you to have such a dream? The movie *The Matrix* provides the closest approximation of the concept of the world as our dream and the ability to change it instantly. I recommend seeing it.

HEALING CHOICE

I choose to see my life as a dream, thereby giving myself the ability to change it for the better and fully realizing my happiness.

HEALING EXERCISE

The following methods can usefully and effectively change your dream. Forgive the people involved, yourself, and the situation. Commit to everyone involved and to the situation so that it can get better. Join with the others, light to light, as many times as you think of it. Integrate the parts of your mind that the others in the situation represent, by seeing you and them melting together. See yourself receiving the energy. Remember to ask for a miracle.

Choose three problems and describe them by giving them three qualities. Then choose three problem people and give them each three qualities. Then choose three chronic problem persons, with whom you have a long-running issue, and give them each three qualities:

Problem	Recent problem person	Chronic problem person
1. _____	_____	_____

Qualities

_____ _____ _____
_____ _____ _____
_____ _____ _____

Problem   Recent problem person   Chronic problem person
2. _____ _____ _____

Qualities

_____ _____ _____
_____ _____ _____
_____ _____ _____

Problem   Recent problem person   Chronic problem person
3. _____ _____ _____

Qualities

_____ _____ _____
_____ _____ _____
_____ _____ _____

With each problem, each recent problem person and each chronic problem person, intuitively respond to complete the following statements:

If I were to know what having this person or situation allows me to do, it is probably_____

If I were to know what excuse this person or situation gives me, it is probably

_____

If I were to know how I get to be right by having this occur, it is probably

_____

If I were to know what this justifies, it is probably _____

_____

If I were to know, how am I like the qualities of this person, or situation? _____

_____

If I were to know what I am hiding by this, it is probably _____

_____

Typically, you will notice that you have just those same qualities, or you will have an opposite, compensatory quality. If you do, melt the compensation and the behavior together. If not, forgive yourself and the other qualities. Now, ask yourself, "What conspiracies is my ego using in these situations or with these people to hold me back?" Here are some common ones to name a few: fear of your purpose conspiracy, guilt conspiracy, jealousy conspiracy, sacrifice conspiracy, heartbreak conspiracy, fear conspiracy, hiding conspiracy, smallness conspiracy, betrayal conspiracy, sex conspiracy. Now complete the following statements:

If I were to know what having this conspiracy allows me to do, it is probably

_____

If I were to know what excuse this gives me, it is probably _____

_____

If I were to know how I get to be right by having this occur and what it justifies, it is probably_____

If I were to know what gift hides under this person or situation, it's probably the
gift of _____

The size of the gift is the size of the conspiracy. If the gift doesn't come to you immediately, meditate or dwell on it until it becomes perfectly clear. Embrace the gift fully. See yourself sharing this gift with the people or situation and at least one other person in your life.

102.

HEALING A TRIANGLE RELATIONSHIP

A triangle relationship is a heartbreak in the making and has the ability to devastate the lives of all three individuals involved. A triangle or even rectangle relationship is created when each person involved fears intimacy. It is part of each individual's pattern, which stems from their childhood Oedipal patterns and broken bonding. The triangle relationship commonly arises as part of a power struggle, a lack of satisfaction, or when there is deadness in the relationship.

Many times, a single person is attracted to someone who is married or already in a relationship. They are tempted by the married person because they believe that this person has all of the qualities that they want in someone for a partnership, except, of course, they are not available. If they start a relationship with this person out of hunger or lack of faith, they end up missing someone with all the right qualities who *is* available.

Triangles are very messy and full of unclear boundaries, the Oedipus complex, and heartbreak. The person with two partners often felt unloved as a child, was in the throes of a major Oedipal pattern, and became so independent that they now place their own satisfaction above the needs of and the potential hurt caused to their partner. They defend against their feelings with more independence and dissociation. And the person whose partner strayed is ripe for heartbreak while attempting to pay off their own old guilt and betrayal. The new partner will also face challenges when the relationship progresses because a partner who is easily led astray will always be looking for new excitement elsewhere. There is also a lack of trust for a partner who left someone else. And the deadness that new partners face when they get to this stage is usually doubled because of the guilt of breaking up a relationship, which triggers off childhood guilt and betrayal.

The person in the center of the two relationships is unable to make up their minds about who they want because, as the triangle relationship progresses, each of their partners seems to be half of their ideal of who they want in a relationship. "If only I could have both…" is a frequent comment. They end up traveling between relationships on a research mission, which either ends in a choice to remain in the trap of searching or to choose one of them, which would feel like sacrifice because this person only has half the qualities they wanted. There is, however, a way to break the pattern with none of the heartbreak, guilt, or ensuing deadness.

HEARTBREAK PRINCIPLE

A triangle relationship is a conspiracy that the ego uses to entangle and trap three people, and it usually leads to deadness, heartbreak, or both.

HEALING PRINCIPLE

Commitment and willingness to take the next step and to knowing who is our true partner will heal the triangle dilemma.

HEALING SUGGESTION

There is a way to heal and transcend the triangle relationship which is one of the ego's best traps. You can heal this by re-bonding with your original family, which set up the competitive dynamic in the first place, and then heal any ancestral problems, which were passed through to you from your parents. You can use commitment, you can take the next step, and you can heal the shadow figures to resolve this problem or major layers of it. It is important to remember that this situation was a choice made by everyone involved in the trap. No one is to blame yet everyone is responsible. The triangle relationship is usually an expression of your fear of intimacy, success, and the next step, as well as punishment for guilt and feelings of past betrayal of others. This past betrayal may have occurred in earlier relationships, or with your parents, for there are always feelings of guilt and betrayal hidden away, especially if a relationship wasn't successful.

HEALING CHOICE

I commit to healing my patterns and my fear of intimacy so that I might fulfill my relationship, my partner, and myself.

HEALING EXERCISE

If you are in a triangle relationship, have no relationship, or have a dead relationship—or even if you just want to improve your relationship, you can begin healing your Oedipal issues by intuitively responding to the following statements. Answer with whatever "pops" into your head.

If I were to know how many core incidents from childhood I would need to clear at this time to heal my relationship issue, it's probably _____

_____

If I were to know when the most important one occurred for me, it was probably at the age _____

If I were to know who was involved, it was probably me and _____

_____

If I were to know what occurred, it was probably _____

_____

Go back in your mind to this incident. Now, ask your higher mind to return everyone to their centers. When that is achieved, ask that everyone be returned to an even deeper center. From the light within you connect to the light within everyone present, and then have each of them connect with everyone else. Now give everyone the gifts that you have come to give them in order to help both you and them heal and move forward. What are the colors of these gifts? See them being filled with the gifts and their colors, then see the gift going back through your family generations on both sides of the family, freeing your ancestors. For each of the other core childhood incidents, repeat the intuitive method above, replacing "next most important incident" for the most important incident, and then continue until they are all dealt with.

The key to getting out of the triangle relationship after this preliminary work is very simple and can be done by whichever member of the triangle you are. If you have the courage, you can clear this now. Commit to the truth. Commit to the next step. Ask for a miracle. Put any partner and the outcome you have in the hands of your God. At present you are unable to make a reasonable decision about what is best for you or what would make you happy. You need the help of your spiritual guide or your own core—truthful inner self-knowledge—which will lead you to the right choice.

Do this inner work and continue your life as usual. Inside, however, commit, choose, pray, and want the answer. Now, any time you think of your situation, commit to the next step, and trust that the answer and the way through is coming to you. Recognize and accept any fears you may have and put it in the hands of God or your spirit. In about a week, as if by a miracle, something will radically and significantly change. The resolution of who is really whose true partner will be clear. If you have two partners, your true partner will follow you as you step ahead, and the other will say goodbye without guilt or recriminations. If you are one of the other triangle partners, your partner will also step forward as you do, or as the case may be, come to say goodbye. There will be no bad feelings—only a belief that this is the natural course for the situation to take. There will always be a connection with this person if they aren't your true partner; there may even be friendship for the remaining parties.

This method leaves all parties feeling innocent, without heartbreak, and ready to take the next step in their lives. It is important to do nothing on the outside level, unless you are absolutely inspired to do it. Any one of the three individuals in the triangle relationship can break everyone free. This is one of the best traps the ego has set up, but there is a way to be free from the problem with grace and ease.

103.

HEALING THE LOST SELVES AND THE WAR STORY

We have all lost parts of ourselves. These are selves so wounded they may be unknown to us, or we may think we have permanently lost them. If we lose many "selves," we can become a "lost soul" drifting through life. Most of us will compensate for our losses by being a hard-charger and an overachiever, but others are cut loose from their moorings and will drift through life, forming only casual relationships. It takes heartbreak of major proportions or a number of heartbreaks in the same place, to cut us loose like this.

A lost self is the result of heartbreak so traumatic that we feel that there is no hope for us. Some of us turn our energies to helping others when we have given up on ourselves, and we become wounded healers on a "save the world" mission. As noble as this may seem, we will never be more than sacrificers until we clear the original heartbreaks. This type of self-sacrifice also leads to burn-out from time to time, in which some of the original pain and energy surfaces. When this occurs, we need to return to the original incident and heal it.

Lost selves are often born in an emotional war zone. The war zone is usually established within a family where parents are fighting, but it takes the whole family, collectively, to create such a powerfully negative environment. Every member of the family becomes a major character in the "war story" and plays an equal part in its unfolding. Being caught in a war story can turn us into a victim, a predator, or a sacrificing helper— and these are roles that can lock us into patterns that remain with us for the rest of our lives. These patterns must be healed if we are to know ourselves and to experience love and success.

HEARTBREAK PRINCIPLE

A lost self can result from living a "war story," which creates a heartbreak so painful that we feel we are not going to survive.

HEALING PRINCIPLE

It is important to recover our lost selves, to give up the war story and any compensations in order to find peace, and to embrace the major gift the trauma was meant to hide.

HEALING SUGGESTION

What did you feel when you read this section? Could you identify with it? Check to see if your lost selves were compensated for or hidden by victim, predator, or false "helper" personalities. It is time to integrate all these lost selves and regain your true direction, rather than follow the goals and directions of roles compensating for major trauma.

HEALING CHOICE

I commit to finding and healing all lost selves, war stories, and the original traumas that generated them.

HEALING EXERCISE

Respond intuitively (with the first answer that enters your head) to complete the following statements. This will help you to discover your lost selves and to heal your war story and heartbreaks:

If I were to know how many traumas I have within me that gave rise to lost selves, it is probably _____

If I were to know how many war stories I have within me, it is probably _____

_____

If I were to know where I buried each group of lost selves that came from traumas or an ongoing war story, it is probably _____

_____

Go to each place within you where those "lost selves" are buried, and have them all melt back into you. For each war story, imagine that you took each one and offered it up to your creative mind. Let it go as a bad decision, choice, or experience. See and feel what you are given in return. For each trauma, intuitively respond to complete the following statements:

If I were to know when the most important trauma occurred, it was probably at the age of _____

If I were to know with whom it occurred, it was probably _____

_____

If I were to know what went on, it was probably _____

_____

If I were to know what gift I was frightened of and sought to control by having this trauma occur, it was probably _____

_____

With each trauma, imagine yourself back at that time, and make a choice to embrace this gift within you. Go back to just before the trauma occurred and share your gift. How do things turn out now?

104.
FROM INTERPRETATION TO UNDERSTANDING

One of the ways in which we hurt ourselves is the way we interpret an event. When we are in pain, we have misinterpreted a situation, someone's actions, or what they have said. By changing our interpretation, we can heal the pain. This is one of the reasons why *clarification* can take care of so many of our problems. When we share our thoughts, feelings, and intentions about or behind whatever we have said or done, and then listen to our partners, we learn to understand each other and where we are coming from. This works in about eighty-five percent of all cases of pain and heartbreak. The other fifteen percent are caused by deeper, more chronic problems and heartbreaks. Clarification will help with more serious problems, but it's usually not enough to heal deeper misunderstandings. One of the methods that I have found most effective is taking people back to original heartbreaking events, where they felt rejected or unwanted. By helping them to understand what they misunderstood, or see that they were not really being rejected—that it was just their *interpretation* of their parents' behavior that led to heartbreak—their pain has been healed. With the benefit of hindsight and maturity we can understand that the problems in the past that caused us the most pain are only problematic and painful because we allowed them to be. We relied on our interpretation of events to guide our feelings, never considering that we may have been mistaken.

When we look back we can usually see that our parents were acting in a painful or independent way because of their own pain or needs.

Some of the longest power struggles or most painful situations can be turned into positive learning events when we have the right perspective. We can use them to turn something tragic into something more acceptable which has a great healing effect.

A classic misunderstanding and example of "denial in action" occurs when we claim that someone started a fight with us, and that we were the completely "innocent bystander." In principle, it always takes two to fight. We often fail to realize that we are also fighting when we use withdrawal or passive aggression. Fighting or arguing doesn't have to be overtly aggressive to be effective.

Pain is an indication that we are off the track. If we are willing to uncover the truth, and to reassess our interpretations of events, we can heal the separation and choose to take the next step. Simply wanting or agreeing to learn the truth empowers and motivates us to move forward. When we are honest and enlightened, we can experience the spiritual peace that exists at the core of our being, and we will finally understand that we cannot be hurt by anything that goes on around us. From this highest spiritual perspective, we know that all fear is a misunderstanding and we will have the confidence to know and feel that there is a way through any situation.

HEARTBREAK PRINCIPLE

All heartbreak comes from some level of misinterpretation.

HEALING PRINCIPLE

As we bring true understanding to an event, we not only heal the pain, but we are also able to re-bond where there was separation.

HEALING SUGGESTION

Most of your hurt or rejection comes from your belief that someone was rejecting you. This is only your interpretation of a situation. Choose instead to recognize that they were just acting in a particular way to get their own needs met, and that *you* rejected *them* for doing it, which was the foundation of your feelings of hurt and rejection. Your upsets come from your fear which comes from your own judgments. When you make judgments you attack and condemn others, thereby causing further fear, because you mistakenly think that someone or something is threatening you.

HEALING CHOICE

I commit to healing all of my misinterpretations so that I can heal myself of fear and pain.

HEALING EXERCISE

Choose three heartbreak situations and one present problem situation and examine them in the light of misinterpretation.

Heartbreak	What I thought was happening	The need they had	The judgment I made	The fear I had
1.				
2.				
3.				

Present upset	What I think is happening	The need they have	The need and fear that I have	The judgment I am making
1.				
2.				
3.				

Use the present situation to communicate in order to end the misunderstanding in all four incidents. If you don't feel confident about the outcome, take ten minutes to relax and imagine yourself as pure, peaceful spirit. The relaxation will help you feel the serenity necessary to see the way through.

105.

CHANGING OUR PURPOSE

A heartbreak is an intense fracture that painfully separates us from life. The energy is so vivid, all-encompassing, and distracting that we don't realize that something more hidden and ultimately destructive is at work. This is the hidden purpose or dynamic that every heartbreak has. Typically, the purpose of our heartbreak was to gain independence and control so that we could not be hurt again. We decided that this meant doing things our way, the way we had wanted to do them all along. Heartbreaks hide our fractures and Oedipus complex and give us an excuse to avoid going forward to face our fears—especially those concerning intimacy. We use heartbreak to prove ourselves right about something, which is, ultimately, an attempt to prove someone else wrong and then to defeat them with the heartbreak. Our self-righteousness covers over hidden feelings of guilt and self-judgment, and our heartbreaks justify our jealousy and give us an excuse for revenge.

When we give up our mistaken purposes, we can return to our real purpose, and that involves finding peace within ourselves. When we have spiritual peace we will always have happiness, fulfillment, love and self-knowledge. We will experience wholeheartedness and a life of abundance and fulfillment.

When we give up our mistaken purpose, we can begin again. We can learn and change in such a way that we will never have a heartbreak again—not because we are "in control," which is always an invitation to discord within a relationship, but because we have reached a new level of understanding and healing that takes us beyond such events. Our willingness to give up our mistaken goal so that we can see the truth allows our next step to commence, and our life sets off in a new adventure. We are called upon to learn and begin anew and embrace our true purpose—our reason for being here.

HEARTBREAK PRINCIPLE

Every heartbreak masks a mistaken purpose, a choice we make for something that could never make us happy.

HEALING PRINCIPLE

When we choose our true, life's purpose over our mistaken purpose in heartbreak, we move past all conspiracies, which have kept us away from love, happiness, and fulfillment.

HEALING SUGGESTION

As you give up the purpose you had in every mistaken, painful event, you can then choose the happiness of your true purpose both as an individual and in your relationships.

HEALING CHOICE

I commit only to my true purpose so that I may find the peace within myself.

HEALING EXERCISE

Choose one heartbreak situation and one current upset in your life. Use the intuitive method (focusing on the first answers that enter your head) to discover and heal your mistaken purpose.

Heartbreak	My hidden, mistaken purpose	My real spiritual purpose in this event and in general
1._____	_____	_____

Current upset	My hidden, mistaken purpose	My spiritual purpose in this event and in general
1._____	_____	_____

When you have time, do this exercise with every heartbreak and with any current upset as it appears.

106.
FORGIVENESS

Forgiveness is a powerful tool for transformation, but the ego tells us that it is a form of weakness. Forgiveness is a tool that frees us, allowing us to reach a peaceful place within ourselves where we no longer hold grievances against others. When we forgive others, we forgive ourselves, because it is our own negative patterns and qualities that we are judging in others. When we forgive we no longer hold another person responsible for meeting our needs or making us happy. When we forgive we value our peace more than holding ourselves and others hostage. We release our demands, knowing that the next step will satisfy our needs and bring us to the next level of success.

Forgiveness can be a difficult lesson for some of us to learn, but as we learn the value of moving forward in life, forgiveness will be an invaluable tool for healing ourselves and for changing our world. If we find that forgiveness is impossible or even difficult, we can forgive using the peace that exists at our spiritual core, or we can ask our God to accomplish the forgiveness through grace. Without forgiveness, we are forced to live lives of fear that are dictated by a past that is regurgitated again and again in many different forms. When we forgive, the situation changes our history and the story of our life changes with that. With true forgiveness we actually forget past transgressions and move forward. If we are unable to do so, we are holding on to some misconception, fear, or fracture. Forgiveness is the solvent that will dissolve any lingering guilt, judgment, self-attack, and grievance, releasing us from all the pain.

Until our patterns are resolved, they will continue to occur. Forgiveness is one of the best ways in which we can create change, and it is a way to make a clean start. The pain of any heartbreak situation can be our springboard into a higher level of learning and creative living, and forgiveness provides the momentum for a new chapter in our lives.

HEARTBREAK PRINCIPLE

The ego tells us that forgiveness involves living a life of continuous sacrifice and heartbreak, so we are afraid to use one of the greatest principles of healing.

HEALING PRINCIPLE

Forgiveness is the principle that dissolves judgment, guilt, grievance, pain, self-attack, and the past, and it brings our heart into wholeness once more.

HEALING SUGGESTION

Review the story of your life and the painful events of the past and the present. Spend some time forgiving these events and the people involved, including yourself. Forgive the God, prophet, or guru of your spiritual path. If some part of your past is stuck, you're using it as some kind of excuse or conspiracy, which is not making you happy. Forgiveness is not one-sided. The extent to which you forgive others is the extent to which you forgive yourself; and the extent to which you forgive yourself is also the extent to which you will forgive others.

HEALING CHOICE

I commit to forgive everyone against whom I have ever had grievances so that I can be totally free and confident.

HEALING EXERCISE

Choose three past heartbreak situations and three present problems. Be willing to recognize your grievances so that you can forgive and free yourself.

Heartbreak	Grievance at that time	Grievance from the past	Grievance against myself
1.			
2.			
3.			

Present problem	Grievance at this time	Grievance from the past	Grievance against myself
1.			
2.			
3.			

Now, choose to forgive the situation and everyone involved so that you might heal the past and know happiness now.

107.
LETTING GO

Letting go is absolutely crucial if we are to move forward after a heartbreak. When we commit to letting go, we will find that we move beyond dependence, sacrifice, independence, and using our heartbreaks as an excuse to be dominant or in control. When we successfully let go, the positive effects will continue through the pain that we are experiencing in the present to heal layer after layer of old needs and heartbreaks beneath that. We can let go of old feelings of guilt and unworthiness to escape the cycle leading to poor self-esteem and unhappiness. When we let go, we feel good about ourselves and we can move forward confidently to a whole new level in life and relationships.

Fully letting go is a new birth rather than a shattering. Letting go of every need and attachment frees us from chains of desire, which imprison us rather than fulfill us in any way. Letting go can be done in a minute or across a lifetime, depending on our courage. The letting-go principle focuses on the fact that whatever pain, need, attachment, person, or situation that we let go of, something better comes to take its place.

There are a number of ways to let go. The most basic of these is experiencing our feelings fully. When we observe and truly experience every feeling without running away from it, we can gradually exhaust the painful feelings until they become peaceful and joyous. By having the courage to feel through to the end of the negative feelings, we will eventually reach the positive ones. On the journey, we may hit an unconscious pocket that could first lead us into deeper, darker emotions before we reach peace. This might last two to three days as we "burn" through our feelings. Sooner or later, the pain will lessen and we will move into a more whole, more associated place where we go with feelings rather than resist them. When we aggressively feel all of the pain and stay aware, we will eventually notice that hope and then some love creeps in to take its place. When we pay attention to love, we move through painful feelings much faster. Experiencing our feelings is one of the oldest, simplest forms of healing, and for some people it is the only way to let go. Experiencing feelings means allowing them free rein. Suppressing them in order to modify or dull them is not the same thing. Nor is hysteria, which is really just an attempt to avoid the feeling at hand. If we had felt all of our pain when it first occurred and stayed with it until it was over, painful patterns would never have been created.

The other forms of letting go have to do with putting the pain and the heartbreak situation or pattern into the hands of our higher mind or spirit. Acceptance, another basic form of letting go, has a way of getting us unstuck from places where we have resisted. Letting go can also happen when we take the next step, successfully moving beyond the issue and pain at hand. Commitment to our partners, situations, or our next steps, releases them painlessly if they are not right—because we move up to the next step. It's helpful to recognize our style of letting go whether we let go once and for all, or do it a little at a time as we work through the layers.

Truly letting go can allow us to heal the unfinished business of both our relationships and our pasts. Many of our problems are actually places where we are afraid to let go and move forward to a new level. The size of our problem is an indication of how big the next step is. Many of us do not want to let go, because while we have the pain, we think we have a good reason to avoid moving forward but it is, in reality, only fear. We may also resist losing a part of ourselves, a part of our identity, no matter how negative or untrue it may be. Actually, as we let go, all of these feelings move out of the foreground and into the background, as we move forward to a newer and truer perspective. When we let go there is more love. Love never takes hostages, so if we are holding on to a relationship or to our pain, it is a sign that we have made our love untrue by our attachment.

HEARTBREAK PRINCIPLE

Holding on is a way of trying to stay attached to someone, as long as we pay the price by feeling the pain.

HEALING PRINCIPLE

Letting go fully moves us out of the pain and the unfinished business of the past that created the heartbreak pattern and into a new chapter in our life.

HEALING SUGGESTION

All pain comes from attachment. Your willingness to let go of the pain and attachment moves you forward. Every problem hides some form of attachment, which is an attempt to have our past needs met in the present. If yesterday you needed a coin to make a phone call, would you continue trying to get that coin today and forever in an attempt to fulfill yesterday's need? It does not make sense, yet, without letting go, this is what you will continue to do. Your satisfaction will remain unavailable unless you heal.

HEALING CHOICE

I commit to letting go of my attachments, past and present, for present freedom and success.

HEALING EXERCISE

Choose three heartbreak situations and three current problems, then complete the following exercise to bring to your awareness what it is that you are holding on to. Choose the form of letting go that will work best for you in each situation. Examples of letting go are: experiencing your feelings, putting the pain, the situation, and the pattern in the hands of your spirit or your God, acceptance, taking the next step, and forgiveness.

Heartbreak	Attachment	Form of letting go I choose to employ
1.		
2.		
3.		

Current problem	Attachment	Form of letting go I choose to employ
1.		
2.		
3.		

Now, take the time to let go of each situation by the method you have chosen.

108.

COMMITMENT

Commitment, which is the decision to give ourselves fully to a person or project, is one of the great healing methods. When we commit, we bring about truth and freedom, yet it is a word that strikes fear into the hearts of many independent people. Most people think that commitment means sacrifice, slavery, and deadness, but commitment is actually one of the most effective antidotes to these traps.

While a breakthrough can heal a single conflict, commitment can heal many conflicts by taking us to the next step or stage in our lives. It is the difference between climbing one mountain and a whole mountain range using much the same effort. Commitment becomes a great time-saver in and "renewer" of our relationship. We do not make just one commitment to our partners at the beginning of our relationships; we make many throughout our relationships as we go through the steps and stages of growing in love. Commitment allows us to focus and build our lives. Without it, our energy and goals are split in many directions, which is just what the ego wants because it delays us. Too many goals are also symbolic of a split mind. As we focus on commitment, we can build our lives in a positive direction. Commitment brings partnership, intimacy, and success.

People often say that they are committed, but their partners are not. This is a classic case of self-deception. When we feel this way, we are viewing commitment as a form of dependence rather than as a tool for freedom and true love. It is evidenced by the fact that when we finally give up and go away in an independent manner, our partners want to get married, or if our partners move toward us in so-called commitment, which is really dependency, now it becomes our turn to flee.

When we truly commit to our partners, it encourages exactly the same level of commitment in our partners. In the rare case of untrue partners, they will leave after we truly commit, but this separation will be achieved without heartbreak, sadness, or any negative feelings.

HEARTBREAK PRINCIPLE

A heartbreak always demonstrates a lack of commitment on the part of both partners.

HEALING PRINCIPLE

Commitment encourages us to leap to a whole new step in our relationships and effects a corresponding level of commitment from our partners.

HEALING SUGGESTION

Whenever there is a major conflict with your beloved, a family member, a friend, or a business associate, commit to them and then see how the relationship jumps to a whole new stage. While there may be resistance to commitment, the extent to which you are in pain or feeling righteous is the extent to which your commitment will bring a true new level of relationship for both of you. It transforms your attitude and behavior, as well as those of your partner in the jump to a new level of partnership.

HEALING CHOICE

I choose to commit to my partner, my career, and my purpose.

HEALING EXERCISE

Examine your past relationships, especially your heartbreaks, for your level of commitment. Do this for your career as well. Knowing what you know now, how would you do it differently? Consider this when you begin your examinations: in your relationships and your career, others give to you to the extent that you give to them.

109.
GIFTS

About sixteen years ago I began to discover the power of gifts as a healing tool in my work. I discovered that behind every problem there is a hidden gift, and that one of the ego's main purposes is to hide this gift. A gift is something for sharing; it is something that creates a flow. Both sharing and flow are qualities that dissolve layers of ego. A gift is a blessing that blesses us and the person with whom we share it. It inspires and fulfills the giver and the receiver. Gifts are effective in healing self-consciousness and self-attack. Discovering and embracing a hidden gift can collapse the problem that is hiding it. When the gift is discovered, accepted, and shared, our pain—even age-old pain—disappears because the purpose of the problem has now been dissolved. Sometimes, pain covers a gift that is exactly opposite to it; for example, heartbreak may cover a gift of true love. Sometimes, the gift and the trap can be similar, in the case of sexual promiscuity hiding a gift of sexuality or sexual healing.

As I worked with family guilt, sacrifice, valuelessness, and pain, I discovered that centering, bonding, and, especially, gift-giving were an effective means of healing old traumas and patterns. Underneath our pain are judgments and grievances, and underneath those are feelings of guilt and failure. Beneath that lie the gifts that we brought in to heal the very situations that caused us pain and heartbreak. Giving these gifts that were hidden under our pain, grievance, and guilt is one of the only ways to defeat one of the most basic conspiracies against fulfilling our life's purpose. The gifts we have for our parents, family, and our partners are soul-level gifts. As these gifts are given, we release the conspiracy to hide them, and we realize that these gifts are ours to share. When we give these gifts, they become part of our being, so wherever we show up, the gifts show up. They are always there, and it becomes natural for us to share them. The more often we do so, the more we can free ourselves from negative patterns that have been with us since childhood, and the easier we will find it to step away from feelings of guilt and failure.

We have an unlimited supply of gifts and as we give gifts to others, more gifts are offered to us. As we give the gift that we have come to give to our love partners, or our beloved, we free them from their pain. As we free them with our gifts, they free us with their gifts. Working with gifts is a relatively quick and easy way to heal messy problems and conspiracies.

Our complaints about our parents and love partners hide a gift or gifts that we were destined to give to them. For instance, in marriage counseling, it is commonplace to hear one of the partners complaining that they aren't getting enough sex. Their partner may have been abused sexually, or their withdrawal is part of an argument or a power struggle. Or there may just be some other reason why sexuality had been repressed or suppressed in that partner. The complainer can either carry on in the same vein, which of course leads to guilt, bad feelings, and further withdrawal on their partner's part, or they can give a gift to their partner. I discovered that complaints mask a place where the complainer isn't giving completely. When the complainer gives a gift in this area, the complaint is gone. Both partners now share the gift, and they can both grow and move forward. Some people claim that they are willing to give the gift of sex at any time, night or day, but complain that their partner is always unavailable. There is, however, a fundamental difference between the *act* of sex and the *gift* of sex. The gift of sex is sexuality and it is energetic. When we give that energy during sex or romance or at virtually any time, it opens our partners who begin to resonate with the same energy. When our partners have been wounded in a certain area, such as in sex, we make a soul-level promise to rescue them by giving our gift. When we give our gift completely, they rapidly heal.

Gifts are energetic qualities that are given without expectation of any return. When they are offered, both partners benefit and grow. When we give and share a gift often enough, our friends or beloved begin to develop the same gift and, correspondingly, we begin to develop their own gifts. The energy is shared, and it spreads, opening up new gifts for each of us. Living our lives around gifts denies the ego's trap of envy and embarrassment, and we are able to hear the calls for help and respond to them. It allows us to lead by example and to experience the riches of true friendship, spiritual peace, and wholeheartedness.

HEARTBREAK PRINCIPLE

Every heartbreak hides a gift that frightens us more than the heartbreak itself. Part of the purpose of the heartbreak is to hide and control this gift and ourselves.

HEALING PRINCIPLE

Finding, embracing, and sharing our hidden gifts frees us and those around us from pain and problems.

HEALING SUGGESTION

One way of discovering your hidden gifts is to ask yourself what someone needs. If your parents are fighting, it means that within you there are gifts that you have for each one of your parents to be free. For your mother you might have the gift of love and for your father you can offer peace and confidence. The gift you can offer them as a couple may be your role as peacemaker. Your greatest gifts are soul-level gifts that you were destined to give to free those closest to you and the world. They are part of your promise to help and to save—in other words, your purpose for being here. They represent a big part of your purpose in life. The extent to which every experience was 100 percent fulfilling in your life is the extent to which you gave all the gifts within you to free yourself and others at that time.

HEALING CHOICE

I commit to recover all my gifts for my benefit and for that of the world around me.

HEALING EXERCISE

Choose three heartbreak situations, then three major complaints that you have in your life or about someone. Then choose three current problem situations. Complete the exercise to reclaim and give your gifts to each situation and to those involved so that you change it.

Heartbreaks	People in pain	Gift within me to free them
1.		
2.		
3.		

Complaints	Lesson	Gift I am to give
1.		
2.		
3.		

Problems	What gifts I am to give	To whom or what
1.		
2.		
3.		

Take time each day to go back to one heartbreak situation and ask yourself what the people, or the situation, needed to heal. Give your gifts.

110.

THE POWER OF CHOICE

Once a heartbreak has occurred, it is essential that we make a new choice. Without that we will withdraw from life and become either more dependent or more dissociated, neither of which is helpful in life or relationships. Most of us don't realize that we can choose how a heartbreak will affect us. Will we lose trust forever, or will we learn and heal so effectively that a heartbreak never happens again? Will we use the heartbreak for birth or to head toward emotional death? Will we use this heartbreak to compound mistaken beliefs or as an opportunity to get rid of negative beliefs and self-concepts?

Most of us go through our lives unaware that we are constantly making choices about how our lives will be. When we are aware we can consciously choose how we would like our lives to be, and we can ask our higher mind to help make our decisions with us. We can decide that we will soon be over our heartbreak. We can choose and ask for miracles in our present situation. We can choose to let go of all attachments that create pain in order to get on with our lives on a whole new level.

Consciously phrase your decisions and choices in the present, in a positive way. For example, "I am getting over this heartbreak" rather than "I will not let this heartbreak get me down."

We may uncover many layers of conflict and each positive choice removes another negative layer. If we are positive, strong, and determined enough, we can clear all of the layers at once. It is also important to be aware that the positive effects of each choice may last only for a few moments before another negative layer emerges. As we make more and more positive decisions we can find ourselves bringing up deeper, more conflicted and painful areas. But if we know what is occurring, we can get through the pain with the prospect of total healing in sight. If we stop when we reach a painful layer, we will mire ourselves in that area of conflict. Continue to choose positively to reach a place of peace and joy.

HEARTBREAK PRINCIPLE

The heartbreak was a mistaken choice that could never make us happy.

HEALING PRINCIPLE

Choice is the power that we can use to move us in the right direction—out of pain and into love and abundance.

HEALING SUGGESTION

Choosing forgiveness, miracles, and the next step frees you from your pain and the past. Choosing grace to accomplish all the work you need to do, allows it to be done through you, rather than *by* you. Choosing your higher mind to make every decision with you allows you to get it completely right. Experiment with choice. For example, choose true love ten times a day for ten days or choose wealth a hundred times a day for ten days. Keep a log of how you feel every day and any results you notice. At the root of every problem there is fear. Choose that the fear be gone any time you think of the problem.

HEALING CHOICE

I commit to know and use the full power of choice in my life.

HEALING EXERCISE

For any problem that arises in your life, state "I choose for any negative effects to be gone from this problem of _____, and I choose a new chapter of love and success instead."

Here are some positive choices to get you through any heartbreak experience or problem situation:

"I choose to forgive myself and _____

_____ for this experience."

"I choose to let go of all revenge relating to this situation."

"I choose to change all negative beliefs that led to this event."

"I choose not to use this event as a sign of suffering, destruction, and death, but as a means of healing and peace."

"I choose that this event is a means to my peace."

"I choose to be finished with this new birth by next week, this week, tomorrow, etc."

"I choose to go through this birth as quickly, effortlessly, and easily as possible."

"I acknowledge that I made a mistake in choosing this event to happen. I now choose the truth."

"I realize there must be a better way than what has occurred. I now choose that better way. Let my higher mind show it to me."

"I choose to let go of all attachments that led to this event so that I might have true love and bonding."

"I choose to be a better, more attractive person as the result of this birth."

"I choose to let my higher mind guide and inspire me in all of my choices."

111.

ASKING FOR A MIRACLE

Every couple that I have ever known has found themselves in a predicament that seemed like the end of the relationship. The cause of the predicament was inevitably misunderstanding, power struggles, deadness, taking a wrong direction, or an unconscious fracture. It is important to know that in the midst of such a situation, we are neither helpless nor comfortless. When we have painted ourselves into a corner, the only direction to go is up.

Throughout my career I have witnessed firsthand the fact that human beings are ultimately spiritual beings and that personal and collective evolution is taking us to this realization. We do not have to do everything ourselves because there is a power either within or outside us that governs our journeys. Whether we believe in a particular religion or faith, or we simply acknowledge our own deeply spiritual and peaceful core—the center of our being—we can rely on a higher authority to guide us. Sometimes we have to stand aside, to stop fighting, in order for this spiritual peace to use its grace to work its miracles.

When we get ourselves into what appear to be impossible, difficult, or foolproof situations we can ask for a miracle. When we do so, we invite all of the help the universe holds for us. We have nothing to lose and everything to learn and gain by putting things in the hands of our higher powers, and when we put our faith in the pure energy of spiritual love, we can only experience the warm glow of success.

HEARTBREAK PRINCIPLE

In the face of impossible odds, many relationships fold and break up.

HEALING PRINCIPLE

In the face of impossible odds, don't hesitate to ask for help from the forces that surround us—the pure love of spirit or God.

HEALING SUGGESTION

If you aren't in the habit of asking for a miracle, you might want to give it a try. You have nothing to lose and everything to gain. When you give up your judgment and choose love or forgiveness instead, when you use your faith and trust to see the truth, while at the same time denying the evidence given by the illusion of reality that is presenting itself to you, you will help bring about a miracle by receiving grace. You can receive a miracle by simply asking for one.

HEALING CHOICE

I commit to learn of my ability to ask for miracles so that I can begin to change the impossible situations of my life.

HEALING EXERCISE

At the beginning of every day, choose the most troublesome problem you or someone around you has, and from the deepest part of your heart, ask for a miracle.

THE LAST
COACHING

This book is not just about heartbreaks; it is also about the mistakes that are made in relationships, which are, of course, the cause of heartbreaks. Relationships are not just bad karma; they are the perfect vehicles for profound healing in your life. Everyone has ongoing patterns to heal, and if we do not stay on top of the patterns, they will stay on top of us. At the first sign that something is "off" in your relationship, you must give up all self-righteousness and be willing to learn if you want things to change. When you remember that what is happening is transference—an old pattern that you've dealt with before but not healed completely—you will also see that it is your forgiveness and joining that will heal another layer now. The person in any situation represents someone that you have come to help, so as you let go of your judgment, you can offer the gift that you came to give them.

Your partner, or the people in any situation, represent a part of your mind that you have projected, *because* you have judged and rejected the same thing in yourself. You project your own fractures externally, on situations, and people around you. You can integrate and win back this part of yourself which will end a conflict within you. You can now use the energy to build your life and your love. Your partner or the people in the conflicted situation are then recognized as a blessing to you; they are there to help you heal.

You can use unhappy situations as a time to remind yourself about what is truly important. When you are on a healing path, you will have a healing attitude, which means that the next thing to come up is just something else for healing. If you do not have a healing attitude, you will not be heading in a healing direction with wholeheartedness as your goal. If you head toward battle instead of the healing path, you won't see others as a reflection of a major part of your mind; you will only see that what they are doing is wrong. You will see yourself as being innocently attacked and betrayed, but you will not understand your mistakes and your own part in the situation. Only if *you* choose to make your relationship better will it get better. If you are fighting or judging, your partner will be fighting, and if they quit and you win, both of you will lose. Healing each step along the way is the only thing that works. When you learn the lessons of healing and commitment, and understand the issues and the stages, you can have weeks, even months of peace and happiness until the next layer arises.

Don't ignore the signals that something is wrong. You must ask your higher mind to show you the way and you must galvanize yourself into action. Ask for grace to create ease in your relationship. You must forgive your partner. Join your partner. Commit to your partner. Commit to the next step. Commit to the truth. Ask for spiritual peace. Ask for miracles. Be willing, because the next layer *will* come up in your relationship. If you have a healing attitude, then you have the confidence to know what works, even in the face of old pain that has turned up once again for healing. Pain is just a new layer of the past asking for forgiveness in the present.

There are no fairytale relationships in life. Every relationship has its honeymoon periods to enjoy and its fractures to heal. Begin any place with anyone in any of your relationships—partner, spouse, lover, family, friend, co-worker, acquaintance—and when you give yourself to that relationship, you will see what needs healing from the past. In each relationship, you can heal the parts that you rejected. You can heal whatever you have against anyone, everyone, against life, and against your God or the world. Every relationship will bring you back to spiritual peace if you allow it to. Love waits for you, and it is calling you to come home. Will you respond? There is a way that is easy to follow when you don't resist it. It is even easier when you ask for help.

It is important to heal your heartbreaks, because mistakes must not determine the course of your life. It is important to have full access to your heart because, without it, you have lost everything that gives meaning and purpose to your life. It is your heart that allows you to give yourself and to receive from others. Without your heart, life becomes something from which you need to protect yourself. There can be no springtime, no exuberance, and no rebirth. Success becomes nothing more than winning, like collecting colored paper in a Monopoly game. Love, bonding, mutuality, and forgiveness become lost when we strive to be independent and to have more than others do. In a hundred years, none of that will matter, but where you recovered your heart, people will live because of you, and the world will be a better place because of your wholeheartedness.

Without your heart you will live in the past, having lost something precious. But that precious something—also known as wholeheartedness—is recoverable through learning, unlearning, and choice. Having your heart allows you to know that you have power in your life and that, ultimately, you can choose the path and quality of your life. You can recover your heart when it has been shattered. You can recover yourself from the destructive effects of defenses such as independence, dissociation, dependence, and sacrifice. I know this personally, and I know this professionally. You can win back your life and your courage to live.

Your heart is your greatest asset in life, and you are the greatest gift to life itself. With you, there can be one more act of kindness and mercy. With you, there can be one more act of friendship and mutuality. With you, one more person can be helped—by your hands, by your words, by your smile, and by your loving eyes. You can receive one more inspiration or give one more blessing. You can smell one more flower or encourage one more friend. You can forgive one more mistake or learn one more lesson. You can remember Oneness, and know yourself as part of that, deserving of every good thing. You can end one more illusion and its inevitable disillusionment. You can bring love and hope back to your life and to the lives of others. You can say one more prayer and help end one more agony. You can reach out one more time and give one more hug. The world will be a better place, because you have walked it. Recover your heart and you become a beacon of hope, a savior to those locked in the hell of heartbreak. You have become a friend to the earth and all her people.

Your new life awaits you. What will you decide? Will you choose suffering and death, or birth and its springtime? Will you take yourself down from your cross so that you can live?

You can decide to give up your pound of nails and, in so doing, you will no longer be helpless in the face of the pain of those you love. You can help them down from their crosses. What will you decide? This is your world. Will you choose to do whatever it takes to continue healing your heartbreaks so that your heart is safe and healed and whole? Or will you choose hell? Look in the eyes of a child you love and then decide, because you do not ever choose for yourself alone.

For details on other books, the full range of audio and video-tapes, and worldwide seminars, please contact us at:

Psychology of Vision Products Ltd
France Farm
Rushall
Pewsey
Wiltshire SN9 6DR
UK
Tel: 44(0)1980 635 121
e-mail: Vision-Products@Compuserve.com
website: www.psychology-of-vision.com